The Psychology of Prejudice and Discrimination

The Psychology of Prejudice and Discrimination

VOLUME 3
BIAS BASED ON GENDER AND SEXUAL ORIENTATION

Edited by
Jean Lau Chin

Foreword by
Joseph E. Trimble

PRAEGER PERSPECTIVES

Race and Ethnicity in Psychology
Jean Lau Chin, John D. Robinson, and Victor De La Cancela
Series Editors

Westport, Connecticut
London

R
303.385
PSY
V.3

Library of Congress Cataloging-in-Publication Data

The psychology of prejudice and discrimination / edited by Jean Lau Chin ; foreword
by Joseph E. Trimble.
    p. cm.—(Race and ethnicity in psychology, ISSN 1543-2203)
    Includes bibliographical references and index.
    ISBN 0-275-98234-3 (set : alk. paper)—ISBN 0-275-98235-1 (v. 1 : alk. paper)—
ISBN 0-275-98236-X (v. 2 : alk. paper)—ISBN 0-275-98237-8 (v. 3 : alk. paper)—
ISBN 0-275-98238-6 (v. 4 : alk. paper) 1. Prejudices—United States. I. Chin, Jean
Lau. II. Series.
BF575.P9P79 2004
303.3'85'0973—dc22   2004042289

British Library Cataloguing in Publication Data is available.

Library of Congress Catalog Card Number: 2004042289
ISBN: 0-275-98234-3 (set)
      0-275-98235-1 (Vol. 1)
      0-275-98236-X (Vol. 2)
      0-275-98237-8 (Vol. 3)
      0-275-98238-6 (Vol. 4)
ISSN: 1543-2203

First published in 2004

Praeger Publishers, 88 Post Road West, Westport, CT 06881
An imprint of Greenwood Publishing Group, Inc.
www.praeger.com

Printed in the United States of America

The paper used in this book complies with the
Permanent Paper Standard issued by the National
Information Standards Organization (Z39.48-1984).

10 9 8 7 6 5 4 3 2 1

Contents

Foreword

Civilized men have gained notable mastery over energy, matter, and inanimate nature generally and are rapidly learning to control physical suffering and premature death. But, by contrast, we appear to be living in the Stone Age so far as our handling of human relations is concerned.

(Gordon W. Allport, 1954, p. ix)

Although written over fifty years ago, the haunting words of the eminent social psychologist Gordon W. Allport may ring true today. His intent then was to clarify the various elements of the enormously complex topic of prejudice. Since the writing of his now well-cited and highly regarded text on prejudice, social and behavioral scientists have made great strides in furthering our knowledge of the field. Since 1950, for example, thousands of books, journal articles, and book chapters have been devoted to studying prejudice and discrimination. Professor Allport would be somewhat pleased with the numbers because that was partly his expectation when he said, "So great is the ferment of investigation and theory in this area that in one sense our account will soon be dated. New experiments will supersede old, and formulations of various theories will be improved" (1954, p. xiii). But has there been that much improvement that we have moved away from a Stone Age understanding of human relations to a higher level of sophistication? The question begs for an answer, but that can wait until later.

Let me back up for a moment to explore another line of thought and inquiry that bears directly on the significance and importance of this wonderful set of books on the psychology of prejudice and discrimination. For as long as I can remember, I have been deeply interested in the origins of, motives in, and attitudes about genocide and ethnocide; as a young child I did not use those horrific terms, as I did not know them then. But I did know about their implied destructive implications from stories passed along by sensitive teachers, ancestors, and elders. The deep social psychological meaning of the constructs later became an intense interest of mine as a graduate student in the turbulent 1960s, an era filled with challenges and protestations of anything regarding civil rights, discrimination, racism, sexism, and prejudice. During that era I threw my mind and spirit into the study of Allport's writings on prejudice—not merely to study them, but to explore every nuance of his scholarly works to expand the depth of my understanding and expecting to come away with fewer questions and more answers. I was not disappointed in my exploration. I was baffled, though, because I recognized more so just how complicated it was to prevent and eradicate prejudice and discrimination.

As I write these thoughts, I am reminded of a sign that was once posted over the porch roof of an old restaurant and tavern in a rural South Dakota community adjacent to an American Indian reservation. The sign was hand-painted in white letters on a long slat of weathered wood; it was written in the Lakota language, and the English translation read, "No dogs or Indians allowed." The store was and is still owned by non-Indians. The offensive, derogatory sign is no longer there— likely torn down years ago by angry protestors from the nearby reservation. While the sign is gone, the attitude and intent of the message still linger in and around the rustic building, except that it is more insidious, pernicious, and guileful now. The prevailing prejudicial and loathsome attitude is a reflection of many of the residents of the small town. Many of the town's residents tolerate Native Americans because they dependent on them economically, but their bigoted and closed-minded convictions are unwilling to accept Native Americans as equals and provide them with freedom of movement and expression.

The wretched, mean-spirited, pernicious attitudes present in that rural South Dakota town symbolize the prevailing changes in attitudes and behavior across North America—the blatant signs are gone, but in many places and for many individuals the prejudicial attitudes persist, sometimes in sly and subtle forms. On other occasions they are overt and repulsive. Chapters in these volumes summarize and explore the social and psychological motives and reasoning behind the persistence of prejudicial attitudes and discriminatory practices. They go beyond the conclusions drawn by Professor Allport and other early writers on the topic and take us into domains represented by those who have experienced prejudice and discrimination firsthand, as did their ancestors. Indeed, a voice not included in early studies on prejudice and discrimination is intensified and deepened as more and more ethnic groups and women are represented in the social and behavioral sciences than in years gone by.

Stories and anecdotes, too, recounted by the rising groups of diverse scholars and researchers, lend a new authenticity to the literature. Some of the accounts provide a different perspective on historical events involving racial hatred that provide more thorough descriptions of the details and perspectives. Revisionist historical approaches have a place in the study of prejudice and discrimination because for so long the authentic voices of the victims were muffled and muted. For example, as a consequence of European contact, many Native American communities continue to experience individual and community trauma, a "wound to the soul of Native American people that is felt in agonizing proportions to this day" (Duran & Duran, 1995, p. 27). The cumulative trauma has been fueled by centuries of incurable diseases, massacres, forced relocation, unemployment, economic despair, poverty, forced removal of children to boarding schools, abuse, racism, loss of traditional lands, unscrupulous land mongering, betrayal, broken treaties—the list goes on. Brave Heart and DeBruyn (1998) and Duran and Duran (1995) maintain that postcolonial "historical and intergenerational trauma" has left a long trail of unresolved grief and a "soul wound" in Native American communities that contribute to high levels of social and individual problems such as alcoholism, suicide, homicide, domestic violence, child abuse, and negative career ideation. The presence of Native American scholars contributed a voice that was suppressed for decades because some feared the consequences if these scholars told their stories. The stories and accounts of past racial events and their corresponding trauma also were not told because there were few visible ethnic scholars available.

Decades ago the topics of prejudice and discrimination largely emphasized race and, more specifically, the racial experiences of black Americans. Over the years the topic has expanded to include the experiences of other ethnic groups, women, the elderly, those with disabilities, those with nonheterosexual orientations, and those with mixed ethnic heritages. The volumes edited by Jean Lau Chin expand the concepts of diversity and multiculturalism to add a broader, more inclusive dimension to the understanding of prejudice and discrimination. The addition of new voices to the field elevates public awareness to the sweeping effects of prejudice and discrimination and how they are deeply saturated throughout societies.

The amount of scholarly attention devoted to the study of prejudice and discrimination closely parallels the growth of ethnic diversity interests in psychology. Until about thirty years ago, psychology's mission appeared to be restricted to a limited population as references to blacks, Asian Americans, Native American and Alaska natives, Hispanics, Pacific Islanders, and Puerto Ricans were almost absent from the psychological literature; in fact, the words *culture* and *ethnic* were rarely used in psychological textbooks. The long absence of culture in the web of psychological inquiry did not go unnoticed. About three decades ago, ethnic minority and international psychologists began questioning what the American Psychological Association meant by its use of *human* and to whom the vast body of psychological knowledge applied. America's ethnic psychologists and those from other countries, as well as a small handful of North American psychologists, argued that American psychology did not include what constituted the world's population. They claimed that findings were biased, limited to studies involving college and university students and laboratory animals, and therefore not generalizable to all humans. Comprehensive literature reviews reinforced their accusations and observations.

Accusations of imperialism, cultural encapsulation, ethnocentrism, parochialism, and, in some circles of dissent, of "scientifically racist" studies, run the gamut of criticisms hurled at the field of psychology during that period. Robert Guthrie (1976), for example, writing in his strongly worded critique of psychology, *Even the Rat Was White*, argues that culture and context were not taken seriously in the history of psychological research. Given these conditions and the myopia of the profession, it is no small wonder that prejudice and discrimination were not given more widespread attention. The topic was not perceived as salient and important enough for extensive consideration. The four volumes in this set are a testament to the amount of change and emphasis that are focused on ethnicity, culture, and the topics of prejudice and discrimination.

The changing demographics in the United States call into question the relevance of a psychology that historically has not included ethnic and racial groups and that fostered a research agenda that was ethnocentric and bound by time and place. This can no longer be tolerated, as the rapid growth of ethnic minority groups in the United States amplifies the need for more attentiveness on the part of the social and behavioral sciences. Consider the population projections offered by the U.S. Bureau of the Census. By 2050, the U.S. population will reach over 400 million, about 47 percent larger than in 2000 (U.S. Bureau of the Census, 2001). The primary ethnic minority groups— specifically, Hispanics, blacks, Asian Americans, and Native American and Alaska Natives—will constitute almost 50 percent of the population in 2050. About 57 percent of the population under the age of eighteen, and 34 percent over the age of 65, will be ethnic minorities.

America never was and likely will not be a melting pot of different nationalities and ethnic groups for another century or two. As the mixture and size of ethnic groups increase, we are faced with the disturbing possibility that an increase in prejudice and discrimination will occur accordingly. Given this possibility, the topics covered in these volumes become even more worthy of serious consideration, especially the ones that emphasize prevention. Given the demographic changes and the topical changes that have occurred in the social and behavioral sciences, the extensive contents of these four volumes are a welcome addition to the field. Editor Jean Lau Chin and her long list of chapter authors are to be congratulated for their monumental effort. The volumes are packed with useful and wonderfully written material. Some is based on empirical findings, some on firsthand experiences. The blend of various writing styles and voice adds to the breadth of coverage of the topic. The many points of view provided by the contributors will help shape the direction of research and scholarly expression on a topic that has been around since the origins of humankind. We can hope that the contributions of these four volumes will move the field of human relations from a perceived Stone Age level of understanding to one where we believe we are moving closer to eliminating prejudice, discrimination, and the vile hatred they engender.

Joseph E. Trimble
Professor of Psychology
Western Washington University
Bellingham, WA
March 21, 2004

REFERENCES

Allport, G. W. (1954). *The nature of prejudice*. Garden City, NY: Doubleday.

Brave Heart, M. Y. H., & DeBruyn, L. (1998). The American Indian holocaust: Healing unresolved grief. *American Indian and Alaska Native Mental Health Research, 8*(2), 56–78.

Duran, E., & Duran, B. (1995). *Native American postcolonial psychology.* Albany, NY: State University of New York Press.

Guthrie, R. (1976). *Even the rat was white: A historical view of psychology.* New York: Harper & Row.

U.S. Bureau of the Census. (2001). *Census of the population: General population characteristics, 2000.* Washington, DC: Government Printing Office.

Introduction

Prejudice and discrimination are not new. The legacy of the Pilgrims and early pioneers suggested a homogenous, mainstream America. Our early emphasis on patriotism in the United States resulted in a false idealization of the melting pot myth. Prejudice and discrimination in American society were overt and permeated all levels of society, that is, legislation, government, education, and neighborhoods. In the 1960s, attempts to eradicate prejudice, discrimination, and racism were explicit—with an appeal to honor and value the diversity within different racial and ethnic groups. This soon extended to other dimensions of diversity, including gender, disability, and spirituality. However, long after the war to end slavery, the civil rights movement of the 1960s, desegregation in the schools, and the abolition of anti-Asian legislation—indeed, in the midst of growing public debate today regarding gay marriage—we still see the pernicious effects of prejudice and discrimination in U.S. society.

Prejudice and discrimination toward differences in race, ethnicity, gender, spirituality, and disability have had negative psychological consequences, and they continue in primarily covert forms. Bias and disparities still exist and result in inequity of services, opportunities, and practices in American society. Combating prejudice and discrimination in today's environment warrants some different strategies. We live in an environment of heightened anxiety due to war and terrorism. Thanks to technological advances in communication, travel, and the

Internet, news and information from all parts of the world are almost instantaneously brought to us. We live in a global economy with a narrowing of borders between countries and groups. Generations of immigrants have resulted in the U.S. population becoming so diverse that there may soon be no single majority group within most major cities. Technological advances have eliminated the biological advantage of males in strength and the biological "limitations" of women of childbearing age in the work environment. Yet, the more things change, the more they stay the same. Irrational and unjust perceptions of other people remain—more subtle, perhaps, but they remain.

This four-volume set, *The Psychology of Prejudice and Discrimination*, takes a fresh look at that issue that is embedded in today's global environment. Images, attitudes and perceptions that sustain prejudice and discrimination are more covert, but no less pernicious. What people say, believe, and do all reflect underlying bias. **We do not claim here to address every existing form of prejudice or discrimination, nor do we cite every possible group targeted today. What we offer are insights into a range from the most to least recognized, or openly discussed, forms of this injustice.** Each chapter offers new perspectives on standing issues, with practical information about how to cope with prejudice and discrimination. The "toolbox" at the end of each chapter suggests steps to be taken at different levels to combat prejudice and discrimination and to achieve change. At the individual level, self-reflection needs to occur by both the victims and perpetrators of discrimination. Practitioners, educators, and all who deliver services potentially impart a bias perpetuating prejudice and discrimination. At the systems level, communities and policymakers must join together and have the will to combat discrimination.

How does one remain "whole" or validate one's identity despite persistent assaults to self-esteem from prejudice and discrimination? How does one raise children or teach amid societal institutions that perpetuate bias? Culturally competent principles and practices are needed to provide a framework for managing diversity and valuing differences.

Volume 1, *Racism in America*, looks at stereotypes, racial bias, and race relations. How do we avoid internalizing racism or accepting negative messages about a group's ability and intrinsic worth? How do we address institutionalized racism that results in differential access to goods, service, and opportunities of society? Volume 2, *Ethnicity and Multiracial Identity*, looks at discrimination toward differences due to immigration, language, culture, and mixed race. Volume 3,

Bias Based on Gender and Sexual Orientation, looks at gender bias, women's issues, homophobia, and oppression of gay/lesbian lifestyles. Volume 4, *Disability, Religion, Physique, and Other Traits*, strives to examine less-spotlighted bias against other forms of difference, and begins the difficult dialogue that must take place if we are to eradicate prejudice and discrimination.

Written for today's people and environment, these volumes are rich with anecdotes, stories, examples, and research. These stories illustrate the emotional impact of prejudice and discrimination throughout history and as it still strikes people's lives today. While the chapters spotlight psychology, they interweave history, politics, legislation, social change, education, and more. These interdisciplinary views reflect the broad contexts of prejudice and discrimination that ultimately affect identity, life adjustment, and well-being for every one of us.

Please take with you the strategies for change offered in the toolbox at the end of each chapter. Change needs to occur at all levels: individual, practitioner/educator, and community. The intent of the toolboxes is to move us from the emotional to the scholarly to action and empowerment. They are intended to encourage and compel readers to begin individual change that will spur community and social action. With each person who reads these volumes, gains understanding, and finds the motivation or method to help make his or her small part of the world a more just and open-minded place, we have moved closer to making our goal a reality.

Jean Lau Chin

CHAPTER 1

Prejudice and Discrimination against Women Based on Gender Bias

Roberta L. Nutt

There is a long history of discrimination against women in U.S. culture and the world that often rests on the foundation of gender bias, which restricts the roles and potential of both women and men. However, for women this discrimination and prejudice often result in role conflict, devaluation, low self-esteem, lack of confidence, depression, discouraged achievement, victimization, dependency, and feelings of helplessness (Nutt, 1999). Most cultures teach women that they are of lesser value than men, and this message is repeated throughout the life span. Characteristics viewed as masculine are more highly valued than those considered feminine, such as assertiveness versus submissiveness, achieving versus caretaking, and strong versus gentle.

In many cultures, when women are not instructed to be invisible, there is an overemphasis on physical appearance and beauty to the detriment of full personal development (Wolf, 1991). Women's voices are frequently silenced, and their thoughts and opinions are not valued (Belenky, Clinchy, Goldberger, & Tarule, 1986; Jack 1991, 1999; Thompson, 1995). Theorists suggest that in recent times in less-traditional cultures, women actually receive paradoxical messages, such as "you should be gentle and nurturing while also being a shrewd business woman in the workplace" (Halas & Matteson, 1978; O'Neil & Egan, 1992), which result in confusion and vulnerability to self-doubt. Then when women encounter prejudice and discrimination, they may collude with the system and believe they deserve it. Hence, women feel devalued by external sources and devalue themselves.

Although a variety of changes have occurred in the United States in the past several decades regarding expectations of women and men (Eagly, Wood, & Diekman, 2000), most researchers still report different gender-role socialization patterns for girls and boys and women and men. These patterns may be even more striking in other countries around the world that have experienced less social change in the late twentieth century, and they also vary by ethnicity, class/economic status, sexual orientation, and religion. Hence, prejudice and discrimination against women are found in many places around the world.

INFANCY

Parents still tend to treat and dress girls and boys differently (Matlin, 1996). In western cultures, girls' clothing suggests delicacy and fragility through color (pastel—often pink) and style (dresses with frills and bows) and less likely lends itself to action-oriented activity or exploration. Girls' rooms are also more often decorated in pastel colors with flowers and lace for decor (Pomerleau, Bolduc, Malcuit, & Cossette, 1990), which further suggests girls' need for protection and an inability to be independent and strong.

Adults also play with girl babies in different ways than they do with boys. They are gentler with girls, as girls are seen as delicate and weaker, and adults are more likely to play roughly and aggressively with the hardier, stronger boys (Grieshaber, 1998; Huston, 1983; Rubin, Provenzano, & Luria, 1974). Girls are praised for being cute and adorable and displaying behavior labeled "sweet." They are more often "helped" and "rescued" (Paludi, 2002).

There is substantial evidence in U.S. culture and many others that boy babies are preferred over girl babies, especially for a firstborn child (Arnold & Kuo, 1984; Basow, 1992; Hamilton, 1991; Pooler, 1991). In some countries, girl babies are even killed or sold (Neft & Levine, 1997), so strong is this preference for boys and discrimination against girls.

CHILDHOOD

In childhood, the different expectations and treatment of girls and boys continues and increases. Girls' activities are more likely to be restricted (Gilligan, 1982; Lytton & Romney, 1991) under the guise of protecting them. Children's books and toys strongly communicate society's expectations of their appropriate gender-role behaviors (Clark, Lennon, & Morris, 1993; Evans & Davies, 2000; Kortenhaus & Demarest, 1993; Robinson & Morris, 1986). Toys for girls usually aim them toward future roles as wives and mothers—dolls, stoves, dishes, etc. They are not typically given the boy-oriented toys like building blocks, chemistry sets, and vehicles that might teach them career values and skills. They are less adventurous and engage in fewer activities. Fairy tales and children's books, with some exceptions, further stereotype girls as passive victims who need rescuing or as caretaking nurturers (Bordelon, 1985; Purcell & Stewart, 1990). Girls are taught to look good (Wolf, 1991) and to rely on men to rescue and take care of them. In addition, girls are underrepresented in children's books despite recent attempts to equalize the ratio (Doyle & Paludi, 1998). Children's books still predominantly portray male and white characters, communicating to white girls and girls of color that women are not important (Reid & Paludi, 1993). These messages result in girls and women not feeling important or competent and able to take care of themselves. The messages lead the larger culture also to view women as not competent or independent, and less is expected of them.

Gender stereotypes are reinforced in the classroom as children enter the school system. Girls are less often called upon in class or encouraged to speak up in public (AAUW, 1992; Sadker & Sadker, 1994), and black girls receive even less attention (AAUW, 1992; Orenstein, 1994). Boys are given more time to answer questions, and they are often asked to elaborate, which leads them to think more deeply. Girls more typically receive a vague or neutral response. Also, when girls have difficulties with a problem, the teacher usually gives them the solution rather than encouragement to figure it out themselves. The Association of American Colleges (Hall & Sandler, 1982) described the U.S. school system as a chilly classroom climate for women, extending from elementary school to college and even graduate school. Teaching style also favors a male style of learning, which further disadvantages most girls (Belenky et al., 1986; Ginorio & Huston, 2000). Consequently, girls feel less valued in the classroom. They participate less, which further erodes self-worth and other people's attitudes toward them as girls. Their voices are silenced and their ideas and opinions are seen as not mattering (Jack, 1991, 1999; Thompson, 1995). Girls learn to defer to boys, give higher value to neatness than creativity, emphasize appearance over intelligence, and fear and avoid science and math (Sadker & Sadker, 1994). Their classroom performance deteriorates.

During this time period, children resist involvement with the "other" sex (Feiring & Lewis, 1987; La Freniere, Strayer, & Gauthier, 1984; Lobel, Stone, & Winch, 1997; Maccoby, 1998; Martin & Fabes, 2001), further isolating girls. The isolation of any group, especially one with lesser power, is directly related to the ease with which that group may receive discrimination. In fact, girls and women are given more latitude in behavior and attire than boys and men because the masculine is more highly valued (Feinman, 1981; Urberg, 1982). Sex harassment of girls by boys is being reported in U.S. elementary schools, and there are countries that do not even allow girls to be educated (for example, in Afghanistan during the Taliban era).

On television, boys favor sports, shows about the supernatural, and entertainment cartoons, while girls are attracted to comedy. As in American children's books, these shows portray more male than female characters (Thompson & Zerbinos, 1997), a finding that has been replicated in Japan (Rolandelli, 1991). Boys and girls are also portrayed primarily in stereotyped, traditional roles (Furnham & Bitar, 1993; Furnham & Twiggy, 1999; Signorielli, 1989). Since, on the average, American children watch eight to fourteen hours of television each week (Wright, et al., 2001), TV's messages have a significant impact. On prime time television, women also are seen less frequently (Signorielli & Bacue, 1999), although there has been some progress in depicting women in the workplace and in nontraditional careers. The lack of sufficient competent female role models in the media disadvantages girls and reinforces prejudice toward women as lesser.

ADOLESCENCE

Gender differences are even further accentuated at adolescence, thereby strengthening gender bias. Pipher (1994) considered adolescence the most critical period of gender-role conflict and change. She stated, "Something dramatic happens to girls in early adolescence. Just as planes and ships disappear mysteriously into the Bermuda Triangle, so do the selves of girls go down in droves" (p. 19). Even girls who have done well academically in elementary school often pull back from academic achievement in adolescence.

Girls who continue to achieve are often criticized, even ridiculed, since high academic performance is considered a masculine trait. Their femininity may be questioned. Girls therefore lose confidence in their academic abilities (Freiberg, 1991; Walker, Reis, & Leonard, 1992), are directed toward traditionally "feminine" and generally lower-paying careers, tend to under-aspire in relation to their abilities, and lose self-confidence and self-esteem (AAUW, 1992; Brody, 1997; Kling, Hyde, Showers, & Buswell, 1999). Girls and women are then perceived as less competent than men, with prejudicial attitudes toward women as a result. Less is expected of them, girls who attempt to escape their traditional roles are sanctioned, and the gender-bias system is reinforced. There is some evidence that black girls may suffer less of this loss of self-esteem because of the influence of parents who actively work to confront racism and support their daughters' self-esteem (Michaelieu, 1997).

As girls reach dating age, they tend to pay more and more attention to appearance and social popularity. They spend large sums of money on clothing, makeup, and fashion magazines, particularly those aimed at teenagers. Although it is biologically appropriate and desirable for adolescent girls to increase their fatty tissue to maintain normal reproductive functioning, girls perceive any increase in body weight or size as problematic in a culture that values a lean "masculine" body for women and devalues and criticizes a more feminine, round, shapely body (Martz, Handley, & Eisler, 1995; McKinley & Hyde, 1996). Not being sufficiently thin, and therefore attractive, creates negative self-evaluation (Cattarin, Thompson, Thomas, & Williams, 2000; Evans, 2003; Thornton & Maurice, 1997), a finding that holds across multiple cultures (Bay-Cheng, Zucker, Stewart, & Pomerleau, 2002; Demarest & Allen, 2000; Henriques & Calhoun, 1999; Pumariega, 1997), although somewhat less among blacks (Cash & Henry, 1995; Hebl & Heatherton, 1998).

This overemphasis on appearance via thinness causes many adolescent girls to submit themselves to stringent dieting, which may take a serious toll on their health, in addition to leading to prevalent eating disorders (Frederick & Grow, 1996; Haworth-Hoeppner, 2000; Striegel-Moore & Smolak, 2000). Kaschak (1992) described this violation of the female body as a combat zone in that "women become the enemies of their bodies in a struggle to mold them as society wishes, to mediate and embody conflicts between the physical and the demands of society" (p. 193). She elaborated that "conflicts surrounding women's desires and appetites, about taking up space, and about adult sexuality are expressed elegantly and painfully in eating disorders in women" (p. 195). Frederickson and Roberts (1997) delineated the consequences of shame, anxiety, and serious mental health problems that result when women's bodies are objectified. Women's guilt about not being physically perfect and desirable and taking up more than their share of space leads to feelings of guilt and self-devaluation. These feelings may be further accentuated in cultures where women are hidden from view by clothing or isolation. Because these attitudes are widespread, they result in prejudice and discrimination toward women who do not meet the cultural ideal of beauty. These women feel shamed and criticized, and their development is limited.

YOUNG ADULTHOOD

In young adulthood, the emphasis on appearance and its connection to relationships in women's lives continues to grow. In describing this classic developmental stage of "identity versus role confusion," Erikson (1964, 1968) postulated that a young woman cannot fully form an identity until she knows the man she will marry. He thereby assumes women must satisfy their relational needs before they can define an identity. His premise suggests that women are only half-people waiting for someone to fulfill and complete them (Kolbenschlag, 1981; Russianoff, 1981). While newer theories have emphasized the importance of connection and relationships to both genders (Jordan, Kaplan, Miller, Stiver, & Surrey, 1991), Erikson's writings are still seriously adopted by many. The assumption that a woman cannot develop a separate, independent identity but rather is defined by the men in her life (husband, male children, father) leads the culture again to believe that women are lesser and incomplete. It provides support for those who would restrict women's roles based on the assumption that women have inherent role restrictions and lesser competencies.

Kolbenschlag (1981), in her aptly titled book, *Kiss Sleeping Beauty Goodbye*, described young women as continually waiting: waiting for the completion of something missing in their lives, waiting for young men to bring purpose and fulfillment to their lives. While waiting, young women restrict themselves from living fully and fully developing their lives. They often put major life issues and decisions "on hold." "The 'tomboy' phase, which often precedes puberty, is, for many young girls, the last eruption of individuated personality before the fall into 'beauty' and the inevitable 'sleep' of the female psyche" (p. 8). "The second persona in the . . . girl's repertoire is that of the desire to live for another. This role will school her in self-forgetfulness,

service and sacrifice, in nurturing rather than initiating behaviors . . .
She will give up everything when the expected one comes, even the
right of creating her own self" (p. 10). At the same time, Miller
(1986) and Spence and Buckner (2000) noted that "in our culture
serving others is for losers, it is low level stuff. Yet serving others is a
basic principle around which women's lives are organized; it is far
from such for men" (p. 61). Kolbenschlag (1981) concluded that
"giving advice to women [about who they should be] has been one
of the most constant industries in Western civilization" (p. 11). The
result is that women are viewed as inferior creatures who are assumed
to be passive and submissive, dependent on others for identity and
protection, and fearful of unexpected events and new challenges.
They are not expected to be able to make their own choices and
therefore need directions from others, which can be used to justify
discrimination against allowing them in positions of responsibility
and authority. While it is certainly true that the numbers of young
women with career aspirations and educational achievement have
grown in recent decades, the messages about women's need for another to complete them continue. Viewing just one episode of the
recent, popular television series *Sex and the City* provides strong evidence for this focus on relationships in women's lives, even for
women in successful careers.

American women are putting more emphasis on education and
career and are waiting longer to marry, but the expected lifestyle for
adult women is still heterosexual marriage, traditional gender roles in
the marital relationship, and the rearing of children (Bridges, Etaugh, &
Barnes-Farrell, 2002; Chaffin & Winston, 1991; Prentice & Carranza,
2002; U.S. Bureau of the Census, 1996), an expectation that holds
across most cultures (Frieze et al., 2003; Funk & Mueller, 1993;
Massey, Hahn, & Sekulic, 1995; Morinaga, Frieze, & Ferligoj, 1993).
Extended family and friends begin to ask pointed questions of a woman
who has not married by twenty-eight or thirty or who is married but
does not have children. "The motherhood mystique asserts that being
a mother is the ultimate fulfillment for a woman. (In contrast, men are
viewed as being fulfilled not merely by becoming fathers but by having
varied, unique lives full of experiences and achievements)" (Unger &
Crawford, 1992, p. 431). This motherhood message creates a
double-bind situation in that while motherhood is widely praised, it
actually receives low status and prestige in most cultures (Mueller &
Yoder, 1997). Prejudice will result when women are viewed primarily
as wives and mothers rather than independent individuals with a

variety of important roles. In its extreme form, this view results in justifying the physical abuse of wives by their husbands in countries around the world (Glick, Sakalli-Ugurlu, Ferreira & de Souza, 2002; Haj-Yahia, 1998, 2002; Harway, Hansen, Rossman, Geffner, & Deitch, 1996; Harway & O'Neil, 1999; Yllo & Straus, 1990).

Recent research has shown some shift in roles of women in heterosexual marriage. As women develop careers and create a stronger sense of competence and independence, they also want and expect more egalitarian roles in marriage (Botkin, Weeks, & Morris, 2000)—more egalitarian than men endorse (Fowers, 1991). However, most couples still view the male partner as the one with more power (Felmlee, 1994). A number of studies have demonstrated that equality of power generally leads to higher marital satisfaction (Acitelli & Antonucci, 1994; Schroeder, Blood, & Maluso, 1992; Shacher, 1991; Sperberg & Stabb, 1998). However, only a minority of marriages have achieved true equality in terms of behavior (Steil, 1997). Extensive research indicates that a disproportionate share of household labor is still performed by women (Baxter, 1992; Beckwith, 1992; Biernat & Wortman, 1991; DeMeis & Perkins, 1996; Starrels, 1994) regardless of race/ethnicity (John & Shelton, 1997) or socioeconomic status (Wright, Shire, Hwang, Dolan, & Baxter, 1992). The average amount of female-typed tasks (meal preparation, cleanup, laundry, housecleaning, grocery shopping, etc.) done by husbands across white, Latino, and black couples in the United States (John, Shelton, & Luschen, 1995) and many other countries (Moore, 1995; United Nations, 1995) is about 20 percent. This is progress, since the amount for all housework in 1965 was 8 percent to approximately a third in the 1990s (Bianchi, Milkie, Sayer, & Robinson, 2000), but it is not yet equity and continues to reflect old prejudices regarding women's and men's roles.

Consistent with earlier descriptions, in the past young women were not encouraged to develop the problem-solving, independent, risk-taking, and abstract way of thinking necessary for career decision-making, maturity, and advancement negotiation (Wade, 2001). Early career theorists even based their writings on a white male model and saw women's career development as inferior or nonexistent (Fitzgerald & Crites, 1980). In the 1940s, researchers believed women had no personal need for achievement but achieved vicariously through their husband and male children (McClelland, 1961). There is still evidence that young women's career aspirations are typically lower than their abilities

(Betz & Fitzgerald, 1987; Eccles, 1987; Walsh & Osipow, 1994), and young women are still often guided into traditional teaching, nursing, and other service careers. They are frequently steered away from science, math, and computers (Arch & Cummins, 1989) or discriminated against when they try to enter a male-dominated career area (Margolis & Fisher, 2002; Steele, James, & Barnett, 2002; Yoder, 2002). While this discrimination is slowly changing as women do enter male-dominated professions, the change is slow (Kaufman, 1995).

Another particular barrier for women in the workplace is sexual harassment. As a result of sexual harassment and the hostile climate it creates, women change jobs and careers, leave educational programs, suffer decreased morale and job satisfaction, and become less productive (Dansky & Kilpatrick, 1997; Fitzgerald & Omerod, 1993; Levy & Paludi, 1997; Munson, Hulin, & Drasgow, 2000; Paludi, 1996). Those who do not believe women belong in the workforce might use sexual harassment to drive women out: an act of discrimination based upon prejudice.

Finally, the mental health system, since its members are also products of the culture, has not treated women fairly. Women are diagnosed and treated in greater numbers than men (Russo & Green, 1993) and are likely to be diagnosed with disorders that frequently represent exaggerations of the female role, such as depression, agoraphobia, histrionic disorders, dependent personality disorder, borderline personality disorder, and eating disorders (Bekker, 1996; Caplan, 1995; Handwerker, 1999; Rudolf & Priebe, 1999). These diagnoses may then be used to discriminate against women and judge them as less competent than men. In therapy, these attitudes yield the greater likelihood that male clients will be given a more positive prognosis and an instrumental "let's fix it" approach, while women are often *directed* to solutions and given less responsibility for change (Fowers, Applegate, Tredinnick, & Slusher, 1996; Klonoff, Landrine, & Campbell, 2000; Rudman & Glick, 2001; Seem & Johnson, 1998).

MIDDLE AND LATER ADULTHOOD

In middle and later adulthood, the earlier described patterns continue. There is an ongoing emphasis on women being valued primarily for their appearance (which stereotypically declines with age) and their caretaking abilities (Bridges et al., 2002; Frederickson & Roberts,

1997; Miller, 1986; Prentice & Carranza, 2002). In her book *The Beauty Myth* (1991), Wolf describes in great detail how images of beauty are detrimental to women. Women sacrifice much money, time, physical pain, and esteem in the pursuit of beauty, often to the detriment of personal and professional development. As stated by Wolf, "Since the Industrial Revolution, middle-class Western women have been controlled by ideals and stereotypes as much as by material constraints" (p. 15). Beauty has been shown to give the women who possess it advantages in both relationships with men and in the marketplace. Complicating this emphasis on beauty is the evidence that the current U.S. standard for beauty is one that no woman can truly achieve (Heyn, 1989; Kilbourne, 1994). This impossible goal devalues women and results in distorted body images, depression, chronic personal dissatisfaction, eating disorders, excessive and dangerous cosmetic surgery, and a lessening of self-esteem (Dunn, 1994; Saltzberg & Chrisler, 1995). Rodin, Silberstein, and Striegel-Moore (1984) labeled this strong and prevalent obsession with weight and dieting as "normative discontent," such that even normal-weight women consider themselves too fat. Such discontent, dissatisfaction, feelings of depression and self-criticism, and devaluation of self make it difficult for a woman to stand up for herself in personal and professional arenas, which leads to the larger society viewing women as weaker and lesser, thereby deserving discrimination and less respect. In fact, Brown (1987) has suggested that women's distortion of body image and fear of fat have resulted from male standards that value smallness, weakness, and the absence of overt power in women.

The socialization messages discussed earlier continue to have negative consequences on women's physical and mental health. Hare-Mustin (1983) observed the harmfulness of gender-role socialization and gender-role conflict and postulated that "the demands of traditional sex roles lead to more problems for women than men. Certain aspects of women's sex roles may influence the development of mental illness, such as holding in negative feelings, behaving to satisfy a male partner, passivity, learned helplessness, exaggerated femininity, and other-directedness" (p. 595). The caretaking role can lead women to overvalue their love relationships, invest too much of their self-worth in their connections and relationships, and give insufficient attention to developing important aspects of themselves and their skills and competencies. As suggested earlier, these emphases may also lead to physical and mental diagnoses that label and devalue women.

At midlife, there is some decline in physical abilities and the loss of reproductive ability (Etaugh, 1993; Hayflick, 1994; Whitbourne, 1985). Stereotypically, this has led to many western cultures devaluing middle age and older women as dried-up, useless, old hags (Cole & Rothblum, 1990; Gergen, 1990; Rostosky & Travis, 1996). The changes that occur with aging, such as wrinkles and gray hair, are perceived to diminish femininity (Heilbrun, 1991) even though they are perceived to enhance masculinity. Heilbrun remarked that "signs of age come upon women in our society like marks of the devil in earlier times" (p. 56). Middle-aged and older women often report feeling invisible, since the feature for which they were most valued, their physical beauty, has declined. They are underrepresented in all varieties of media. In a study spanning 1940 through the 1980s, the 100 highest-grossing movies not only underrepresented women compared to men, they also tended to portray them more negatively (Bazzini, McIntosh, Smith, Cook, & Harris, 1997). Similarly, only 3 percent of characters portrayed by older actors on prime time television were women, again presented more negatively (Vernon, Williams, Phillips, & Wilson, 1991). In magazines, older women's age is disguised by airbrushing (Chrisler & Ghiz, 1993); and, except for advice on dentures, laxatives, and incontinence and needs for medical attention, older women are ignored in advertising (Bailey, Harrell, & Anderson, 1993; Grambs, 1989).

More recent writing has begun to celebrate the liberation, freedom, and independence of middle age (Bergquist, Greenberg, & Klaum, 1993; Friedan, 1993; Grambs, 1989; Greer, 1992; Helson & Wink, 1992; Jong, 1994; Niemela & Lento, 1993; Rountree, 1993; Sang, 1993; Sheehy, 1992). Many women in their fifties appear to be in the "prime of life." They report their lives as positive, financially comfortable, engaged in social issues, autonomous, and highly satisfying.

Upon reaching midlife, many women "wake up" to the socialization messages (Kolbenschlag, 1981) and begin to make changes in their lives. Over the past two decades, many women in the United States who have raised their families have been entering the work force, sometimes for the first time, or are continuing their education (Alington & Troll, 1984). They are enjoying their new lifestyles and accomplishments (Mitchell & Helson, 1990) and increased freedom of self-definition (Friedan, 1993), although some retain anger and frustration about time they feel they have lost, and also at the internal and external barriers, prejudice, and discrimination in personal and professional life around both the sexism and ageism they experience on their way to their new goals.

Many women at midlife report heightened sexual desire and pleasure and increased marital satisfaction after children have left home and they are free of fears of unwanted pregnancy (Leiblum, 1990; Mansfield & Koch, 1998). Similar results have been reported for lesbian couples (Cole & Rothblum, 1990). They feel more control over their lives in all areas (Mitchell & Helson, 1990) and a sense of joy in living.

Hence, there appears to be a disparate view of middle and late adulthood between the culture and the participants. While the culture—at least U.S. culture—may devalue women as they age and deem them invisible, the women themselves report increased freedom and life satisfaction.

THE SENIOR YEARS

There is ongoing evidence that in later years, there is some tendency toward role reversal between women and men (Neugarten, 1968; Sinnott, 1984). As stated in the prior section, women tend to become more independent and in charge of their lives while men tend to become more relationally oriented and may regret the connections they missed. Unfortunately, since appearance is not considered enhanced by age in women, in many ways their value decreases (Healey, 1986). In her classic article, Sontag (1972) suggested that there was a double standard of aging that devalued women (Canetto, Kaminski, & Felicio, 1995). The resulting cultural prejudice leads to discrimination against older women. They are often viewed as inept, with little of value to say.

Due to gender differences in life expectancy and the tendency for women to marry older men, there are many more widows than widowers in the United States (Etaugh, 1993; Hess & Waring, 1983). The rates are even higher for Latina and black women (Markides, 1989). Widowhood for many women has traditionally been described as a time of loneliness, social isolation, poverty, and depression (Lopata, 1979; Matlin, 1996). However, women's better skills in interpersonal relationships provide some advantages during this time period, although parts of society may shun and reject older people (Whitbourne & Hulicka, 1990), particularly single women.

The stereotype that older women live in poverty is partially supported by the fact that women's retirement benefits have been only 60 percent of the amount men receive (Arber & Ginn, 1994; Belgrave & Haug, 1987), since women have consistently received less pay on the average than men, may have interrupted their working life for childrearing, and are expected to live longer (Patterson, 1996; Ryder, 2000). While the prevailing assumption in the United States is that the majority of the elderly are living in nursing homes, this lifestyle is true for only 5 percent of people over sixty-five, although 70 percent of these people are women. The percentage of people in nursing homes rises to approximately 20 percent by age eighty, predominantly women (Russo, 1990). Since widows value their autonomy and independence, they prefer to live alone in their own homes. Financial security in widowhood, however, varies by ethnicity and social class, with higher poverty rates for blacks, Native Americans, and Latinas (Hardy & Hazelrigg, 1995; Logue, 1991; Silverman, Skirboll, & Payne, 1996).

In spite of stereotypes, prejudice, and discrimination, most women live active and happy lives in their senior years, with a continued emphasis on learning and growing (Friedan, 1993). They broaden their social networks (Arber & Ginn, 1994; Hessler, Jia, Madsen, & Pazaki, 1995; Shumaker & Hill, 1991; Shye, Mullooly, Freeborn, & Pope, 1995) and are involved in many outside activities. They report stronger beliefs in self-efficacy than do men of similar age (Bosscher, Van Der Aa, Van Dasler, Deeg, & Smit, 1995). Elderly women have much life experience to offer to the broader society (Siegel, 1993).

CONCLUSION

This chapter has attempted to present both the prejudice and discrimination committed against women based upon gender bias while also describing progress made within the last several decades. There is still ample evidence in U.S. culture and other cultures of discrimination against women based upon the view of them as valued less than men, but there is also growing evidence of women leading fuller and richer lives as the complexity of their roles grows.

The discrimination is based upon several principles that span the lifetime. These include (1) valuing women primarily for their appearance, (2) expecting women to live through others and sacrifice personal needs for others, (3) valuing men more highly than women, (4) lower academic and career expectations of women, (5) feelings of passivity and learned helplessness, and (6) general disempowerment and loss of self-esteem. The number of women (and men) challenging these principles at all levels is resulting in change, but not change at a rate many would wish.

Toolbox for Change

For	Images/perceptions	Strategies for change
Individual	I am an unattractive woman because I don't look like the models in magazines.	Examine evidence regarding normal weight; read evidence of thinness messages in advertising and other media.
	I feel guilty when I make more money than my husband.	Confront stereotype that financial success is a masculine characteristic.
	If I say what I really think, no one will like me.	Realize that my opinion is as important as anyone else's.
	I must wear high-heeled shoes to be feminine.	Examine evidence of harm done to women's feet by high-heeled shoes.
	I feel like a bad person if I take time for a leisurely bubble bath when I could be cleaning the house or sewing for my family.	Every person deserves personal time and rest and relaxation.
Community/ society	Every woman's most important job is to fit a cultural ideal of beauty.	Boycott products that suggest women's appearance is their most important characteristic.
	Only men are suited for the responsibility of high political office.	Actively support the fund-raising and campaigns of women candidates.
	Girls are not as good as boys at sports.	Develop sports teams—baseball, football, hockey, etc.—based upon skill, not gender.
	Women are too emotional to serve as effective police officers or military personnel.	Create equity in the military so that women have equal responsibilities and equal opportunities.
Practitioners/ educators	Girls are just not good at math and science.	Encourage girls to develop math and science skills and boys to develop their empathic sides.
	It is more important for girls and women to learn to care for their families than develop workplace skills.	Teach both girls and boys workplace and home skills; Design reading assignments with diverse role models.

Toolbox for Change

For	Images/Perceptions	Strategies for change
	An assertive woman is a "bitch."	Validate women's voices and ability to stand up for themselves.
	Boys and men will achieve more in their lives, so they deserve more attention.	Recognize that both girls and women and boys and men have a need to achieve and have equivalent potential; encourage girls to talk in class.
	A woman cannot form an identity separate from the man she marries.	Recognize that every person is capable of forming a strong self-identity.
	Traditional "masculine" characteristics are more valuable than "feminine" characteristics.	Provide gender issues workshops for all practitioners and educators.
	Girls and women must be thin to be beautiful.	Educate the public about the dangers of eating disorders, especially via media.

REFERENCES

Acitelli, L. K., & Antonucci, T. C. (1994). Gender differences in the link between marital support and satisfaction in older couples. *Journal of Personality and Social Psychology, 67*, 688–698.

Alington, D. E., & Troll, L. E. (1984). Social change and equality: The roles of women and economics. In G. Baruch & J. Brooks-Gunn (Eds.), *Women in mid-life* (pp. 181–202). New York: Plenum.

American Association of University Women (AAUW). (1992). *The AAUW report: How schools shortchange girls.* Washington, DC: The American Association of University Women Educational Foundation.

Arber, S., & Ginn, J. (1994). Women and aging. *Reviews in Clinical Gerontology, 4*, 349–358.

Arch, E. C., & Cummins, D. E. (1989). Structured and unstructured exposure to computers: Sex differences in attitude and use among college students. *Sex Roles, 20*, 245–254.

Arnold, F., & Kuo, E. C. (1984). The value of daughters and sons: A comparative study of the gender preferences of parents. *Journal of Comparative Family Studies, 15*, 299–318.

Bailey, W. T., Harrell, D. R., & Anderson, L. E. (1993). The image of middle-aged and older women in magazine advertisements. *Educational Gerontology, 19,* 97–103.

Basow, S. A. (1992). *Gender stereotypes and roles* (3rd ed.). Pacific Grove, CA: Brooks/Cole.

Baxter, J. (1992). Power attitudes and time: The domestic division of labor. *Journal of Comparative Family Studies, 23,* 165–182.

Bay-Cheng, L. Y., Zucker, A. N., Stewart, A. J., & Pomerleau, C. S. (2002). Linking femininity, weight concern, and mental health among Latina, black, and white women. *Psychology of Women Quarterly, 26,* 36–45.

Bazzini, D. G., McIntosh, W. D., Smith, S. M., Cook, S., & Harris, C. (1997). The aging woman in popular film: Underrepresented, unattractive, unfriendly, and unintelligent. *Sex Roles, 36,* 531–543.

Beckwith, J. B. (1992). Stereotypes and reality in the division of household labor. *Social Behavior and Personality, 20,* 283–288.

Bekker, M. H. J. (1996). Agoraphobia and gender: A review. *Clinical Psychology Review, 16,* 129–146.

Belenky, M. F., Clinchy, R. M., Goldberger, N. R., & Tarule, J. M. (1986). *Women's ways of knowing.* New York: Basic Books.

Belgrave, L., & Haug, M. (1987). *Interaction of health and pension: The effects on women's early retirement.* Proceedings of the 1987 Public Health Conference on Records and Statistics.

Bergquist, W. H., Greenberg, E. M., & Klaum, G. A. (1993). *In our fifties: Voices of men and women reinventing our lives.* San Francisco: Jossey-Bass.

Betz, N. E., & Fitzgerald, L. F. (1987). *The career psychology of women.* Orlando, FL: Academic Press.

Bianchi, S. M., Milkie, M. A., Sayer, L. C., & Robinson, J. P. (2000). Is anyone doing the housework? Trends in the gender division of household labor. *Social Forces, 79,* 191–228.

Biernat, M., & Wortman, C. B. (1991). Sharing of home responsibilities between professionally employed women and their husbands. *Journal of Personality and Social Psychology, 60,* 844–860.

Bordelon, K. W. (1985). Sexism in reading materials. *Reading Teacher, 38,* 792–797.

Bosscher, R. J., Van Der Aa, H., Van Dasler, M., Deeg, D. J., & Smit, J. H. (1995). Physical performance and physical self-efficacy in the elderly: A pilot study. *Journal of Aging and Health, 7,* 459–475.

Botkin, D. R., Weeks, M. O., & Morris, J. E. (2000). Changing marriage role expectations: 1961–1996. *Sex Roles, 42,* 933–942.

Bridges, J. S., Etaugh, C., & Barnes-Farrell, J. (2002). Trait judgments of stay-at-home and employed parents: A function of social role and/or shifting standards? *Psychology of Women Quarterly, 26,* 140–150.

Brody, J. E. (1997, November 4). Girls and puberty: The crisis years. *The New York Times,* p. B8.

Brown, L. S. (1987). Lesbians, weight, and eating: New analyses and perspectives. In Boston Lesbian Psychologies Collective (Ed.), *Lesbian psychologies* (pp. 294–309). Urbana, IL: University of Illinois Press.

Canetto, S. S., Kaminski, P. L., & Felicio, D. M. (1995). Typical and optional aging in women and men: Is there a double standard? *International Journal of Aging and Human Development, 40,* 1–21.

Caplan, P. J. (1995). *They say you're crazy: How the world's most powerful psychiatrists decide who's normal.* Reading, MA: Addison Wesley.

Cash, T. F., & Henry, P. E. (1995). Women's body images: The results of a national survey in the U.S.A. *Sex Roles, 33,* 19–28.

Cattarin, J. A., Thompson, J. K., Thomas, C., & Williams, R. (2000). Body image, mood, and televised images of attractiveness: The role of social comparison. *Journal of Social and Clinical Psychology, 19,* 220–239.

Chaffin, R. J., & Winston, M. (1991). Conceptions of parenthood. *Journal of Applied and Social Psychology, 21,* 1726–1757.

Chrisler, J. C., & Ghiz, L. (1993). Body image issues of older women. *Women & Therapy, 14,* 67–75.

Clark, R., Lennon, R., & Morris, L. (1993). Of Caldecotts and kings: Gendered images in recent American children's books by black and non-black illustrators. *Gender & Society, 7,* 227–245.

Cole, E., & Rothblum, E. (1990). Commentary on "Sexuality and the mid-life woman." *Psychology of Women Quarterly, 14,* 509–512.

Dansky, B., & Kilpatrick, D. (1997). Effects of sexual harassment. In W. O'Donohue (Ed.), *Sexual harassment: Theory, research, and treatment.* Boston: Allyn & Bacon.

Demarest, J., & Allen, R. (2000). Body image: Gender, ethnic, and age differences. *Journal of Social Psychology, 140,* 465–472.

DeMeis, D., & Perkins, H. W. (1996). "Supermoms" of the nineties: Homemakers and employees' mothers' performance and perceptions of the motherhood role. *Journal of Family Issues, 17,* 776–792.

Doyle, J., & Paludi, M. A. (1998). *Sex and gender: The human experience* (4th ed.). New York: McGraw-Hill.

Dunn, K. (1994). Why do women remake their bodies to fit the fashion? In K. M. Hicks (Ed.), *Misdiagnosis: Woman as a disease* (pp. 95–97). Allentown, PA: People's Medical Society.

Eagly, A. H., Wood, W., & Diekman, A. (2000). Social role theory of sex differences and similarities. In T. Eckes & H. M. Trautner (Eds.), *The developmental social psychology of gender* (pp. 123–174). Mahway, NJ: Erlbaum.

Eccles, J. S. (1987). Gender roles and women's achievement-related decisions. *Psychology of Women Quarterly, 11,* 135–172.

Erikson, E. H. (1964). The inner and outer self: Reflections on womanhood. *Daedelus, 93,* 582–606.

Erikson, E. H. (1968). *Identity, youth, and crisis.* New York: Norton.

Etaugh, C. (1993). Women in the middle and later years. In F. L. Denmark & M. A. Paludi (Eds.), *Psychology of women: A handbook of issues and theories* (pp. 213–246). Westport, CT: Greenwood Press.

Evans, L., & Davies, K. (2000). No sissy boys here: A content analysis of the representation of masculinity in elementary school reading textbooks. *Sex Roles, 42,* 255–270.

Evans, P. C. (2003). "If only I were thin like her, maybe I could be happy like her": The self-implications of associating a thin female ideal with life success. *Psychology of Women Quarterly, 27,* 209–214.

Feinman, S. (1981). Why is cross-sex-role behavior more approved for girls than for boys? A status characteristic approach. *Sex Roles, 7,* 289–300.

Feiring, C., & Lewis, M. (1987). The child's social network: Sex differences from three to six years. *Sex Roles, 17,* 621–636.

Felmlee, D. H. (1994). Who's on top? Power in romantic relationships. *Sex Roles, 31,* 275–295.

Fitzgerald, L. F., & Crites, J. O. (1980). Toward a career psychology of women: What do we know? What do we need to know? *Journal of Counseling Psychology, 27,* 44–62.

Fitzgerald, L. F., & Omerod, A. (1993). Sexual harassment in academia and the workplace. In F. L. Denmark & M. A. Paludi (Eds.), *Psychology of women: Handbook of issues and theories.* Westport, CT: Greenwood Press.

Fowers, B. J. (1991). His and her marriage: A multivariate study of gender and marital satisfaction. *Sex Roles, 24,* 209–221.

Fowers, B. J., Applegate, B., Tredinnick, M., & Slusher, J. (1996). His and her individualism? Sex bias and individualism in psychologists' responses to case vignettes. *Journal of Psychology, 130,* 159–174.

Frederick, C. M., & Grow, V. M. (1996). A mediational model of autonomy, self-esteem, and eating disordered attitudes and behaviors. *Psychology of Women Quarterly, 20,* 217–228.

Fredrickson, B. L., & Roberts, T. (1997). Objectification theory: Toward understanding women's lived experiences and mental health risks. *Psychology of Women Quarterly, 21,* 173–207.

Freiberg, P. (1991). Self-esteem gender gap widens in adolescence. *APA Monitor, 22*(4), 29.

Friedan, B. (1993). *The fountain of age.* New York: Simon & Schuster.

Frieze, I. H., Ferligoj, A., Kogovsek, T., Rener, T., Horvat, J., & Sarlija, N. (2003). Gender-role attitudes in university students in the United States, Slovenia, and Croatia. *Psychology of Women Quarterly, 27,* 256–261.

Funk, N., & Mueller, M. (Eds.). (1993). *Gender politics and post-communism: Reflections from Eastern Europe and the former Soviet Union.* New York: Routledge.

Furnham, A., & Bitar, N. (1993). The stereotyped portrayal of men and women on British television. *Sex Roles, 29*, 297–310.

Furnham, A., & Twiggy, M. (1999). Sex-role stereotyping in television commercials: A review and comparison of fourteen studies done on five continents over 25 years. *Sex Roles, 41*, 413–437.

Gergen, M. M. (1990). Finished at 40: Women's development within the patriarchy. *Psychology of Women Quarterly, 14*, 471–494.

Gilligan, C. (1982). *In a different voice: Psychological theory and women's development.* Cambridge, MA: Harvard University Press.

Ginorio, A., & Huston, M. (2000). *¡Si, se puede! Yes, we can: Latinas in school.* Washington, DC: American Association of University Women's Educational Foundation.

Glick, P., Sakalli-Ugurlu, N., Ferreira, M. C., & de Souza, M. A. (2002). Ambivalent sexism and attitudes toward wife abuse in Turkey and Brazil. *Psychology of Women Quarterly, 26*, 292–297.

Grambs, J. D. (1989). *Women over forty: Visions and realities* (Rev. ed.). New York: Springer.

Greer, G. (1992). *The challenge: Women, ageing and the menopause.* New York: Knopf.

Grieshaber, S. (1998). Constructing the gendered infant. In N. Yelland et al. (Eds.), *Gender in early childhood.* New York: Routledge.

Haj-Yahia, M. M. (1998). A patriarchal perspective on beliefs about wife beating among Palestinian men from the West Bank and the Gaza Strip. *Journal of Family Issues, 19*, 595–621.

Haj-Yahia, M. M. (2002). Beliefs of Jordanian women about wife-beating. *Psychology of Women Quarterly, 26*, 282–291.

Halas, C., & Matteson, R. (1978). *Paradoxes: Key to women's distress. I've done so well—why do I feel so bad?* New York: Ballantine.

Hall, R. M., & Sandler, B. R. (1982). *The classroom climate: A chilly one for women?* [Project on the Status and Education of Women]. Washington, DC: Association of American Colleges.

Hamilton, M. C. (1991). *Preferences for sons or daughters and the sex role characteristics of the potential parents.* Paper presented at the meeting of the Association for Women in Psychology, Hartford, Connecticut.

Handwerker, W. (1999). Cultural diversity, stress and depression: Working women in the Americas. *Journal of Women's Health and Gender Based Medicine, 8*, 1303–1311.

Hardy, M. A., & Hazelrigg, L. E. (1995). Gender, race/ethnicity, and poverty in later life. *Journal of Aging Studies, 9*, 43–63.

Hare-Mustin, R. T. (1983). An appraisal of the relationship between women and psychotherapy: 80 years after the case of Dora. *American Psychologist, 38*, 593–601.

Harway, M., Hansen, M., Rossman, B. B. R., Geffner, R., & Deitch, I. (1996). Families affected by domestic violence. In M. Harway (Ed.),

Treating the changing family: Handling normative and unusual events (pp. 163–190). New York: Wiley.

Harway, M., & O'Neil, J. M. (Eds.). (1999). *What causes men's violence against women?* Thousand Oaks, CA: Sage Publications.

Haworth-Hoeppner, S. (2000). The critical shapes of body image: The role of culture and family in the production of eating disorders. *Journal of Marriage and the Family, 62,* 212–227.

Hayflick, L. (1994). *How and why we age.* New York: Ballantine Books.

Healey, S. (1986). Growing to be an old woman: Aging and ageism. In J. Alexander, D. Berrow, L. Domitrovich, M. Donnelly, & C. McLean (Eds.), *Women and aging* (pp. 58–62). Corvallis, OR: Calyx.

Hebl, M. R., & Heatherton, T. F. (1998). The stigma of obesity in women: The difference is black and white. *Personality and Social Psychology Bulletin, 24,* 417–426.

Heilbrun, C. (1991). *The last gift of time: Life beyond sixty.* New York: Dell.

Helson, R., & Wink, P. (1992). Personality change in women from the early 40s to the early 50s. *Psychology and Aging, 7,* 46–55.

Henriques, G. R., & Calhoun, L. G. (1999). Gender and ethnic differences in the relation between body esteem and self-esteem. *Journal of Psychology, 133,* 357–368.

Hess, B., & Waring, J. (1983). Family relationships of older women: A women's issue. In E. W. Markson (Ed.), *Older women: Issues and prospects* (pp. 227–251). Lexington, MA: Lexington Books.

Hessler, R. M., Jia, S., Madsen, R., & Pazaki, H. (1995). Gender, social networks and survival time: A 20-year study of the rural elderly. *Archives of Gerontology and Geriatrics, 21,* 291–306.

Heyn, D. (1989, July/August). Body hate. *Ms.,* pp. 35–36.

Huston, A. (1983). Sex typing. In P. H. Mussen (Ed.), *Handbook of child psychology* (Vol. 4). New York: Wiley & Sons.

Jack, D. C. (1991). *Silencing the self: Women and depression.* Cambridge, MA: Harvard University Press.

Jack, D. C. (1999). Silencing the self: Inner dialogues and outer realities. In T. Joiner & J. C. Coyne (Eds.), *The interactional nature of depression: Advances in interpersonal approaches* (pp. 221–246). Washington, DC: American Psychological Association.

John, D., & Shelton, B. A. (1997). The production of gender among black and white women and men: The case of household labor. *Sex Roles, 36,* 171–193.

John, D., Shelton, B. A., & Luschen, K. (1995). Race, ethnicity, gender, and perceptions of fairness. *Journal of Family Issues, 16,* 357–379.

Jong, E. (1994). *Fear of fifty.* New York: Harper Collins.

Jordan, J. V., Kaplan, A. G., Miller, J. B., Stiver, I. P., & Surrey, J. L. (1991). *Women's growth in connection: Writings from the Stone Center.* New York: Guilford Press.

Kaschak, E. (1992). *Engendered lives: A new psychology of women's experiences.* New York: Basic Books.

Kaufman, D. R. (1995). Professional women: How real are the recent gains? In J. Freeman (Ed.), *Women: A feminist perspective* (5th ed., pp. 287–305). Mountain View, CA: Mayfield.

Kilbourne, J. (1994). Still killing us softly: Advertising and the obsession with thinness. In P. Fallon, M. A. Katzman, & S. C. Wooley (Eds.), *Feminist perspectives on eating disorders* (pp. 395–418). New York: Guilford Press.

Kling, K. C., Hyde, J. S., Showers, C. J., & Buswell, B. N. (1999). Gender differences in self-esteem: A meta-analysis. *Psychological Bulletin, 125,* 470–500.

Klonoff, E. A., Landrine, H., & Campbell, R. (2000). Sexist discrimination may account for well-known gender differences in psychiatric symptoms. *Psychology of Women Quarterly, 24,* 93–99.

Kolbenschlag, M. (1981). *Kiss Sleeping Beauty goodbye.* Toronto, Canada: Bantam.

Kortenhaus, C. M., & Demarest, J. (1993). Gender role stereotyping in children's literature: An update. *Sex Roles, 28,* 219–232.

La Freniere, P., Strayer, F. F., & Gauthier, R. (1984). The emergence of same-sex affiliative preferences among preschool peers: A developmental/ethological perspective. *Child Development, 55,* 1958–1965.

Leiblum, S. R. (1990). Sexuality and the midlife woman. *Psychology of Women Quarterly, 14,* 495–508.

Levy, A., & Paludi, M. A. (1997). *Workplace sexual harassment.* Englewood Cliffs, NJ: Prentice-Hall.

Lobel, T. F., Stone, M., & Winch, G. (1997). Masculinity, popularity, and self-esteem among Israeli preadolescent girls. *Sex Roles, 36,* 395–408.

Logue, B. J. (1991). Women at risk: Predictors of financial stress for retired women workers. *Gerontologist, 31,* 657–665.

Lopata, H. Z. (1979). *Women as widows.* New York: Elsevier.

Lytton, H., & Romney, D. M. (1991). Parents' differential socialization of boys and girls: A meta-analysis. *Psychological Bulletin, 109,* 267–296.

Maccoby, E. E. (1998). *Sex differences in behavior: The debate continues.* Cambridge, MA: Belknap Press of Harvard University Press.

Mansfield, P. K., & Koch, P. B. (1998). Qualities midlife women desire in their sexual relationships and their changing sexual response. *Psychology of Women Quarterly, 22,* 285–303.

Margolis, J., & Fisher, A. (2002). *Unlocking the clubhouse: Women in computing.* Cambridge, MA: Massachusetts Institute of Technology Press.

Markides, K. S. (1989). Consequences of gender differentials in life expectancy for black and Hispanic Americans. *International Journal of Aging and Human Development, 29,* 95–102.

Martin, C. L., & Fabes, R. A. (2001). The stability and consequences of young children's same-sex peer interactions. *Developmental Psychology, 37*, 431–446.

Martz, D. M., Handley, K. B., & Eisler, R. M. (1995). The relationship between feminine gender role stress, body image, and eating disorders. *Psychology of Women Quarterly, 19*, 493–508.

Massey, G., Hahn, K., & Sekulic, D. (1995). Women, men, and the "second shift" in socialist Yugoslavia. *Gender & Society, 9*, 359–379.

Matlin, M. W. (1996). *The psychology of women* (3rd ed.). Fort Worth, TX: Harcourt Brace.

McClelland, D. (1961). *The achieving society.* New York: Van Nostrand.

McKinley, N. M., & Hyde, J. S. (1996). The Objectified Body Consciousness Scale. *Psychology of Women Quarterly, 20*, 181–215.

Michaelieu, Q. (1997). Female identity, gendered parenting and adolescent women's self-esteem. *Feminism & Psychology, 7*, 328–333.

Miller, J. B. (1986). *Toward a new psychology of women* (2nd ed.). Boston: Beacon.

Mitchell, V., & Helson, R. (1990). Women's prime in life. Is it the 50's? *Psychology of Women Quarterly, 14*, 451–470.

Moore, D. (1995). Gender role attitudes and division of labor: Sex or occupation-type differences? An Israeli example. *Journal of Social Behavior and Personality, 10*, 215–234.

Morinaga, Y., Frieze, I. H., & Ferligoj, A. (1993). Career plans and gender-role attitudes of college students in the United States, Japan, and Slovenia. *Sex Roles, 29*, 317–334.

Mueller, K. A., & Yoder, J. D. (1997). Gendered norms for family size, employment, and occupation: Are there personal costs for violating them? *Sex Roles, 36*, 207–220.

Munson, L., Hulin, C., & Drasgow, F. (2000). Longitudinal analysis of dispositional influences and sexual harassment: Effects on job and psychological outcomes. *Personnel Psychology, 53*, 21–46.

Neft, N., & Levine, A. (1997). *Where women stand: An international report on the status of women in 140 countries, 1997–1998.* New York: Random House.

Neugarten, B. L. (Ed.). (1968). *Middle age and aging: A reader in social psychology.* Chicago: University of Chicago Press.

Niemela, P., & Lento, R. (1993). The significance of the 50th birthday for women's individuation. *Women & Therapy, 14*, 117–127.

Nutt, R. L. (1999). Women's gender-role socialization, gender-role conflict, and abuse: A review of predisposing factors. In. M. Harway & J. M. O'Neil (Eds.), *What causes men's violence against women?* (pp. 117–134). Thousand Oaks, CA: Sage Publications.

O'Neil, J. M., & Egan, J. (1992). Abuses of power against women: Sexism, gender role conflict, and psychological violence. In E. P. Cook (Ed.),

Women, relationships and power: Implications for counseling (pp. 49–78). Alexandria, VA: American Counseling Association Press.

Orenstein, P. (1994). *School girls: Young women, self-esteem, and the confidence gap.* New York: Anchor.

Paludi, M. A. (Ed.). (1996). *Sexual harassment on college campuses: Abusing the ivory tower.* Albany: State University of New York Press.

Paludi, M. A. (2002). *The psychology of women* (2nd ed.). Upper Saddle River, NJ: Prentice Hall.

Patterson, M. (1996). Women's employment patterns, pension coverage, and retirement planning. In C. Costello & B. Krimgold (Eds.), *The American woman 1996–97: Women and work* (pp. 148–165). New York: Norton.

Pipher, M. (1994). *Reviving Ophelia: Saving the selves of adolescent girls.* New York: Ballantine.

Pomerleau, A., Bolduc, D., Malcuit, G., & Cossette, L. (1990). Pink or blue: Environmental gender stereotypes in the first two years of life. *Sex Roles, 22,* 359–367.

Pooler, W. S. (1991). Sex of child preference among college students. *Sex Roles, 25,* 560–576.

Prentice, D. A., & Carranza, E. (2002). What women and men shouldn't be, are allowed to be, and don't have to be: The contents of prescriptive gender stereotypes. *Psychology of Women Quarterly, 26,* 269–281.

Pumariega, A. J. (1997). Body dissatisfaction among Hispanic and Asian-American girls. *Journal of Adolescent Health, 21,* p. 1.

Purcell, P., & Stewart, L. (1990). Dick and Jane in 1989. *Sex Roles, 22,* 177–185.

Reid, P. T., & Paludi, M. A. (1993). Psychology of women: Conception to adolescence. In F. L. Denmark & M. A. Paludi (Eds.), *Psychology of women: A handbook of issues and theories.* Westport, CT: Greenwood Press.

Robinson, C. C., & Morris, J. T. (1986). The gender-stereotyped nature of Christmas toys received by 36-, 48-, and 60-month-old children: A comparison between nonrequested and requested toys. *Sex Roles, 15,* 21–32.

Rodin, J., Silberstein, L. R., & Striegel-Moore, R. H. (1984). Women and weight. A normative discontent. In T. B. Sonderegger (Ed.), *Psychology and gender: Nebraska Symposium on Motivation* (pp. 267–307). Lincoln: University of Nebraska Press.

Rolandelli, D. R. (1991). Gender role portrayal analysis of children's television programming in Japan. *Human Relations, 44,* 1273–1299.

Rostosky, S. S., & Travis, C. B. (1996). Menopause research and the dominance of the bio-medical model 1984–1994. *Psychology of Women Quarterly, 20,* 285–312.

Rountree, C. (1993). *On women turning 50: Celebrating mid-life discoveries.* San Francisco: Harper.

Rubin, J. Z., Provenzano, F. J., & Luria, Z. (1974). The eye of the beholder: Parents' views on sex of newborns. *American Journal of Orthopsychiatry, 44*, 512–519.

Rudman, L. A., & Glick, P. (2001). Prescriptive gender stereotypes and backlash toward agentic women. *Journal of Social Issues, 57*, 743–762.

Rudolf, H., & Priebe, S. (1999). Subjective quality of life in female inpatients with depression: A longitudinal study. *International Journal of Social Psychology, 45*, 238–246.

Russianoff, P. (1981). *Why do I think I am nothing without a man?* New York: Bantam.

Russo, N. F. (1990). Overview: Forging research priorities for women's mental health. *American Psychologist, 45*, 368–373.

Russo, N. F., & Greene, B. (1993). Women and mental health. In F. L. Denmark & M. A. Paludi (Eds.), *Psychology of women: A handbook of issues and theories.* Westport, CT: Greenwood Press.

Ryder, E. A. (2000). *Our voices: Psychology of women.* Belmont, CA: Wadsworth.

Sadker, M., & Sadker, D. (1994). *Failing at fairness: How America's schools cheat girls.* New York: Scribners.

Saltzberg, E. A., & Chrisler, J. C. (1995). Beauty is the beast: Psychological effects of the pursuit of the perfect female body. In J. Freeman (Ed.), *Women: A feminist perspective* (5th ed., pp. 306–315). Mountain View, CA: Mayfield.

Sang, B. E. (1993). Existential issues of midlife lesbians. In L. D. Garnets & D. C. Kimmel (Eds.), *Psychological perspectives on lesbian and gay male experiences* (pp. 500–516). New York: Columbia University Press.

Schroeder, K. A., Blood, L. L., & Maluso, D. (1992). An intergenerational analysis of expectations for women's career and family roles. *Sex Roles, 26*, 273–291.

Seem, S. R., & Johnson, E. (1998). Gender bias among counseling trainees: A study of case conceptualization. *Counselor Education and Supervision, 37*, 257–268.

Shacher, R. (1991). His and her marital satisfaction: The double standard. *Sex Roles, 25*, 451–467.

Sheehy, G. (1992). *The silent passage.* New York: Random House.

Shumaker, S. A., & Hill, O. R. (1991). Gender differences in social support and physical health. *Health Psychology, 10*, 102–111.

Shye, D., Mullooly, J. P., Freeborn, D. K., & Pope, C. R. (1995). Gender differences in the relationship between social network support and mortality: A longitudinal study of an elderly cohort. *Social Science and Medicine, 41*, 935–947.

Siegel, R. J. (1993). Between midlife and old age: Never too old to learn. *Women & Therapy, 14*, 173–185.

Signorielli, N. (1989). Television and conceptions about sex roles: Maintaining conventionality and the status quo. *Sex Roles, 21*, 341–360.

Signorielli, N., & Bacue, A. (1999). Recognition and respect: A content analysis of prime-time television characters across three decades. *Sex Roles, 40*, 527–544.

Silverman, M., Skirboll, E., & Payne, J. (1996). An examination of women's retirement: African American women. *Journal of Cross-Cultural Gerontology, 11*, 319–334.

Sinnott, J. D. (1984). Older men, older women: Are their perceived roles similar? *Sex Roles, 10*, 847–856.

Sontag, S. (1972, September 23). The double standard of aging. *Saturday Review*, pp. 29–38.

Spence, J. T., & Buckner, C. E. (2000). Instrumental and expressive traits, trait stereotypes, and sexist attitudes: What do they signify? *Psychology of Women Quarterly, 24*, 44–62.

Sperberg, E. D., & Stabb, S. D. (1998). Depression in women as related to anger and mutuality in relationships. *Psychology of Women Quarterly, 22*, 223–238.

Starrels, M. E. (1994). Husbands' involvement in female gender-typed household chores. *Sex Roles, 31*, 473–491.

Steele, J., James, J. B., & Barnett, R. C. (2002). Learning in a man's world: Examining the perceptions of undergraduate women in male-dominated academic areas. *Psychology of Women Quarterly, 26*, 46–50.

Steil, J. M. (1997). *Marital equality: Its relationship to the well-being of husbands and wives*. Thousand Oaks, CA: Sage.

Striegel-Moore, R., & Smolak, L. (2000). The influence of ethnicity on eating disorders in women. In R. Eisler et al. (Eds.), *Handbook of gender, culture, and health*. Mahwah, NJ: Erlbaum.

Thompson, J. M. (1995). Silencing the self. *Psychology of Women Quarterly, 19*, 337–353.

Thompson, T., & Zerbinos, E. (1997). Television cartoons: Do children notice it's a boy's world? *Sex Roles, 37*, 415–432.

Thornton, B., & Maurice, J. (1997). Physique contrast effect: Adverse impact of idealized body images for women. *Sex Roles, 37*, 433–439.

Unger, R., & Crawford, M. (1992). *Women and gender: A feminist psychology*. New York: McGraw-Hill.

United Nations. (1995). *The world's women 1995. Trends and statistics*. New York: United Nations Publications.

Urberg, K. A. (1982). The development of the concepts of masculinity and femininity in young children. *Sex Roles, 6*, 659–668.

U.S. Bureau of the Census. (1996). *Marital status and living arrangements: March 1994*. Washington, DC: U.S. Government Printing Office.

Vernon, J. A., Williams, J. A., Jr., Phillips, T., & Wilson, J. (1991). Media stereotyping: A comparison of the way elderly women and men are portrayed on prime-time television. *Journal of Women & Aging, 2,* 55–68.

Wade, M. E. (2001). Women and salary negotiation: The costs of self-advocacy. *Psychology of Women Quarterly, 25,* 65–77.

Walker, B. A., Reis, S. M., & Leonard, J. S. (1992). A developmental investigation of the lives of gifted women. *Gifted Child Quarterly, 36,* 201–206.

Walsh, W. B., & Osipow, S. H. (1994). *Career counseling for women.* Hillsdale, NJ: Erlbaum.

Whitbourne, S. K. (1985). The psychological construction of the life span. In J. E. Birren & K. W. Schaie (Eds.), *Handbook of the psychology of aging* (pp. 594–618). New York: Van Nostrand Reinhold.

Whitbourne, S. K., & Hulicka, I. M. (1990). Ageism in undergraduate psychology texts. *American Psychologist, 45,* 1127–1136.

Wolf, N. (1991). *The beauty myth.* New York: William Morrow.

Wright, E. O., Shire, K., Hwang, S., Dolan, M., & Baxter, J. (1992). The non-effects of class on the gender division of labor in the home: A comparative study of Sweden and the United States. *Gender & Society, 6,* 252–282.

Wright, J. C., Huston, A. C., Vandewater, E. A., Bickham, D. S., Scantlin, R. M., Kotler, J. A., et al. (2001). American children's use of electronic media in 1997: A national survey. *Journal of Applied Developmental Psychology, 22,* 31–47.

Yllo, K. A., & Straus, M. A. (1990). Patriarchy and violence against wives: The impact of structural and normative factors. In M. A. Straus & R. J. Gelles (Eds.), *Physical violence in American families* (pp. 383–399). New Brunswick, NJ: Transaction Publications.

Yoder, J. D. (2002). 2001 Division 35 Presidential Address. Context matters: Understanding tokenism processes and their impact on women's work. *Psychology of Women Quarterly, 26,* 1–8.

CHAPTER 2

Powerpuff Girls: Fighting Evil Gender Messages or Postmodern Paradox?

Carole Baroody Corcoran
Judith A. Parker

GIRL (INTERRUPTED) POWER

Trust me. You don't even have to own a television set for the invasion to happen. If you are close to a child under ten who has been labeled "female" in the United States, chances are very good that the Powerpuff Girls already rule your world. For the uninitiated, the Powerpuff Girls are a marketing empire aimed at young girls. Created by a male cartoonist in 1998, the Powerpuff Girls aired on the Cartoon Network. By the release of their successful big-screen feature film in 2002, Powerpuff retail merchandising profits had already exceeded a billion dollars (Havrilesky, 2002).

> This animated series featured three flying girls Blossom, Buttercup, and Bubbles—who, under the mentor ship of Professor Utonium, worked to keep the town of Townsville free of danger. According to the show's premise, Professor Utonium was trying to create three perfect little girls but accidentally added the powerful Chemical X. Instead of sweet, girly-girls, he got three cute but tough super heroes. (Fisherkeller, 2002, p. 189)

In a land populated by pink princesses who each seem to own a double-digit horde of Barbies (my child is bombarded with gifts of Barbies, which make up a constantly growing pile in our closet), what could possibly be wrong with three cartoon girl superheroes, you may ask? Let's look at the subtext of the cartoon's premise. Instead of "God created woman" (perfect "girly" females), we have "man played God" (science). Given the inevitable mortal screw-up, we end up with the familiar biological mutation "a mad scientist-created monster"—in this case, aggressive, destructive, adorable, saucer-eyed girls. The Powerpuff Girls embody *man*-made mistakes, but hey, at least these three flukes of nature are cute *and* tough! Still, Blossom, Buttercup, and Bubbles would never pose as a serious threat to Professor Utonium. After all, the Powerpuff Girls possess amazing superpowers due to a freak accident, a hazardous exposure to an unnatural, masculinizing agent. This is in stark contrast to a much more interesting "mad scientist" narrative that we will examine later in a Missy "Misdemeanor" Elliott music video.

Today, despite popular culture's successful marketing of merchandise (from toys and clothing to music) bearing bold slogans like "Girls Rule" and "Girl Power," boys know from the get-go that girls lack boys' authentic power. In truth, the Powerpuff Girls are "powder puff pussies," who, like gender-reversed powerpuff football players, never pose a threat to real (that is, male) power. Indeed, these B-girls are male-defined and thus necessarily have no source of power that is actually their own. Moreover, in our so-called post-feminist, post-patriarchal new world, "being a girl," by definition, requires that female children act blissfully unaware of their *powerlessness.* Like the paradox of being cute *and* tough, girls are expected to embrace and embody an obvious and inherent *contradiction* without question or notice.

As a young radical feminist who came of age in the late 1960s and early 1970s, I decided later to search the Internet for the perspective of my younger sisters in struggle. Interestingly, the first thing I found confirmed and echoed my age-related concerns. This online editorial on "grrl" power and third-wave feminism refers to the Powerpuff Girls when noting the tendency for young women to reject the label "feminist" while living out feminist ways of being that are a direct result of hard-won benefits made possible by older feminists. The editorial states,

> For older feminists, the reluctance of young women to take on a feminist identity is something to reckon with. The discourse of girl power evolving within the new strands of feminism requires more and deeper discussion in order to reach a "third wave" of feminism beyond Buffy, Dark Angel, Ally McBeal, Motoko Kusanagi, Lara Croft, the Powerpuff girls, and Charlie's Angels. (Women in Action, 1998–2003)

In a similar vein, in an insightful *Salon* article exploring feminism, girl power, and the Powerpuff Girls, Havrilesky (2002) articulated the source of my fears better than I could at the time:

> That our heroes' girl-ness is beside the point might just be the most revolutionary aspect of the show. In some ways, these likable squeeze toys have pulled off the ultimate branding feat: They represent girl power without having to mention it. Given a recent Gallup poll that found that only 25 percent of women today consider themselves feminists, the Powerpuff Girls may reflect a shift from embracing political and social labels to choosing between carefully packaged products that have ideologies encoded deep within their shiny exteriors.

But real power cannot be found in packaged products. Instead, it demands a sense of agency, as in a mode of exerting power and, in doing so, an instrumentality that confers control. Thus, Powerpuff Girls lack *agency*, and they don't even know it! Their "girl power" exists as a quirk that derives from the needs of an external agent: their creator, a man. According to the story, the ill-fated experiment to produce perfect test tube girls (from a formula of sugar and spice) was motivated by the professor's weariness with the cold, cruel (male?) state of the world. Blossom, Bubbles, and Buttercup's intended existence was to serve as lovely cheerleaders, an antidote for the postmodern blues that ailed their chemically careless male sponsor and patriarch, a much older and wiser white man.

In order to decipher whether the "power" in Powerpuff Girls was a slick media recycling act, an old-school version of "girly powder puff fluff" that I chafed under as a child, I reached the point of no return. I had to watch the Powerpuff Girls.

TOWNSVILLE'S RULES GIRLS?

Given my shift, my six-year-old child was mildly shocked but ecstatic to find that she at long last had successfully gained my permission to watch an episode of *Powerpuff Girls*. Previously I had told her she could watch them when she was "old enough," after her preschool teacher advised me that the Powerpuff Girls were "bad and said swear words" (I was already getting into hot water with my child for using the swear word *stupid*). As TV-aversive parents know, despite a lack of commercial television viewing, my child was already well-versed in Powerpuff Girldom. Indeed, it ruled her kindergarten playground, and at age five she had wheedled me into buying her a cup at a convenience store that was so hideous-looking I couldn't

fathom why she wanted it so badly. After much pleading to my repeated refusals, I relented because she agreed to dump out the sugary
chemical liquid that was in the container. I was clueless about the
Powerpuff Girls but knew enough to feel duped when I realized later
that I had bought into some marketing ploy aimed at young girls.
Partly, this bug-eyed, bulging, demon-headed cup with what looked
like horns fooled me by not looking like all the other merchandising products aimed at my daughter. Those were cloying, sugary
sweet, and thus easy to spot and not buy without needing to know
whether they were Jasmine, Anastasia, or *that* Mermaid—the one who
made her Tita (grandmother) furious because she gave up her voice
for a man!

As we began viewing our maiden *Powerpuff Girls* episode, I was
momentarily perplexed and then quickly annoyed as I watched repeated bouts of girl-on-girl violence. (This action makes up the first
major portion of the episode.) "I thought they were supergirls. When
are they going to rescue someone?" I asked, barely disguising my disapproval. The plot in this particular episode involves Buttercup's first
lost tooth and subsequent discovery of the tooth fairy. With dollar
signs flashing from her eyes, she quickly realizes that by violently attacking Blossom and Bubbles, she can knock out their teeth (and then move
onto others) and stash a huge sack of coins under her bed, courtesy of the
tooth fairy.

Eventually the somewhat bemused professor gently intervenes.
Professor Utonium reminded me of the benign "Father knows best"
tradition of television "pops" from my childhood, sort of a Steven
Douglas (the single father played by actor Fred McMurray on *My
Three Sons*) only with more of Ozzie Nelson's goofiness thrown in
(teen idol Ricky Nelson's dad on *Ozzie and Harriet*). A recurring
plot device for the *Powerpuff Girls'* episodes, I would learn, involves
the damsels being rescued from their latest superpower mishaps by
the professor. Indeed in this episode, Buttercup comes to see the
error of her ways and, in the end, stops using her superpowers to beat
up her sisters and the town's villains for a profit.

Upon viewing my second *Powerpuff Girls* episode, I encountered
Townsville's boss, the mayor (in addition to a second standard plot
line). It turns out that the Powerpuff Girls *do* indeed save the day,
but only when they are summoned into action by a special phone, a
hotline directly wired from the mayor's office. The mayor, short in
stature and totally inept, like Mr. Magoo or Elmer Fudd, is prone to
bouts of weeping and is a bumbling sexist. Yet, he presides over

Townsville, thanks to three obsequious kindergarten girls and a silicone-enhanced secretary. "Is he the villain?" I asked, noting the patronizing manner that made his little darlings beam with delight. His faithful secretary, Ms. Bellum, or Sara, towers over her boss with a flowing red mane and voluptuous body—Sans Bellum! Picture the animated sexpot Jessica Rabbit (from *Who Framed Roger Rabbit?*) decapitated but somehow with an undisturbed coif. With just two potential female role models available (the other is their "plain Jane" school teacher), the Powerpuff Girls naturally worship Ms. Bellum. This faceless Gal Friday is infinitely smarter than Townsville's ruling patriarch, as is her trio of young protégés. However, all these females go to absurd lengths to play coy and/or dumb in order to preserve the mayor's authority, along with the illusion that this oaf is in charge. The mayor is like the man behind the curtain in *The Wizard of Oz*, only (thanks to the untiring efforts of his dames) his fraud is never exposed.

I had watched two *Powerpuff Girls* episodes, and both clearly illustrated critical features of patriarchy. "Oh, great," I thought as I watched Buttercup gleefully bust her sister's chops in the first episode, "just like 'real' girls"—who inevitably must turn on each other (here replete with cat fights) and compete to earn the favor of the head man, a powerful and frequently incompetent white male. I'll return later to the third episode we watched, which explicitly addresses feminism. There I also learned that girls should not confront, let alone beat up, their boy peers and that, perhaps more pertinently, it is a girl's responsibility to keep other girls in line. By now, I was not at all surprised to learn that according to the Cartoon Network figures, boys account for the majority (56 percent) of the *Powerpuff Girls'* children's audience (Havrilesky, 2002).

I was reminded of the feminist classic *The Creation of Patriarchy*, where Gerda Lerner (1986) articulated so well the requirement that girls and women must (and indeed do) play a crucial role in the perpetuation of male domination as the status quo. To wit:

> The system of patriarchy can function only with the cooperation of women. This cooperation is secured by a variety of means: gender indoctrination; educational deprivation; the denial to women of knowledge of their history; the dividing of women, one from another, by defining "respectability" and "deviance" according to women's sexual activities; by restraints and outright coercion; by discrimination in

access to economic resources and political power; and by rewarding class privileges to conforming women. (p. 217)

By definition, in a patriarchy, men (not women) rule, and most assuredly, *girls* never rule! How is it that these "girls rule" messages, superficially praising girls' power, instead inculcate norms of "pseudo power" for young females? Girls and adolescent females are not completely unaware of their limited agency. Rather, it seems that they must receive strict training to learn complicity in accepting this illusory notion of empowerment.

A question posed by Havrilesky (2002) alludes to the Powerpuff Girls' precarious state:

"Why take on a political label when you can wear a cool-looking T-shirt that says the same thing, but without any of the negative associations? Is she a feminist? Oh, no! She just loves those Powerpuff Girls!"

Why then is it so attractive to many (white) girls to accommodate a reality where boys rule, whites rule, merchandising rules, and girls have to pretend that they've got some kind of power they don't really have? What are the incentive and payoff for girls not imagining and not exercising their real powers? In a description of Blossom, Buttercup, and Bubbles' appeal, Havrilesky (2002) again may provide some clues. She says of the Powerpuff Girls:

> For hyper-analytical adults and avid third-wave feminists, they're animated proof that strong female characters can kick ass and take names without compromising their femininity. For children, and those grown-ups weary of gender-centric postulation, the teensy heroines do viewers the favor of skipping fancy-schmancy politics in the service of good humor.

Hmm, perhaps that's why I was fascinated when I turned to the Powerpuff Girls for instruction and, ultimately, deconstruction. Except for my own telling tendency to substitute "powder" for "power," at least Blossom, Buttercup, and Bubbles linguistically marked a site where power and girls coexisted in the same breath. But once decoded, what I found was a postmodern paradox: *The Powerpuff Girls have power only to the extent that they are complicit in supporting Professor Utonium's patriarchal laboratory world and only if they wield their superpowers in service of Townsville's official patriarch, the mayor.* However, my greatest surprise was in my discovery of just how well these supergirl media icons embodied the contradictory gender power messages aimed at very young *female* children and particularly the ones my own child is encountering.

GENDER PATROL: POWERPUFF GIRLS RUN
AWAY FROM BOYS!

Even if you are a strong, confident female child, kindergarten can be a rude awakening. I was reminded of my own 1950s grade school capability of "beating the boys" when two years ago, my athletic five-year-old described being the frequent target of male play-ground harassment. Her eyes lit up when I suggested that perhaps she and the girls should pull a "switcheroo," given that she was stronger and could run faster than the most aggressive offending boy. *I was pointing out a contradiction for her.* In a "switcheroo," I explained, the girls would catch the boys and "body lock" them so tight that *they* couldn't move and perhaps the boys could see how they liked it. The next day she came home crestfallen. Despite consid-erable effort, she could not find a single girl who was willing to participate in her "switcheroo" plan. Further, and perhaps more infu-riating, she was soundly chastised by the self-appointed "head" Powerpuff Girl, who informed her that *Powerpuff Girls ran AWAY from boys!*

As the work of Thorne (1986, 1993) demonstrates particularly well, the playground continues to function as a critical site for gender politics. Gender play involves constructing and enacting power asym-metries in children's gender relations as well as learning their cultural meanings. Thorne's analysis of gender play includes the concept of "border work," a mechanism for reinforcing "other" phobia, that is, interactions that strengthen group gender boundaries and create a sense of "the boys" and "the girls" as separate and opposing sides. Playground games like cross-gender chasing and capture, or "coo-ties," construct borders that effectively reinforce the boundaries be-tween boys and girls through both contact and avoidance (Thorne, 1993). These activities teach hierarchy and power differences that reflect stereotypical gender relationships in our culture at large. For example, Thorne found that boys are more aggressive and likely to invade girls' games. Her observations showed that girls' play tends to be more sexually defined and that they are also teased and violated more than (and by) boys. Overall, boys' play interaction patterns assert spatial, physical, and social dominance over girls, which, along with a healthy dose of entitlement, resembles proscribed traditionally gendered behavior expected of many adult men (Henley, 1977). More recent research findings are consistent and supportive. For example, Martin's (2003) work explains how preschoolers' bodies become gendered, along with the institutional practices that construct physical differences very early in life.

But let's go back to the playground and my child's failed attempt to enlist a Powerpuff Girl as an ally to pull a "switcheroo." It turns out that the next day she decided to chase and capture a boy (she chose her tormentor) *on her own*. Although she did not gain any Powerpuff Girl points (which thankfully was not her goal), after witnessing her behavior, the "boss" of the Powerpuff Girls began ordering the other Powerpuff Girls to chase and capture the boys. This dubious "victory" may have been due to age and gender-related shifts in playground dynamics rather than my child's individual bravery. However, it still provides her with a good, tangible example of the merits of her *agency*.

Last year, upon entering the first grade, my child informed me that she refused to be a "cootie girl" and play the current "hot" playground game. In this contemporary strain of "girls have cooties," boys who encounter any girl call her a cootie girl and run away. A cootie girl then could chase the boy in hopes of giving him cooties. As Thorne (1993) noted from her observations of gender play, chasing games often evolve into pollution rituals such as "cooties." Apparently, although boys and girls can give cooties to each other, girls are the key contaminators in the game. Girls can pass "cooties" on to other girls, but "cooties" are rarely, if ever, passed from boy to boy (another [homophobic as well] *contradiction* I pointed out to my child). In examining the dynamics of contamination and how it never occurs by male gender membership status alone, Thorne (1993) points out that "there is also a notable gender asymmetry, evident in the skewed patterning of cooties; *girls as a group are treated as an ultimate source of contamination*, while boys *as* boys—although maybe not as Chicanos or individuals with a physical disability—are exempt" (p. 192).

Together, my child and I came up with a "super cootie" game that would empower the girls and reward any boys who would break free of their gender group boundaries, but like the switcheroo, our plan required first the collaboration of at least one girl ally before my daughter could attempt to elicit a boy ally. I did know of one particular boy whom she and her (female) best friend both liked but did not "*like* like," because he was "not like" a boy. The rules are different now that she is in second grade. She's already experienced almost three years of intense public school indoctrination (and separatism) necessary to carefully construct and strictly enforce the required race, class, gender, and sexual orientation rules. Still, I'm convinced that pointing out gender (as well as other) asymmetries and planning corrective strategies to address power imbalances will serve her well, if not next year in the third grade, then perhaps in graduate school.

FROM COOTIE GIRLS TO COOTCHIE MAMAS: THE DOUBLE-BARRELED DOUBLE STANDARD

Almost from the very beginning of kindergarten, my daughter endured daily a period of being taunted to the point of tears on the bus by a popular boy. We had to rehearse "comebacks" and reactions that she decided "weren't mean" (since she had informed me that my initial responses were mean). Thus, as a five-year-old girl, she had to learn to defend herself in order to not continue to be an "easy" target. Later, I learned that the teasing started because she assertively rebuffed her tormentor's repeated attempts to kiss and hold her. The negative consequences that followed her refusal to allow unwanted male contact are disturbing as well because of their pervasiveness in schools (AAUW, 1993). To me, her suffering was a kindergarten variety of sexual harassment.

My child's experience was certainly not atypical for a female in kindergarten. It was normative as her "initiation" into this contradictory world of heterosexual gender politics. I was horrified when I realized as a mother that I had arrived at this "boys will be boys" point in the gender role socialization script, where my part was to help introduce and normalize the idea that invasive, callous, and mean behaviors could/should be construed as something positive—attraction! Was I expected to helpfully explain to my child that this uninvited negative attention was actually an indication of heterosexual romantic interest and regard for her? Indeed, that if a boy is aggressive or coercive, she should learn to tolerate it, but also perhaps be flattered? This is hardly a template for "girl power" or "girls rule," however "postfeminist" her Powerpuff world may construe itself to be.

A behavior pattern of (sexual) dominance and entitlement is acceptable strictly "for boys and men only," and it constitutes the privileged male side of the sexual double standard. My child's encounter with a first "boyfriend" is merely the precursor to the older and ageless version of the restrictions imposed on females by the double standard, replete with age-appropriate perils. Put simply, this dualism produces "material girls" who can only be "good" (virgin/madonna) or "bad" (bitch/whore). Often overlapping with the girl-on-girl aggression mentioned earlier, the danger and titillation provided by tales from the dark side of these dichotomies continues to flourish and is evident by the currently selling spate of "bad girl" books. With provocative titles like *Odd Girl Out: The Hidden Culture of Girls' Aggression* (Simmons, 2002); *The Secret Lives of Girls: What Good Girls Really Do—Sex Play, Aggression and Their Guilt* (Lamb, 2001); *Fast Girls: Teenage Tribes and the Myth of the Slut* (White, 2002); and *Queen Bees and Wannabes: Helping Your Daughter Survive Cliques, Gossip, Boyfriends and Other Realities of Adolescence* (Wiseman, 2002), the latest crop of "bad girl" books varies widely in terms of genre, origins of primary source material, intended audience, and much more, including the quality of ideas and scholarly merits.

Still, if we look for the barest common thread among all of them, it is that these narratives testify to the robust nature that the sexual double standard clearly enjoys as we enter a new millennium.

(HETEROSEXUAL) WHITE BOYS RULE

Despite three decades of unprecedented change in gender role definitions in the United States, the social constructions of gender remain adversarial (for example, the *opposite* sex), particularly when it comes to sexual behaviors and violence sanctioned and even glorified in males but not females. Known by the somewhat benign and highly recognized term, this stubborn, cock-eyed dictum called "the double standard" has lost none of its power or luster, particularly given the gender progress made in other areas (Hall, 2004).

The sexual double standard automatically confers tremendous (not to mention dangerous) power to all young males who consequently are socialized to learn to experience the male sex drive as something akin to hero Keanu Reeves's uncontrollable runaway bus from hell in the 1994 movie *Speed*. The flip side results in Sandra Bullock (the sexually self-negating young female) assuming a no-win, dangerous position that includes total responsibility for the task of steering and somehow putting the brakes on this reckless, impossible male force of nature. Indeed, the sexual double standard rewards such futile attempts at female agency with a romantic kiss at best from the real hero and, at worst, deserved punishment, most often by blaming a victim for her demise, regardless of whether or not she exercises *sexual agency*.

Like the "does she or doesn't she?" double standard itself, the overriding aim of some of the previously mentioned "fallen girl" books is to chronicle and perhaps caution but *not* to problematize or disrupt the patriarchal roots that produce, maintain, and reify these virgin/ whore, mutually exclusive slots for girls. However, on a more positive note, refreshingly feminist versions of these tales are beginning to appear, for example, books such as *Slut! Growing Up Female with a Bad Reputation* (Tanenbaum, 1999) and *Cunt: A Declaration of Independence* (Muscio, 1998).

Certainly much has been written (scholarly or otherwise) attesting to both the necessity and various means by which mandatory heterosexuality, homophobia, the sexual double standard, and male violence against women function to protect, preserve, and perpetuate patriarchy (Pharr, 1988). Alternatively, there is scant evidence of enough erosion or progress within these entrenched power systems (in realms such as politics, education, religion, economics, and sexuality) to accurately describe our current world as post-patriarchal. This is not to say that these sturdy pillars upholding and enforcing white, wealthy, male hegemony are fixed and intractable. Rather, when so much power is at stake, it would be naive, though certainly welcomed and convenient for the major beneficiaries, to think that these long-held social doctrines can be easily changed without facing major resistance and backlash on the part of the status quo.

This is exactly why a claim that, for example, the Powerpuff Girls represent a significant postmodern change in cultural gender roles warrants critical analysis. As Bourque (2001) points out, in examining gender, power, and leadership (forms of agency), the media play a significant role, particularly since the denial of sexual inequality is an important *perceptual* issue. She supports her stance with a quote from Rhode (1997), who writes, "Women's growing opportunities are taken as evidence that the 'woman problem' has been solved. This perception has itself become a central problem. The 'no problem' problem prevents Americans from noticing that on every major measure of wealth, power and status, women are still significantly worse off than men."

Havrilesky (2002) raises these very issues of the media, double standards, sexual inequality, and male rule in her discussion of the Powerpuff Girls and girls' contemporary notions of power:

> Can a new generation of gender-blind Powerpuffs conquer inequality simply by optimistically refusing to recognize its existence? For many girls

today, this approach seems to work. They don't cry out against inequality; they simply take for granted that the world will treat them fairly—and in some cases the world seems to follow suit. . . . Power isn't something that many women feel they should have to struggle for. And for them, dressing sexily or behaving cute is beside the point—those things should enhance their power, not diminish it. It's tough to disagree with such a refreshing self-actualized approach, particularly since it eliminates the need to put a male face on oppression.

(WHITE) GIRLS RULE?

The Powerpuff Girls are "white," or perhaps more accurately, racially unmarked or "neutral." Just to make sure, I checked with my then-six-year-old, who told me that they were "white and kind of pink, actually" but certainly not black. My child is multiracial and was raised to be aware and proud of her black, Cherokee, and German heritages. She is just another mestiza in my family, where not only skin color and tone, but also religion, ethnicity, sexual orientation, disability, and gender differences are consciously noted and discussed, yet such diversity is the accepted family norm. So, my child never had reason or occasion to *seriously* question her racial identity until after attending kindergarten for one week, when she came home from school and reported that she was not brown enough, but (wondering aloud) if she was browner, would I have to work all the time and would we have to have no money?

In recent years, "whiteness" has emerged as a focus worthy of academic study and debate (Fine, Weis, Powell, & Wong, 1997). In articulating how the power inherent in whites' construction of their identity as "cultureless" bolsters (whether intentional or not) white racial superiority, Perry (2003) provides a useful description of the dominant group's perspective: "Unaware of their privileged position as the norm, whites' seemingly ubiquitous claim of culturelessness . . . suggests that one is either 'normal' and 'simply human' (therefore the standard to which others should strive) or . . . 'postcultural' (therefore, developmentally advanced)" (p. 363). As Twine's (1996) work on "brown skinned white girls" delineates so well, class and culture allow for a construction of white-identity suburban communities. Once outside the family fold, like her fair-skinned mother with her newly acquired class privilege, my child immediately learned that a color- and power-evasive paradigm (Frankenberg, 1993) was available to her: one that enabled her to socially construct a white identity.

Without her family's imposed critical consciousness, my child could easily remain unaware that poorer or darker-skinned girls (excluded "others") never enjoyed the options she had by virtue of her phenotype and economic status to "pass."

Still, despite her advantaged position as "white-skinned brown girl," my female child could not escape the teasing brought on by her female and male kindergarten peers, including taunts that she was not "a girl" or "ladylike" due to serious gender infractions like being the only *female* child to wear shorts under her skirt and exhibiting too much physical prowess in gym class and on the playground. I'll never forget the sad look on her face while she told me, "Mommy, sometimes I just don't feel like a boy or a girl." Because my automatic response was "well, good!" in solidarity, I chose to reveal to her my own humiliating ordeal in 1959, when I decided *on my own* in first grade to wear pants to school, then a strict taboo. My rebellious spirit (at the time it was labeled bad judgment) resulted in public shame, a summons to the principal's office, a phone call to my parents, and ultimately, being sent home from school.

Although girls can now wear pants to school, I'm not convinced that violating gender norms is any easier today as a child, and certainly there are still enough negative consequences to keep most boys and girls in line when it comes to gender conformity. As Risman's (1998) research on the complexities for children who grow up in families with changed gender role expectations illustrates, "beyond these abstract [egalitarian] belief statements these children depend on their own lived experiences for understanding gender. And they 'know' that boys and girls are very different" (p. 232). As Sandra Bem (1993) makes clear, the widespread uncritical acceptance of biological determinism and firm belief in the "naturalness" of socially constructed categories such as race, gender, and sexual orientation makes it difficult for adults—not to mention children—to challenge and resist racist, sexist, or homophobic cultural messages. In fact, unequal treatment by gender begins so early, now frequently prior to birth, that it seems natural. Subsequently these socially constructed gender differences become a post hoc validation of existing social inequalities for females and males (Butler, 1990).

Added to that are the results of more than a decade of developmental research, particularly the extensive qualitative studies conducted on adolescent girls by Carole Gilligan and her Harvard colleagues (Gilligan, 1982, 1993; see Basow & Rubin, 1999, for comprehensive reviews of these and other important findings). In the

United States, white middle-class females by the age of ten face more and more *contradictions* and developmental *crossroads*, as they are termed (Brown & Gilligan, 1992). During this period, female adolescents describe facing considerable difficulties from trying to negotiate societal demands to adhere to traditional gender roles that are even stricter than what they faced as girls. For the majority, their attempts to conform are reflected in new pressures such as a strong emphasis on pleasing others, being nice, perfectionism, and increased attention to physical attractiveness. This "relational crisis" faced by white, middle-class girls has been construed as a loss of "voice" or a struggle between "authentic and inauthentic" selves. While feminist psychologists may disagree about the research conceptualizations reflected in these labels, there is consensus that for girls who enjoy the benefits of race and class privilege, this developmental period is accompanied by increased risks for developing depression, eating disorders, and a drop in self-confidence compared to childhood levels of self-esteem (Gilligan, Rogers, & Tolman, 1991; AAUW, 1991). This body of work suggests that even as my child constructs a more privileged "white" identity, there's a bumpy road ahead, and the pressure on girls seems to be occurring at increasingly earlier ages.

In an exceptionally rich article, Harad (2003) uses literary criticism, literature, and tales from junior high school to provide feminist insights that inform the patriarchal functions of female adolescence. She recalls the famous "nymphet" Lolita (from Vladimir Nabokov's 1955 novel of that name) and uses Lolita as archetypal of what she calls "the sexy girl":

> [A]n ordinary middle class white girl transformed by the obsessive gaze of a middle-class middle-aged man into the essence of femininity . . . who haunts the days of girls. Girls who are suddenly captured by powerful, silent rules about how to be a girl. Girls who have suddenly lost their right to simply be "people." Girls who grow up to be women who are still afraid of being bitches or sluts, or who have to adopt those labels as badges of pride in order to act on their desires. And who still watch each other warily, waiting for a mistake, a betrayal. (p. 87)

In a patriarchy, objectification becomes a critical task of adolescence and thus must be accomplished in the transition from girl to woman. As Harad (2003) notes with respect to Lolita and power, "Although her powers may be great, they depend wholly on recognition by [that type of] man. Lolita herself has little chance of manipulating these powers for her own purposes" (p. 86).

Lolita's power is derived from her attractiveness to men; therefore she lacks agency and any power derived from her own sexual desire. In adolescence, girls learn that power is granted only by male desire and recognition; or as Lee (2003) notes in her work on menarche and adolescence:

> Femininity means moving from assertive actor to developing woman, learning to respond to the world indirectly. . . . Women are encouraged to accommodate male needs, understand themselves as others see them and feel pleasure through their own bodily objectification, especially being looked at and being identified as objects of male desire. (p. 88)

Recent work like that of Michele Fine and Debra Tolman (Fine & Macpherson, 1991; Tolman, 2003) explores the "disconnect" a girl learns to experience from her body and erotic desire. If white adolescent girls, like their male adolescent counterparts, were encouraged to have a construction of their bodies and sexuality that was both powerful and positive, then the double standard and mandatory heterosexuality, two vital lynchpins of patriarchy, would be seriously threatened. Despite cultural pressure and messages to the contrary that already surround my seven-year-old female child, I am trying to teach her to derive power not from how desirable she is to males, but from her own physicality and sexuality—in short, to recognize and possess real agency instead of illusory power. Already difficult, I know this will hardly be an easy task and that we will both face mounting resistance as she enters adolescence.

BLACK GIRLS ARE (UN)RULY

Close your eyes for a minute and just imagine that the Powerpuff Girls are black instead of white. What do you see? For one thing, they wouldn't be named Blossom, Buttercup, and Bubbles! No, they would have boisterous names like Tawanna, Laquisha, and Shamika. Instead of keeping the town of Townsville free of danger, they would be the danger—*baaad*-ass female gangstas on a crime spree in New Jill City.

Unlike the negative portrayal of white, upper-middle-class suburbanites as girls whose agency is presumably confined to shopping malls, black girls do have real agency, not as a liberated choice but as a necessity for survival. Summoned as a strategy for successful resistance in a white man's world, it is not a characteristic that we would expect to be portrayed positively. Further, given the double and sometimes triple whammy of a disadvantaged position with respect to gender, race, and perhaps also class, if anything, black girls undoubtedly must contend with many more contradictory messages than white girls. Indeed, silence may be used as a powerful act of political resistance for black girls as well as others (Mahoney, 2001).

When black girls or women are considered at all, it is a marginal, negative portrayal that often is only considered and thus framed to serve the needs of whites regardless of gender. Black females provide a necessary and convenient contrast only to support the case for the virtues of white women and girls. As Fordham (1993) and others have made painfully clear, in the history of the United States, the ideal of womanhood has been defined as being morally superior, chaste, dainty, and of course, white. This bourgeois depiction of the feminine "ideal" is sometimes described as "the cult of domesticity," a term from the Victorian era. Such a definition is inherently racist and can only exist by dehumanizing black women, or as Zora Neale Hurston (1969) put it, as "mules." Unfortunately, this pure, genteel vision of the perfect white female was built upon the backs and knees (not to mention spirits) of black women who toiled first as slaves and then as domestic workers. Black women continue to disproportionately occupy these positions, as do other women of color.

Despite the violent and oppressive legacy of slavery, racism, sexism, and classism that has characterized the black female experience throughout U.S. history, black girls and women remain almost totally invisible in the research literature. Further, as many black feminists have pointed out, often when research does exist, it is not created or framed with the perspectives, concerns, or interests of black females in mind. In an insightful paper, Henry (1998) examined the contradictory consciousness and untenable position that black girls must negotiate in their schooling. She also critiqued the treatment of the black female in research literature:

> Moreover, underlying some of this literature may lurk a hypothesis of "black-girl-as pathologized-female."

> Black girls often serve as a comparative minority cohort in many educational studies; even in literature which is of great significance in helping us understand issues of race, class, gender and culture, most often, Black females are relegated to footnotes, occasional lines, a few meager paragraphs, or a couple of pages. (p. 154)

It is not surprising that when the scant research on black adolescent girls does indicate that they possess more positive characteristics than their white counterparts, these findings receive cursory treatment and tend to serve only as a convenient backdrop to aid attempts at understanding the source of white adolescent girls' relative shortcomings. Extant research does indicate that black girls have better self-esteem, healthier body images, and in general, more agency (Leadbeater & Way, 1996). However, unlike their "racially neutral," economically privileged white counterparts, "those loud black girls" (Fordham, 1993) end up being cast as the image of a very different crisis, namely, aggressive and violent behavior—the racialized, sexualized representation of female adolescent sexuality. Certainly just the degrading language used to describe black girls and young women (freak, bitch, ho, teaser, baby-mommas, etc.) captures well not only their racist and sexist intent, but also the scapegoating role these pernicious stereotypes continue to serve.[1]

SHE BLACK SHE BRAVE (SHEBONICS)

In a study that serves as an outstanding (and, unfortunately, too rare) example of the cogency and insight gained by framing an analysis from a black feminist perspective, Emerson (2002) explores "negotiating black womanhood" in music videos. Her sample includes representations of young black females that are examples of objectification and exploitation, but she also found portrayals of young black women's agency.

> The most interesting video in which this occurs is Sock It to Me (1997), in which Missy Elliott collaborates with the rappers Lil' Kim and Da Brat. It has an outer space fantasy theme, and in the visual narrative, Missy and rapper Lil' Kim appear in red and white bubble space suits as explorers on a mission. As soon as they land on an uncharted planet, they are pursued by an army of monstrous robots under the control of the evil "mad scientist," portrayed by Missy's collaborator and producing partner Timbaland. . . . Just as Missy and Kim appear to be in danger of succumbing to Timbaland's goons, fellow rapper, Da Brat . . . comes to the rescue on a jet ski type spacecraft. They speed off through space, fighting off the mad scientists' crew, and arrive safely at Missy's mother ship, prominently marked with the letter M. (Emerson, 2002, p. 127)

At long last, we have three B-girl super *she*roes who would give the Powerpuff Girls and a whole posse of male "mad scientists," whatever

their race, a run for their money! The contrast between this mad scientist narrative and the one that begins this chapter is powerful, to
say the least. Consider also the interpretation and value of agency in
Missy Elliott's narrative compared with my earlier exercise in imagining the Powerpuff Girls as blacks. Here we have young black females venturing off on their own to brave new worlds, outnumbered,
yet still escaping the threat of male domination through agency *and*
sisterhood!

GIRLS RULE OR GIRLS RULE GIRLS?

Unfortunately, but perhaps not coincidentally, the Powerpuff Girls
are white. Still, they are sisters who are presented, at the very least,
as feminist icons. So what happens if Blossom, Buttercup, and Bubbles do operate outside their usual realm of patriarchal influence?
Unlike Missy and her feminist crew, the girls learn that sisterhood is
powerfully misguided and dangerous when they fall under the (nefari-
ous) influence of feminism. The third episode my child and I just
happened to watch was, to my amazement, called "Equal Fights."
I found the episode transcripts and character descriptions cited below
on an unofficial website (http://www.ppgworld.com/ppgcomics/).

At the start of this cartoon, the Powerpuff Girls encounter a woman
villain named Femme Fatale robbing a bank. Described as "the feminist
of all feminists, Femme Fatale hates men with a passion and will only
accept money in the form of Susan B. Anthony coins."

Our feminist villain is clad in heels and white jumpsuit with the
biological symbol of the female sex (a circle with a cross pointing
down) emblazoned on it in blue. She carries a firearm shaped like a
female symbol, where the end of the cross is the muzzle. Femme Fatale
sports long blond hair and headgear with matching motif. The circle of
the female sign sits atop her head, with the horizontal bar of the
cross forming a mask over her eyes and the vertical bar stopping over
her nose.

No macho meathead can stop her, but to Femme Fatale's surprise,
three girl tykes manage to wallop and capture her. However, en
route to being put in jail, Femme Fatale convinces the Powerpuff
Girls that they have been belittled, taken advantage of, and under-
compensated; in solidarity, the trio set her free. Among other things,
the sudden miniature militants Blossom, Buttercup, and Bubbles then
refuse to clean their room, confront a playground bully, empower the

elementary school girls, zap a Ken doll with their laser vision, and finally tell off the mayor when he pleads for their help because of "some 'crazy tomato' robbing the mint of all the Susan B. Anthony coins."

Luckily for the always-incapable mayor, he also keeps his position due to that decidedly nonfeminist, hot, sexy, and headless woman who does his job. Thus it is Ms. Bellum, the secretary the girls so look up to, who takes it upon herself to restore the three formerly hardworking superheroes to their senses. She summons the help of the other (traditional) female character in Townsville, Ms. Keane, their concerned schoolteacher, along with a few other female characters created just for the occasion. It is the women, led by Sara Bellum, who must confront and deprogram Bubbles, Buttercup, and Blossom and make them realize the absurdity of their feminist claims of sexism and unequal treatment in Townsville. Returned to their "normal, rational" thinking, the Powerpuff Girls quickly recapture Femme Fatale and throw her in the slammer. Their critical thinking so seriously impaired under feminist brainwashing, once free they realize that this greedy feminist doesn't even know who Susan B. Anthony was and are lucid enough to provide this post-feminist history lesson:

> **Buttercup:** Once upon a time, women weren't allowed to do much of anything.
> **Bubbles:** Susan B. Anthony knew that that was wrong.
> **Blossom:** In 1872, she broke the law by voting. And even though she was found guilty, the feds wanted to go easy on her.
> **Girls:** Because she was a girl!
> **Blossom:** And not send her to jail.
> **Femme Fatale:** (*stammering*) Well, you—you know, she was this . . . well, *men* . . . girls should . . . oh, man!
> **Buttercup:** Susan B. Anthony didn't want special treatment. She wanted to be treated equally.
> **Bubbles:** She demanded that she be sent to jail, just like any man who broke the law.
> **Blossom:** And that's exactly what we're gonna do to you.

The episode closes with this final line from Femme Fatale in her cell, her white jumpsuit now replaced by convict stripes: "You can't do this to me! [*whining*] Horizontal stripes make me look fat."

Of course, in a cartoon that pokes fun at gender roles and stereotypes, the rule of order must be upheld and maintained by females untainted by the folly of feminism. But the real world operates that way, too.

Examples spring to mind from any work arena where male superiors frequently reward women who help keep other women in line. In my day, more often than not, you had to break rank to join the very few fortyish-aged women (renegades) promoted to the rank of full professor. You also knew your salary would never match that of certain female colleagues who languished profitably at the rank of associate professor (with much more service but still less pay than their male colleagues). At least that's how it was in the bad old days, and I hope times have changed for my junior colleagues in the tangled groves of academe. Yet I still hear tales of "queen bees" and "ice maidens" who thrive at their sisters' expense in all varieties of employment sectors.

This is what females are socialized to do to get ahead of other females (but not males) in patriarchal systems. How many feminists my age started out like I did as a child, wishing they could be boys and thinking how they either didn't like or didn't fit in with girls? But so early? I don't remember heavy girl-against-girl combat as a painful source of betrayal already in place by the second grade (like it is for my child). Reading all those "mean girls" books were like flashbacks from a bad trip that I needed no reminder of from my junior high days.

Harad (2003), I think, has it right when in response to questions about how or why feminism is relevant to young women, she answers in the affirmative by saying simply "junior high is still hell." Of course, for me that hell resulted in a promise to myself to someday study the worst period of my life if I survived it. I kept my word. Ignoring wise advice to use the university subject pool, or at least the laboratory school, for my master's thesis, I headed back to hell—a working-class junior high school—to collect data on peer popularity and perceptions of masculinity (agency) and femininity (communion) in female and male adolescents. My thesis (and then dissertation) findings defied all the predictions carefully derived from the mid 1970s theoretical literature on sex role development. Rather, at the start of junior high school in seventh grade, despite gender, students perceived as popular by their peers were perceived as possessing high levels of both feminine and masculine traits (using the Personal Attributes Questionnaire) (Spence & Helmreich, 1978). By tenth grade, peer ratings of popular males' degree of masculinity and femininity (both high) had not changed. In contrast, by the first year of high school, popular females were still perceived to be high in femininity but not masculinity (agency), regardless of their peer raters' genders. Since the two studies were not longitudinal, any interpretations of girls and boys' changes over time demanded caution. However, over twenty-five years later, these findings sound depressingly current to me. According to her much more recent account, involving a very angry group of junior high girls, apparently Harad (2003) couldn't stay away from hell either. In a quote from her interaction with the girls, she reveals,

> What they feared most, the girls insisted, was not the power of men or boys or teachers or criminals, but the power of other girls, who invented and enforced the labels. . . . In a tie for number one on their (dreaded labels) list: "slut" and "bitch/feminist". . . . They're the same thing, the girls explained. . . . These, then, were the girls' greatest fears: to be seen as having too much desire, too much anger, too much power—and to be cast out of the circle of "normal girls" for these sins. (p. 83)

In discussing the girls' fears and labeling them "depressingly familiar" to those aware of old school feminism, Harad makes explicit the connection between the old women's movement and the current lessons girls face in adolescence. Harad (2003) indicates that what they indeed share are "familiar though unspoken assumptions that oppose power and desire and are driven by the need to be desirable to but protected from the desire of men and boys" (p. 83). We need to reassure young girls that while junior high is indeed hell, feminism is far from it.

GIRL POWER IS POWER EVASIVE (NOT GENDER BLIND)

> Still, the real impact of "The Powerpuff Girls" may lie in its unrelenting focus on giddy fun for the sake of fun, its hints of a new era of popular art that plays with gender instead of struggling under the weight of it, thereby creating an imaginary world as appealing as it is unbound by archaic stereotypes. (Havrilesky, 2002)

The Powerpuff Girls are consistently purported to be "gender blind," a concept that I think reflects the confusion between two ideas—that gender shouldn't matter versus that gender doesn't matter. What struck me was how the "power blind" and the "gender blind" notions of the Powerpuff Girls and "girl power" feminism were more accurately "power evasive" (like claims of being "colorblind" to race) (Frankenberg, 1993). Without recognizing and analyzing the lack of agency and the source of desire from a critical feminist perspective, I thought that much was lost in the translation of younger (and not so young) women's take on the Powerpuff Girls. This seemed to allow for the "post-feminist" interpretation of "girls rule" that I encountered so frequently in the writings I discovered through my Internet search.

Consider an opinion piece I found online (Sartrell, 2000) that begins with this bold observation: "Gender: It's back with a vengeance, but also with a twist. Fox television has launched The Boyz Channel and The Girlz Channel, sex-differentiated cable networks. Toys R Us is creating separate girls' and boys' zones in their stores. And in elementary classrooms and schoolyards across the country, the boys and girls seem, as much as ever, to be from different species: the girls talk, draw, read; the boys yell, punch, can't sit still."

Sartrell then discusses the alleged failure of 1960s children in their own childraising experiments to find evidence of gender as a social construction or gender difference being rooted in patriarchy. Instead of gender as an evil patriarchal plot, she claims we discovered the source:

> [T]hat there was something (gasp) in the hormones. Our boys wanted to go bow hunting with Nerf products or fight with Star Wars Light Sabers. Men kept getting nominated for president of the United States and going to movies that consisted mostly of explosions. Finally we gave up and started reinstituting painful truisms like "boys will be boys."

No power differences here, just potent hormones like Chemical X. But here's the real twist: Sartrell asserts that although feminism failed in eliminating gender difference, it was successful in redefining femininity. Her evidence and perfect symbol of "girl-ry" progress is provided by those Powerpuff Girls, along with the merchandise girls now purchase in addition to Barbies. According to Sartrell, referring to modern girls: "Much of what they're buying has "Girl Power" or "Grrlz Rule" emblazoned across it. Bad sass attitude is a superficial sign of a deep change in our popular culture and in the lives of our children."

She predicts that these future girls with their "wider selection of off-the rack personae" and a major popular culture market in place as support will bring about radical unprecedented change as women. Apparently it's those pesky raging male hormones that render them immune to feminism. In fact, the focus of Sartrell's opinion piece is itself a familiar (power-evasive) twist. Namely, we need to focus our energy and attention not on girls but on boys instead.

A more thoughtful "post-feminist" analysis is evident in Havrilesky's (2002) well-written online *Salon* article that actually looks closely at the messages behind our three superheroes. When I first read it, I kept wondering how such a piece with clear insights could completely avoid these power issues. By doing so, the contradiction of the Powerpuff Girls is transformed into a dilemma brought on by tough and sexy heroines (Havrilesky, 2002): "Is Lara Croft powerful because she can take you down or because you'd like her to go down on you?"

Thus, when Havrilesky (2002) wonders whether the popularity of Blossom, Buttercup, and Bubbles reflects a genuine cultural shift in gender roles, it's not because they lack agency and that their power is derived as objects of male desire versus subjects of their own sexual desire, "but rather our inability to stomach female anger unless it's sugarcoated in cuteness and scored with a pervasively chirpy, nonthreatening tone." Thus, as noted earlier, once we embrace "gender blindness" and remove the "male face of oppression," she advises that "the more salient question for budding feminists may not be whether it's acceptable to be powerful and pretty at the same time, but whether being powerful without being pretty is even an option. When Janet Reno's appearance garners more sniping than her policies, and Britney Spears' looks get more glowing reviews than her songs, it's difficult to see how real power in the absence of beauty could ever be enticing to a new generation of girls, even with the help of Powerpuffs."

Of course, I believe it is our responsibility to teach the reality of our feminist experiences, knowing what's at stake and the importance of distorting our image, successes, and failures. Otherwise, young women and girls are receptive to what older feminists may see as ridiculous "post-patriarchal fallacies" under the guise of "girl power" from other (closeted? reluctant? white? middle-class? heterosexual?) "post-feminists," and the guys can sit back and enjoy the profits of their clever merchandising. It reminds me of Townsville, where feminists are uninformed, greedy villains who impart delusional thinking to unwitting young girls who must be straightened out by subservient "real" sexy women who are sometimes missing their heads. Meanwhile, both the incompetent sexist men (the mayor) and the well-intentioned, absent-minded men (the professor) can, thanks to the girls, kick back, relax, and enjoy—without ever lifting a finger. Ahh . . . now that's patriarchy!

SISTERHOOD IS POWERPUFF-FUL?

When we cheer on a little girl who knocks a villain's teeth out, are we cheering female power, or is it all an inside joke, an exercise in absurdity that plays on existing injustices? (Havrilesky, 2002)

For the last year or so, I have been tinkering with a model and trying to illustrate how various factors come together in patriarchy to capture and constrain girls as young women. Like Marilyn Frye's (1983) image of a birdcage, I was thinking of elements of female adolescence as the vertical bars (objectified versus embodied, agentic versus non-agentic, self-derived desire versus other-derived desire, etc.). These bars of course could only be held firmly in place by encircled horizontal bars: compulsive heterosexuality, the double standard, and male violence against girls and women. Without these bars, for example, girls possessing embodied, agentic self-derived desire would not find themselves entrapped just as surely as girls who are passive, objectified with male-derived desire also do. The shape of your cage also changes in configuration as a function of status: race, class, religion, body size, physical attractiveness, and so on. Taken from this model, I developed 2 x 2 tables, crossing levels of agency (high versus low) and desirability to males (high versus low) to depict how conceptions of power delimit and define possibilities for girls and young women. For a feminist workshop dealing with media images and adolescent girls, I planned an exercise for participants to classify popular females in music—Britney Spears, Courtney Love, Gwen Stefani, Ani DiFranco, Missy Elliott, Beyonce, Lil' Kim, Janet Jackson, and so on—accordingly. Depending on variations in race and class or age, the categories still translate into tired stereotypes with familiar labels such as *bitch, slut, virgin, shrew,* or *dyke*. It was after the presentation at a feminist colleague's house that I came across the article written by Harad (2003) on Lolita and junior high girls, where she states,

> In the commonplace formula, a slut is "easy" and relatively powerless. A bitch is powerful but sexless and undesirable—to men and boys, at least. This means the only way to be a bitch/feminist and sexual is to be a lesbian, a possibility so frightening to the girls that they wouldn't even mention it until I did so. Homophobia combines with the narrow options for expressing heterosexual desire to pit girls against one another, competing, controlling, and labeling someone else's flaws so their own won't be noticed. (p. 83)

She calls for correctives of feminist theory, the history of feminism, and more feminist stories, and I couldn't agree more. What strikes me as problematic about the Powerpuff Girls is that they are disingenuous. The cartoon and presumably their young audience don't seem to be aware of the content and context of feminism that I find necessary to put tongue in cheek.

Feeling hopelessly out of date and weary, like Professor Utonium, but with only one child and no superpowers, I head off to another feminist conference with no childcare and wonder what so-called post-feminists will do with their kids in a few years if they are not part of a heterosexual couple or (with gay marriage in the news) homosexual couple with two incomes. Then I worry, remembering that with few feminists, there will soon be few such conferences. In addition to watching episodes of the Powerpuff Girls, writing this chapter forced me to reflect on my own past and try to look through my young child's eyes at how girls and women are represented today. To be honest, I don't really like what I see. What became increasingly clear to me was that girls were negotiating a barrage of contradictory messages; and that with the help of representative images like Blossom, Buttercup, Bubbles, and Ms. (Sara) Bellum, I think I have gained a better understanding of why that is. In that first online article I found (Women in Action, 1998–2003) on grrl power and third wave feminism, the editorial refers to contradictions as a reason why young women reject the label "feminist":

> Some women's studies scholars will argue that the perception that young women of today enjoy much more rights and freedom is just that—a perception. While they may indeed have more choices, in both the public and private spheres, they are also subjected to tremendous pressure because of the incongruities in how they grew up, the values they were taught, the standards of performance imposed on them, and the persona or image they need to maintain. Young, urban-based, university-educated women of this generation are socialised into a certain consciousness that embraces certain values inculcated by family, peers, school, church, and media, on the one hand, and rejecting many others, on the other. For example, many young women have a liberal view of their bodies and sexual expressions, including premarital sex. A view, it should be added, shared by their peers and families, although the former might be celebrating such openness of young women with their bodies and their sexuality, and the latter may be fretting about this. Yet, such an attitude of ease with one's body and sexuality is exactly one of the struggles feminists have fought for in the last three decades.

I think of my college students of late in feminist studies classes who label the slightest female irritation as a symptom of PMS, an epidemic that somehow failed to even exist when I was their age and surely wasn't needed to explain why we feminists were pissed off. I was tempted to dismiss the "stigma of the f-word" as yet another luxury for white, upper-middle-class women, like their cell phones and new cars with built-in CD players. But I knew there was more to it—recalling how before starting this paper I typed in *girl* as my key search term for a Psyclit database search and not one journal article came up.

In female desire and sexuality, there is an inherent contradiction. Tolman (2003) captures this well when she points out the role scholars play in supporting the status quo:

> That few feminists have explicitly identified adolescent girls' sexual desire as a domain of theory or research suggests the extent to which girls' own sexual feelings are resisted in the culture at large. At best psychologists seem to be colluding with the culture in simply assuming that adolescent girls do not experience sexual desire; at worst, by not using the power and authority conferred upon them to say what is important in human experience and growth, psychologists participate in the larger cultural resistance to this feature of female adolescence and thus reify and perpetuate this resistance. (p. 100)

So I return to my original question: Is there any real substance behind the latest wave of the "girl movement"? Is it an always-overdue "call to arms" or just more evidence of Powerpuff cutesy girl fluff?

> Isn't this the era of girls who rule, rock, and kick ass? Aren't grown women embracing a girly ethos because of how exhilarating girlhood is these days? Aren't we all wearing powerpuff t-shirts just to grab us a taste of female youth? (Pomerantz, "Grinding the Concrete")

My travels into the Powerpuff world have convinced me of my previous suspicions and provided concrete evidence that the Powerpuff Girls lack agency, and so does the contemporary notion of "girl power." At the start of this paper, I was skeptical of how girls and young women could be unaware of their powerlessness. In closing, my skepticism has had to shift to the apparently widely held belief that girls and young women have real *de facto* agency and thus power.

> And while it is easy to get caught up in the thrill of scene-makers, let's face it—the Riot Grrl movement of the early 1990s has been done to death. Third wave feminism may now want to turn its attention to a different kind of feminist politics, the kind that is not so obvious or observable. In so doing, third wave has the potential to expand on all the possible ways in which girls can begin to think about themselves as

powerful, political, and part of the process of change. (Pomerantz, "Grinding the Concrete")

The above quotation from Pomerantz refers to girl skateboaders. It is taken completely out of context to illustrate my point, and I actually liked the article. I only mention this because I don't want to feed the image that feminists my age are anti-"girls just wanna have fun." Rather, my concern is that my child will not be able to have fun if she assumes she has power while institutional gains we fought for are being quietly dismantled without awareness and hence resistance.

In rather stark contrast, however, it seems that not all young feminists are as tickled pink by the present rise of "girldom." For example, in an essay with the ungirly title "A Call for Young Women to Get Mad!" in the online journal *feminista!*, Delanie Woodlock (2000) debunks pop-feminism's infatuation with the nonthreatening concept of girl power, such as the depiction of Buffy the Vampire Slayer as a feminist icon. In the following quote, Woodlock directly challenges the same cultural icons that other young women her age praise:

> They say we are in a post-feminist era, which seems true if we look to popular culture. There is not much feminism out there. Porn is chic. S/M is sex. "Buffy the Vampire Slayer" is a feminist icon, and young women have girl power to improve their lives. Bad girls, sluts and porn stars are the new elite, "the new girl order." . . . [The legacy] . . . lives on with girl power pop-feminism, which is giving us a culture where young women are set up for a fall and are fooled into believing there are no obstacles to their freedom.

I wanted to close with a quote from Delanie Woodlock (2000) in solidarity because when I read her piece I could identify with her on a very personal level. I thought she sounded like me at her age: furious and writing poems and plays about madness and women with ants not in their kitchens but in their brains. I want to tell her to hang in there because I can picture her surrounded by the chorus of rolling eyeballs now and perhaps for years to come. Like in high school when the film *MASH* came out and my solemn prediction that there would someday be a comedy about the Vietnam War was met with considerable disbelief and ridicule. So please listen when she says, "Young women do have power. Not the pseudo-girl power promoted so readily by patriarchy, but a real passionate, mad power. Fueled by generation upon generation of women who have fought before us, we

Activity 1: Change your mind! Read women's lives and history

Read books from the first, second, and third waves of feminism. For example, try these favorites:

- Miriam Schneir (Ed.): *Feminism: The Essential Historical Writings*
- Una Stannard: *Mrs. Man*
- Simone de Beauvoir: *The Second Sex*
- Tillie Olsen: *Silences*
- Shulamith Firestone: *The Dialectic of Sex: The Case for Feminist Revolution*
- Betty Friedan: *The Feminine Mystique*
- Germaine Greer: *The Female Eunuch*
- Gloria Anzaldúa: "How to Tame a Wild Tongue," in Gloria Anzaldúa, *Borderlands/La Frontera: The New Mestiza*
- Angela Y. Davis: *Women, Race, & Class*
- Gloria T. Hull, Patricia Bell Scott, and Barbara Smith (eds.): *All the Women Are White, All the Blacks Are Men, but Some of Us Are Brave: Black Women's Studies*
- Daisy Hernandez and Bushra Rehman (Eds.): *Colonize This! Young Women of Color on Today's Feminism*
- Edwidge Danticat: *Behind the Mountains*

Activity 2: Change your community! Imagine different outcomes

Try to remember a situation that occurred in your community (such as family, school, neighborhood) where you felt discriminated against because of your age or, conversely, where you felt you had unearned privilege because of your age. Were you able to take an action to create more equity for yourself and other people in that situation? Freewrite for five minutes as you try to imagine other ways to deal with that situation now.

Activity 3: Change your world! Organize for change

Part 1:
Research the lives and accomplishments of four great leaders for civil rights and workers' rights: Septima P. Clark, Ella Baker, Fannie Lou Hamer, and Dolores Huerta. Watch the video *Fundi: The Story of Ella Baker.*

Toolbox for Change

Focus on different ways of developing a movement for social change.
Talk about the distinctions among these terms: *mobilizing, organizing, spheres of influence.*

Part 2:
Role-play for (and against) change. Have student groups collaborate on the action planning worksheet to develop a proposal for change at your college (institution/organization). Then have each student group present its proposal for a change at the college to the teachers/graduate students (other "higher-ups in the hierarchy") who are acting the roles of college administrators (board members, committee) who are receptive, evasive, defensive, critical, dismissive—difficult!—at the same time they are always expressing appreciation for students' ideas and encouraging further efforts that occupy the students' time. After your "hearing" with the administrators, your group needs to refocus on a problem you want to address and develop a proposal to overcome some of the obstacles you have already encountered in your effort to achieve your goal.

have within us—between us—a real chance of reclaiming ourselves. Young women, it is our responsibility to continue the fight for women's freedom, to refuse to accept a future of limited control over our own lives. Rise up, connect with your sisters, let them feel our resistance" (Woodlock, 2000).

Action Planning Worksheet

1. What action do you want to take to interrupt or combat ———?
2. What resources or materials, if any, would you need to achieve your goal?
3. How can you get those resources?
4. What behaviors or steps would taking this action entail?
5. What is the realistic timeline for carrying out the steps involved in this action plan?
6. What hazards or risks are involved?
7. Is this action worth taking that risk? (If not, go back to number 1 or think through what could be done to minimize that risk.)
8. What obstacles might you encounter?
9. What could you do to overcome these obstacles?
10. What supports do you have?
11. Where could you find more support?

12. How can you measure/evaluate your success? (How can slow change be differentiated from failure?)

(Adapted from Adams, Bell, & Griffin, 1997)

NOTE

1. See West (2004) for an excellent article on the oppressive images of Mammy, Jezebel, and Sapphire.

REFERENCES

Adams, M., Bell, L. A., & Griffin, P. (Eds.). (1997). *Teaching for diversity and social justice: A sourcebook.* New York: Routledge.

American Association of University Women Education Foundation (AAUW). (1991). *Shortchanging girls, shortchanging America.* Washington, DC: AAUW.

American Association of University Women Education Foundation (AAUW). (1993). *Hostile hallways: The AAUW survey on sexual harassment in America's schools* (No. 923012). Washington, DC: Harris/Scholastic Research.

Basow, S. A., & Rubin, L. (1999). Gender influences on adolescent development. In N. Johnson, M. Roberts, & J. Worell (Eds.), *Beyond appearance: A new look at adolescent girls* (pp. 25–52). Washington, DC: American Psychological Association.

Bem, S. L. (1993). *The lenses of gender: Transforming the debate on sexual inequality.* New Haven, CT: Yale University Press.

Bourque, S. C. (2001). Political leadership for women: Redefining power and reassessing the political. In S. C. Bourque & C. M. Shelton (Eds.), *Women on power: Leadership redefined* (pp. 84–113). Boston: Northeastern University Press.

Brown, L. M., & Gilligan, C. (1992). *Meeting at the crossroads: Women's psychology and girls' development.* Cambridge, MA: Harvard University Press.

Butler, J. (1990). *Gender trouble: Feminism and the subversion of identity.* New York: Routledge.

Emerson, R. A. (2002). "Where my girls at?" Negotiating black womanhood in music videos. *Gender & Society, 16,* 115–135.

Fine, M., & Macpherson, P. (1991). Over dinner: Feminism and adolescent female bodies. In M. Fine (Ed.), *Disruptive voices.* Albany: State University of New York Press.

Fine, M., Weis, L., Powell, L. C., & Wong, L. M. (Eds.). (1997). *Off white: Readings on race, power, and society.* New York: Routledge.

Fisherkeller, J. (2002). Growing up with television: Everyday learning among young adolescents. Philadelphia, PA: Temple University Press.

Fordham, S. (1993). "Those loud black girls": (Black) women, silence, and gender "passing" in the academy. *Anthropology and Education Quarterly, 24*(1), 3–32.

Frankenberg, R. (1993). *White women, race matters: The social construction of whiteness.* Minneapolis: University of Minnesota Press.

Frye, M. (1983). *The politics of reality: Essays in feminist theory.* New York: The Crossing Press.

Gilligan, C. (1982). *In a different voice.* Cambridge, MA: Harvard University Press.

Gilligan, C. (1993). Letter to readers, 1993. In *In a different voice* (2nd ed.), Cambridge, MA: Harvard University Press.

Gilligan, C., Rogers, A. G., & Tolman, D. L. (Eds.). (1991). *Women, girls and psychotherapy: Reframing resistance.* Binghamton, NY: Haworth Press.

Hall, R. L. (2004). Sweating it out: The good news and bad news about women in sport. In J. Chrisler, C. Golden, & P. D. Rozee (Eds.), *Lectures on the psychology of women* (pp. 56–74). New York: McGraw-Hill.

Harad, A. (2003). Reviving Lolita; or, because junior high is still hell. In R. Dicker & A. Piepmeir (Eds.), *Catching a wave: Reclaiming feminism for the 21st century* (pp. 81–98). Boston: Northeastern University Press.

Havrilesky, H. (2002). Powerpuff girls meet world. *Salon.* Retrieved July 2, 2002, from http://www.salon.com/

Henley, N. M. (1977). *Body politics: Power, sex and nonverbal communication.* Englewood Cliffs, NJ: Prentice-Hall.

Henry, A. (1998). "Invisible" and "womanish": Black girls negotiating their lives in an African-centered school in the USA. *Race, Ethnicity and Education, 1*(2).

Hurston, Z. N. (1969). *Mules and men.* New York: Negro Universities Press.

Lamb, S. (2001). *The secret lives of girls: What good girls really do—Sex play, aggression and their guilt.* New York: The Free Press.

Leadbeater, B. J., & Way, N. (Eds.). (1996). *Urban girls: Resisting stereotypes, creating identities.* New York: New York University Press.

Lee, J. (2003). Menarche and the (hetero)sexualization of the female body. In R. Weitz (Ed.), *The politics of women's bodies: Sexuality, appearance, and behavior* (pp. 82–99). New York: Oxford University Press.

Lerner, G. (1986). *The creation of patriarchy.* New York: Oxford University Press.

Mahoney, M. A. (2001). The problem of silence in feminist psychology. In S. J. Freeman, S. C. Bourque, & C. M. Shelton (Eds.), *Women on power: Leadership redefined* (pp. 61–83). Boston: Northeastern University Press.

Martin, K. A. (2003). Becoming a gendered body: Practices of preschools. In R. Weitz (Ed.), *The politics of women's bodies: Sexuality, appearance, and behavior* (pp. 219–239). New York: Oxford University Press.

Muscio, I. (1998). *Cunt: A declaration of independence.* New York: Seal Press.

Perry, P. (2003). White means never having to say you're ethnic: White youth and the construction of "cultureless" identities. In J. A. Holstein & J. F. Gubrium (Eds.), *Inner lives and social worlds* (pp. 362–380). New York: Oxford University Press.

Pharr, S. (1988). *Homophobia: A weapon of sexism.* Little Rock, AR: Chardon.

Pomerantz, S. Grinding the concrete (third) wave. Available at http://www.ppgworld.com/

Rhode, D. (1997). *Speaking of sex.* Cambridge, MA: Harvard University Press.

Risman, B. (1998). Ideology, experience, identity: The complex worlds of children in fair families. In *Gender vertigo: American families in transition.* New Haven, CT: Yale University Press.

Sartrell, C. (2000). It's time for us to rethink boyhood. Available at http://www.crispinsartwell.com/media/gender.html

Simmons, R. (2002). *Odd girl out: The hidden culture of girls' aggression.* New York: Harcourt.

Spence, J. T., & Helmreich, R. L. (1978). *Masculinity and femininity: The psychological dimensions, correlates, and antecedents.* Austin: University of Texas Press.

Tanenbaum, L. (1999). *Slut! Growing up female with a bad reputation.* New York: Seven Stories Press.

Thorne, B. (1986). Girls and boys together . . . but mostly apart. In W. W. Hartup & Z. Rubin (Eds.), *Relationships and Development* (pp. 167–184). Hillsdale, NJ: Lawrence Earlbaum Associates.

Thorne, B. (1993). *Gender play: Girls and boys in school.* New Brunswick, NJ: Rutgers University Press.

Tolman, D. L. (2003). Daring to desire: Culture and the bodies of adolescent girls. In R. Weitz (Ed.), *The politics of women's bodies: Sexuality, appearance, and behavior* (pp. 100–121). New York: Oxford University Press.

Twine, F. W. (1996). Brown skinned white girls: Class, culture and the construction of white identity in suburban communities, *Gender, Place & Culture, 3*(2), 205–224.

West, C. M. (2004). Mammy, Sapphire, and Jezebel: Developing an "oppositional gaze" toward the images of black women. In J. Chrisler, C. Golden, & P. D. Rozee (Eds.), *Lectures on the psychology of women* (pp. 236–252). New York: McGraw-Hill.

White, E. (2002). *Fast girls: Teenage tribes and the myth of the slut.* New York: Scribner.

Wiseman, R. (2002). *Queen bees and wannabes: Helping your daughter survive cliques, gossip, boyfriends and other realities of adolescence.* New York: Crown Publishers.

Women in Action (WIA). (1998–2003). Grrl power and third wave feminism. Isis International–Manila. http://www.isiswomen.org/pub/wia/wia203/editorial.htm

Woodlock, D. (2000). A call for young women to get mad! Women in Action. Available at http://www.isiswomen.org/pub/wia/wia203/editorial.htm

CHAPTER 3

Life Experiences of Working and Stay-at-Home Mothers

Judith LeMaster
Amy Marcus-Newhall
Bettina J. Casad
Nicole Silverman

In 1997, the country was transfixed by the death of eight-month-old Matthew Eappen while in the care of his nanny. In the months after his death, and during the trial of the nanny, much criticism was focused on the working mother of the child, Dr. Deborah Eappen, a Boston physician ("Parents of Baby," 1998). At the same time, the Clinton administration developed programs (such as Temporary Aid to Needy Families of 1997) designed to get poor mothers off welfare and into the workforce. More recently, a famous radio personality argued that mothers who worked outside of the home were negligent (or in the case of poor women, in a "tragic" situation). This intersection of events prompted a well-known newspaper columnist to comment on the implied double standard that low-income mothers are expected to work outside of the home, even when daycare is poor, and middle-class mothers are expected to stay home, even when excellent provisions for their children are available.

Are these viewpoints about mothers common today? Is there a double dilemma such that mothers are criticized if they stay home and take care of their children and criticized if they go back to work and put their children in daycare?

Russo (1976) used the term *motherhood mandate* to argue that society expected mothers to be available to their children and to be the primary caretakers. In the last three decades, the roles carried out by mothers have shifted as more mothers have entered the workforce.

What do we know about the perceptions that members of society hold for stay-at-home and working mothers? Do these perceptions differ from the reality that stay-at-home and working mothers experience? Do these perceptions and realities differ among mothers from different cultural/ethnic backgrounds? Are mothers satisfied with the life choices they have made? Are there patterns to the life choices that mothers make? Do mothers' expectations, real experiences, and life choices lead to prejudice and/or discrimination against them because of their motherhood status? These are the primary questions that will be addressed in this chapter. More specifically, this chapter reviews the current literature on (1) perceptions and stereotypes of working and stay-at-home mothers, (2) the real-life experiences of working and stay-at-home mothers, and (3) various models women choose when navigating the paths of career and family.

The most common family type in the United States in the twenty-first century is the dual-earner family, where both men and women work outside the home to provide financial support for the family (White & Rogers, 2000). Today, only 3 percent of American families have the traditional arrangement of a stay-at-home mother and a working father who is the sole breadwinner (Gilbert & Rader, 2001). More and more women are working outside the home, with women currently making up over half of the U.S. workforce (U.S. Department of Labor, 2003). Many working women also are mothers. Indeed, over half of mothers with children under age one work outside the home (Erel, Oberman, & Yirmiya, 2000). Although working mothers have become a common part of today's society, societal views have not kept pace with this change and do not reflect reality. That is, many Americans still expect mothers to stay at home to care for their children while fathers work to provide for the family (Ganong & Coleman, 1995).

SOCIAL ROLE THEORY

Women Should Be Mothers; Men Should Be Providers

One explanation for why society still holds traditional views of families is provided by social role theory (Eagly & Steffen, 1984). Social role theory suggests that because men have historically been the primary breadwinners and women the primary caretakers of children, people still associate men with work and women with motherhood (Eagly, Wood, & Diekman, 2000). When women choose to engage in roles other than motherhood, like paid employment, and men choose to engage in roles other than financial provider, like being stay-at-home fathers, people tend to react negatively (Doherty, 1998).

Society's lingering expectation that women focus on caring for children rather than focus on a career has been called the "motherhood mandate" (Russo, 1976). The motherhood mandate suggests that women should want to become mothers. Their motherhood role is viewed as the most important aspect of their identities, whereas their worker role is a secondary identity. According to this standard, "good" mothers are expected to be constantly available for their children and to sacrifice their careers for family.

Similar to the motherhood mandate for women, society judges men according to the provider role (Bernard, 1981). Men are expected to provide for the financial needs of their families. If they cannot fulfill their provider role, their competence is questioned. Fathers who want to play an active role in childcare, for example by working part-time, are likely to be viewed as less competent than fathers who work full-time (Etaugh & Folger, 1998).

Mothers Should Be Feminine; Fathers Should Be Masculine

As illustrated in the example of fathers working part-time, people often make assumptions about individuals' personality traits based on stereotypes (Eagly & Steffen, 1984; Harris, 1991). Men and women are presumed to have certain personality traits and behaviors because of their traditional social roles as fathers and mothers (Eagly & Steffen, 1984). The personality traits commonly associated with fathers and mothers include (1) communality, or the ability to work well with and care about others; (2) agency, or being task-oriented and competent; (3) femininity, or having qualities traditionally associated with women; and (4) masculinity, or having qualities traditionally associated with men.

To successfully fulfill their caretaker role, mothers are assumed to be communal, which includes being nurturing, warm, caring, and willing to sacrifice their careers for family (Ganong & Coleman, 1995). Men are not expected to be communal or nurturing, because these traits are presumably not required of the provider role. Working mothers have been viewed as less communal and less committed to their families (Bridges & Etaugh, 1995) and less nurturing (Bridges & Orza, 1992; LeMaster, Marcus-Newhall, Casad, & Silverman, In press) than stay-at-home mothers. In contrast to communality, men are presumed to be agentic, or competent and task-oriented, because these traits are required for successful financial providing (Eagly et al., 2000). Women are not expected to be agentic because these traits are presumably not required of the motherhood role.

Women are expected to have feminine personality traits such as kindness, sensitivity, and patience (Prentice & Carranza, 2002). Stay-at-home mothers are considered more feminine than employed mothers (Bridges & Etaugh, 1995). For example, stay-at-home mothers were rated by college students as more soft-spoken than employed mothers (Riedle, 1991). When women violate the expected norms of the feminine personality traits by working outside the home, they are liked less and receive less approval than women who possess these feminine personality traits (Marcus-Newhall, LeMaster, Casad, & Shaked, In press). Fathers employed part-time were considered more feminine than mothers employed full-time. For example, fathers who worked part-time to care for their children were rated as more communal than mothers who worked full-time (Etaugh & Folger, 1998).

Men are expected to have masculine personality traits, such as competitiveness, assertiveness, and ambition (Prentice & Carranza, 2002). Just as fathers employed part-time are viewed as more feminine (Etaugh & Folger, 1998), employed mothers are perceived as more masculine, such as being more self-sufficient and having stronger leadership abilities, than stay-at-home mothers. However, employed mothers also are perceived as less feminine than stay-at-home mothers (Riedle, 1991).

Mothers Are Devalued as Workers

People tend to make assumptions not only about personality traits based on stereotypes but also about behaviors based on stereotypes (Harris, 1991). These assumptions affect how people actually behave (Olson, Roese, & Zanna, 1996). For example, people have stereotypes about what personality traits are required to perform a particular job. Real estate agents are expected to be extroverted, or outgoing, whereas librarians are expected to be introverted, or quiet and reserved. These stereotypes about careers led people to rate individuals whom they thought were extroverted as more suitable for the real estate job and individuals thought to be introverted as more suitable for the librarian job (Snyder & Cantor, 1979). This finding suggests that people's expectations regarding the behaviors required to perform a job may lead to discrimination in hiring. If a stay-at-home mother decides to apply for a job, the employer may expect the mother to be low in competence and unable to perform the job simply because she is a mother.

There are several real-life examples of how people's expectations about personality and behavior lead them to treat others in a discriminatory manner. For example, in a Michigan court case, a judge granted custody to a paternal stay-at-home grandmother rather than the child's biological mother. The mother worked outside the home, attended school, was unmarried, and put her child in daycare, which the judge apparently thought made her an unsuitable mother (Ganong & Coleman, 1995). In another example, a female senior manager was denied promotion to partner because she was not "feminine enough" and needed a "course at charm school" where she could learn to "walk more femininely, talk more femininely, dress more femininely . . ." even though she had the top sales among the eighty-eight candidates for the position (*Price Waterhouse vs. Hopkins*, 1985, as cited in Fiske, Bersoff, Borgida, Deaux, & Heilman, 1991, p. 1050).

Although the expectations of working and stay-at-home mothers appear to be discrepant from actual behaviors, what does the research show about the actual experiences of working and stay-at-home mothers?

PERCEPTIONS DO NOT MATCH REALITY: WORKING AND STAY-AT-HOME MOTHERS' ACTUAL EXPERIENCES

The roles carried out by mothers shifted as more mothers entered the workforce. Women are more likely to balance multiple roles as partners, mothers, and workers. Difficulty with balancing multiple roles has been labeled "work–family conflict," which is defined as incompatible pressures in one's roles such that participation in one role is made more difficult by participation in another role (Greenhaus, Parasuraman, Granrose, Rabinowitz, & Beutell, 1989). Terms such as *role strain* and *role conflict* often are used interchangeably with work–family conflict. Interestingly, research examining work–family conflict has produced contradictory conclusions. Some researchers have found that balancing several roles and responsibilities can be rewarding (Zambrana & Frith, 1988) and lead to increased well-being

(Barnett & Marshall, 1993), whereas other studies have found that fulfilling multiple roles can be demanding and overwhelming and result in work–family conflict (Kossek & Ozeki, 1998). Whether mothers experience work–family conflict is determined by the quality of their multiple roles rather than the number of roles (Barnett & Hyde, 2001). Factors such as high-stress jobs, traditional sex-role attitudes, and help with the housework influence role equality (Amaro, Russo, & Johnson, 1987; Krause & Markides, 1985). As one can imagine, mothers who have less-stressful jobs, hold less-traditional sex-role attitudes, and have help with the housework tend to experience less work–family conflict.

One result of combining the roles of motherhood and employment is psychological distress. There is an upper limit to the benefit of engaging in multiple roles; too many roles can lead to psychological distress (Barnett & Hyde, 2001). Individuals in low-prestige jobs experience greater psychological distress than individuals in high-prestige jobs (Matthews, Raikkonen, Everson, Flory, Marco et al., 2000). Some studies indicate that employed wives are more distressed than employed husbands (Gore & Mangione, 1983). Whether women experience psychological distress depends on several factors, including role quality, job support, and spousal support.

Another result of having multiple roles is the potential for workplace discrimination. Combining family life and employment is beneficial for men, often resulting in higher salaries, career advancement, and greater career satisfaction. However, when women combine family life and employment, they often have lower salaries, hindered career advancement, and less career satisfaction (Friedman & Greenhaus, 2000; Phillips & Imhoff, 1997).

Discrimination: Explaining Why Men and Women Are Treated Differently in the Workplace

Why might this differentiation between men and women occur? One explanation is that women tend to devalue their own work, something called the "depressed-entitlement effect." In a laboratory study, women paid themselves less than men paid themselves for the same task (Jost, 1997). This may be because men and women often report being ambivalent about women as financial providers for the family (Thompson & Walker, 1989). Women often are not viewed as financial providers in dual-earner families, even if they earn a higher salary than their husbands (Cook, 1993). These beliefs are likely due to the historical role of men as the sole financial providers for their families (Eagly et al., 2000). Expectations often influence behavior (Harris, 1991). Beliefs in men's role as the financial provider may lead women to expect lower salaries than men and for employers in turn to provide lower salaries.

A second explanation for workplace discrimination is that some employers expect that most or all young women in the workplace will want to marry, have children, and leave their careers. Because of the commitment of time, resources, and training, employers may avoid hiring women who might leave their careers in the early stages. Even when hired, supervisors and co-workers may question young women's commitment to their careers, hindering potential mentoring relationships and advancement. When women temporarily interrupt their careers to have children, their future income and chances for promotion are negatively impacted (Booth, 2002; Friedman & Greenhaus, 2000). Women who use company benefits such as flexible work schedules, family care leave, and childcare services risk being perceived negatively, having their job commitment questioned, and being placed on the "mommy track" (Kossek & Ozeki, 1998; Schwartz, 1998).

A third explanation for workplace discrimination is that employed women may be seen as violating their traditional feminine gender role and the motherhood mandate. When women appear too aggressive or tough, which is often required for top jobs, they risk being evaluated negatively (Furr, 2002). As stated in the 1989 Supreme Court case *Price Waterhouse v. Hopkins*, "An employer who objects to aggressiveness in women but whose positions require this trait places women in an intolerable Catch 22: out of a job if they behave aggressively and out of a job if they don't" (as cited in Fiske et al., 1991, p. 1055).

Ethnic Differences in Work–Family Conflict

Thus far our discussion of the differences between men's and women's experiences with work–family conflict has primarily, if not exclusively, focused on those who are white and middle class. But what do we know about differences and/or similarities between white women and ethnic minority women? Do the same patterns exist or are there differences that should be taken into account when thinking about issues for ethnic minority working and stay-at-home mothers? Although the majority of research on working mothers has been conducted with white women, there is a growing body of research concerning the experiences of black, Asian American, Latina, and Native American working mothers. Although certain aspects of role strain may be common to working mothers of all ethnic backgrounds, there are important differences in the ways that ethnic groups experience role strain. These similarities and differences have important implications.

Black Working Mothers

Black women have been working outside the home longer than white women (Bridges & Orza, 1996; Gilbert & Rader, 2001). As a result, balancing multiple roles of motherhood and employment may come more easily to black mothers. Due to economic necessity, black mothers often did not have the choice to stay home full-time with their children, as did many white mothers, and often were the heads of the household. However, employment is also is a way that black women have tried to overcome social and economic inequalities in the United States. Black mothers with infants are more likely to work than are their white counterparts with the same socioeconomic status (Granrose & Cunningham, 1988). Black women also are more likely to work after marriage and childbirth than white women. Because many black mothers are the heads of their households, they may feel less ambivalence toward being financial providers than white women (Myers, 1989). In addition, black men tend to be more accepting of wives' employment than are white men (Broman, 1991; Orbuch & Custer, 1995; Rushing & Schwabe, 1995).

The research that addresses work–family conflict among black mothers reveals that they often receive strong support from their families for their roles as working mothers (Benin & Keith, 1995; Broman, 1991). For example, Benin and Keith investigated social support among employed black and white mothers. They specifically investigated types of family support such as help with childcare and transportation, which directly help mothers balance their work and family responsibilities, thereby reducing their feelings of role strain. Although both groups reported moderate levels of support from their families, family was a particularly important source of support for black mothers. In fact, black mothers were more likely to receive additional support by living with their own mothers. In addition, black couples tend to have more egalitarian relationships than white couples (Broman, 1988). Black husbands tend to be more involved in household tasks and childcare than white husbands, providing additional support for black mothers (Orbuch & Custer, 1995; Hossain & Roopnarine, 1993).

Asian American Working Mothers

Research on Asian American working mothers' experiences with role strain is growing. It has been found that as Asian immigrant women enter the workforce, they often become the co-providers or breadwinners of their families; yet this new role may have unintended negative consequences. For example, employed Asian immigrant women may experience role strain as employment often intensifies their responsibilities as employees, wives, and mothers. In addition, many face discrimination in the workplace as well as a higher likelihood of marital conflict, divorce, and even spousal abuse because the husbands often feel that their traditional beliefs about being the financial providers have been threatened. Researchers have suggested that employed Asian immigrant wives may not feel empowered, in part, because their wages may be too low to make them feel self-sufficient. Korean immigrants, for example, tend to be reluctant to adjust their traditional gender role beliefs, which have been attributed to their ". . . cultural homogeneity, their economic segregation, and their high affiliation with Korean ethnic churches" (Min, 2001, p. 309). It is important to note that researchers also have found that Asian immigrant women tend to view their work in a positive light (Espiritu, 1999). As noted by one researcher, ". . . like many ethnic, immigrant, poor, and working-class women, working-class Asian women view work as an opportunity to raise the family's living standards and not only as a path to self-fulfillment or even upward mobility as idealized by the white feminist movement. As such, employment is defined as an extension of their family obligations—of the roles as mothers and wives" (Espiritu, 1999, p. 642).

Other researchers investigated the ways in which culture, ethnicity, and nationality affect women's attitudes toward employment. One study compared middle-class Japanese and American women's perceptions of working mothers. Although both groups of women in the study were full-time housewives, neither Japanese nor American women fully endorsed the statement "I could be happy as a full-time housewife" (Engel, 1988, p. 367). The researchers suggested that although Japanese women may be changing their perceptions of working mothers, their overall attitudes are still more conservative than those held by American women. Furthermore, Japanese women believed more strongly that a mother's employment outside the home fundamentally hindered marital and child development. Whereas Japanese women believed that wives or mothers should not work outside of the home without their husbands' approval, American women believed that wives or mothers should not work outside the home unless they themselves wished to. American mothers also believed in mothers' capability of balancing work and family. These findings were explained in part by the discrepancy between the Japanese values of collectivism and the American values of individualism (Engel, 1988).

Latina Working Mothers

The experiences of working and non-working Latina mothers are reminders of the negative effects of prejudice and discrimination. For example, one study found that many Latina women had experienced discrimination in their jobs; such negative experiences in the workplace have been associated with decreased psychological well-being and increased role strain. The researchers also identified an in-home contributor to Latina women's experiences with role strain—having a Latino partner. Latino partners tended to be less supportive of their wives or female partners working outside the home. Some researchers have suggested that traditional sex-role beliefs and cultural expectations may increase the role burdens of Latina women (Amaro et al., 1987; Hondagneu-Sotelo & Avila, 1997). However, researchers have found that Latina mothers do not succumb to the pressures of cultural stereotypes. In one study, Latina mothers did not believe they should be solely responsible for maintaining the household while also working outside of the home. Instead, they valued egalitarianism in their relationships and expected their husbands to help with household tasks and childcare responsibilities (Herrera & Del Campo, 1995). Married Latina women tend to be less satisfied working outside of the home if they hold traditional gender-role beliefs (Krause & Markides, 1985), which illustrates the importance of holding gender role beliefs that are consistent with actual behavior.

Researchers also have found that certain factors are associated with higher risk for psychological distress and depression among Latina women. In general, perceived spousal support, help with the housework, having a prestigious occupation, and fluency with the English language are associated with lower levels of depression and psychological distress and an overall higher self-reported health status

(Krause & Markides, 1985; Rivera, Torres, & Carre, 1997). In contrast, having a high-stress job, a low income, and experiencing discrimination in the workplace are related to depression and psychological distress (Amaro et al., 1987).

Latino subgroups have been found to have different experiences with role strain and psychological distress. Whereas one study found that Cubans experience less role strain than Mexican American women, other studies have found that Cuban American women and Mexican American women experience better health than Puerto Rican women (Rivera et al., 1997). The finding that members of different Latino subgroups have varied experiences with role strain and psychological distress has important implications. As noted by several researchers (Amaro et al., 1987; Rivera et al., 1997; Zambrana & Frith, 1988), it is increasingly important to be aware of the differences among Latino subgroups and to avoid treating them as one homogenous group.

Native American Working Mothers

The research on role strain among Native American women also is limited. Previous researchers have noticed that Native American women often are not included in studies about work. This may be due, in part, to difficulty locating Native American participants (Byars & McCubbin, 2001).

Despite the difficulty in locating Native American women, a few studies have investigated Native American working women's experiences with role strain. Researchers have been interested in the relationship between gender role and psychological well-being among employed Native American women (Napholz, 1995, 2000). Gender role orientation refers to the extent to which a person displays both masculine and feminine personality traits. In one study, Native American working women who showed more feminine traits had overall poorer psychological well-being, as they tended to have lower self-esteem, greater depression, and greater difficulty with balancing multiple roles. This finding was partially explained by the possibility that displaying more masculine traits or a combination of masculine and feminine traits made a woman more flexible and therefore more capable of balancing different roles and responsibilities. Napholz (1995) suggested that Native American women who displayed more feminine traits had a harder time dealing with work and family roles than women who showed both feminine and masculine traits.

In another study, Napholz (2000) brought Native American women together to form a support network. Many of the women faced multiple roles and responsibilities, such as conflicting work and family obligations. In addition, many women were struggling to develop a better sense of themselves within the context of modern Native American society. By sharing their own personal experiences, the women in the support network were able to identify the causes of their role strain as well as generate personal resources and strategies for reducing their role strain. For example, many women reported feeling guilty about working outside of the home and not spending enough time with their families. They also reported feeling pressured and confined by traditional Native American female roles. Through the support network, the women received the support and resources necessary to relieve their feelings of guilt by learning to let go of "mistakes made in the past and [instead, make] choices that [facilitate] both individual and family growth" (Napholz, 2000, p. 259). By setting boundaries with others, the women were able to become more attentive to their own needs. In addition, reclaiming their connection to Native American culture, such as "drumming, singing, dancing, and spiritual practice" (Napholz, 2000, p. 265), was an important source of belonging and psychological well-being for Native American women. The women in this study were able to redefine their roles within Native American culture to better achieve balance in their lives (Napholz, 2000).

Implications for Research

For several reasons, it is important to examine the similarities and differences among white, black, Asian American, Latina, and Native American women's experiences with role strain. The research shows that the majority of women, regardless of their ethnicity, find it difficult to balance their work and family responsibilities. This finding can be used to better understand how role strain for working mothers can be reduced. Several factors, such as receiving family support and help with the housework, benefit most working mothers, regardless of their ethnicity.

Although researchers have found similarities in the ways women of different racial backgrounds experience role strain, there are key differences that may have important implications. For example, in one study with Native American women, several participants did not complete a part of the survey that is commonly used to assess depression.

As noted by the researcher, this may indicate the "need for more culturally sensitive instruments for Native American women" (Napholz, 1995, p. 70). The researcher further suggested that "because of the community-based definition of self, many traditional therapeutic interventions emphasizing individual volition and responsibility . . . may prove inappropriate [for Native American women] without a cultural translation" (Napholz, 1995, p. 71). Part of the value of studying role strain among various ethnic groups is the ability to develop research tools, policies, and interventions that will be beneficial and culturally sensitive for women of diverse ethnic backgrounds.

Thus, our expectations about working and stay-at-home mothers and our information about their "real" experiences in these roles tend to be based on white, middle-class mothers, who are depicted as the "norm." When researchers have studied mothers' experiences, they usually have looked at white, middle-class mothers' experiences. Future work needs to take this into account and be aware that the white, middle-class working and stay-at-home mothers' experiences may or may not be similar to those of ethnic minority mothers.

BALANCING WORK AND FAMILY CONFLICT: SEQUENCING CHOICES

Given mothers' experiences with work–family conflict, it is important to understand the way women balance the demands of work and family life. Although their choices may be constrained by economic and cultural factors, women can decide whether or not to marry and have children. Further, they make take on these roles at different points in their lives.

How do mothers make their decisions about when to work, get married, and have children? What are the effects of the order of these choices? No research of which we are aware has examined the expectations or realities that are experienced by mothers according to the sequence of choices they make about work, marriage, and children. In this section, we provide a framework for these sequencing patterns as well as discuss the advantages and disadvantages of each of these patterns. It should be noted that most of the research cited in this section involved white, heterosexual participants.

The experiences of newscaster Connie Chung represent one possible sequencing pattern. In 1990, Chung announced that she was taking time off from her career as a news anchor for CBS to start a family. Chung had achieved a remarkable degree of success in a very competitive and challenging field. During this time, the women's movement was encouraging women to pursue their own careers and see themselves as having more options than marriage and mother- hood. Women, particularly educated women, were responding by postponing marriage (*The Wall Street Journal*, as cited in Gilbert, 1993). Indeed, Chung had not married until about age forty. She dis- covered to her dismay that she was having a difficult time becoming pregnant and eventually adopted an infant (Schindehette, Carswell, Sheff, & Micheli, 1990). A few years earlier than Connie Chung's well-publicized efforts to conceive, the popular press had described two stories in great detail. One was drawn from research that showed a critical shortage of marriageable men for women over thirty (Bennett, Bloom, & Craig, 1986, as cited in Faludi, 1991). The second involved an apparent increase in infertility. DeCherney and Berkowitz (1982) reported that women's chances of conceiving dropped sharply after age thirty. The popular press declared that women were taking a terrible risk in postponing childbearing beyond age thirty. Faludi (1991) suggests that women were being warned on all sides of the dangers involved in either postponing marriage or childbearing or trying to combine career with family.

Women who took this advice and married and had children earlier in their lives faced their own difficulties. A great deal of research out- lined the mental and physical benefits of employment and the psycho- logical risks of full-time homemaking (Crosby, 1991; Ferree, 1984; Golding, 1989; Lennon, 1998; Nolen-Hoeksema, 1990; Shehan, 1984). Not all women choose to marry young and stay home with their children. In fact, women are represented in the workforce in record numbers. Gilbert (1993) reported that 59 percent of married women with children under the age of six were in the workforce and, of these, 70 percent worked full time. Sixty-seven percent of married women with children under eighteen were employed, and 73 percent of those were employed full time. These women contributed approxi- mately 40 percent of the household income.

Women, it seemed, faced a dilemma. Full-time homemakers felt isolated at home when caring for families (Lennon, 1998). Women who returned to the workforce after taking time off from careers felt penalized by having lost productive career-building years (Crittenden, 2001). Women who postponed marriage and childbearing until the late thirties or early forties were being warned of a shortage of mar- riage partners and drastically reduced rates of fertility. Women faced a dilemma.

SEVEN MODELS/PATTERNS OF SEQUENCING

Although there are many ways for women to organize their lives, there are seven basic patterns characterizing the modern woman that can be identified. These are by no means the only patterns but rather serve as prototypes of many others. Each model is described here, along with a discussion of its advantages and disadvantages that have been determined from past research. It should be noted that the authors of this chapter are not endorsing one pattern over another, nor are they suggesting that women have made good or bad decisions based on the life sequences they have chosen.

The Woman Who Marries Young and Stays Home

The first of these is the traditional role of the unemployed married woman in the nuclear family. Although this role is now in the minority (U.S. Department of Labor, 2003), it still holds a powerful place in the culture's mythology (Ganong & Coleman, 1995). There are clearly advantages for the young woman who chooses this path. She will select her husband during a time when she has the largest population of unmarried men from whom to choose. The tendency for women to marry men who are more successful on some dimension (such as financial success, termed "the marriage gradient" by Bernard, 1972) has been well documented (Peplau & Gordon, 1985), and these women will be less likely to encounter fertility problems (DeCherney & Berkowitz, 1982). If this woman should have trouble conceiving, she has time for medical intervention before her "biological clock" runs down. When she has children, she need not feel torn between the demands of her home and those of the workplace. The husband often benefits from the advantage of having a full-time homemaker who devotes herself to his nurturance and that of the children (Bernard, 1972). The husband is relieved of most of the tasks of running a home and managing a family. His responsibility is limited to providing financial support. In this marriage, the wife's role as full-time homemaker is clearly defined. Both the wife and the husband are likely to agree that he is the head of the family and has the greater authority (Bernard, 1981; Cook, 1993; Steil & Weltman, 1991).

This role, however, comes at a price. Researchers have suggested that full-time homemakers are at higher risk of depression than are employed women (Crosby, 1991; Ferree, 1984; Golding, 1989; Lennon, 1998; Nolen-Hoeksema, 1990; Shehan, 1984). The tasks that the full-time homemaker does are often dull, repetitive, and without reward (Oakley, 1974). When her children leave home, the full-time homemaker may be more likely to suffer from the "empty nest" syndrome than her employed counterpart (Bart, 1971). If her marriage ends in divorce, she is at risk for poverty (Price & McKenry, 1988). Further, she will find it harder to leave an abusive relationship because she is financially dependent on her husband (McHugh, Frieze, & Browne, 1993).

The Stay-at-Home Mom Goes to Work or School

This pattern is related to the first, in the sense that the woman who follows this pattern has lived some part of her adult life as a full-time wife and mother, and then returns to the workplace or school. She shares some of the advantages of the full-time homemaker. She has selected her husband at a time when many men are available. Because she has not yet begun her career, she does not face the limitations of the marriage gradient that the career woman does (Bernard, 1972). She will be less likely to have trouble with fertility (DeCherney & Berkowitz, 1982). The husband may enjoy many of the advantages of a traditional marriage.

This pattern has disadvantages as well. Women following this path will enter the workforce later in life and may never achieve the level of success of their childless counterparts (Crittenden, 2001). The bulk of household tasks is likely to remain with the wife, even though she is working. Hochshild (1989) found that most employed women put in a full day of work on the job and then returned home to perform a second full day of housework and childcare, a phenomenon she called the "second shift." She also found that women felt caught between the demands of work and the demands of family.

Although Hochshild's findings are controversial, many studies indicate that, even though working women have decreased the number of hours they devote to housework and men have increased the number of hours they spend doing these chores, equity has not been achieved (Gilbert, 1993; Pleck, 1992). Further, husbands in these marriages may still have more power, even though wives are contributing significantly to the household income. In fact, studies have shown that marital power remains with the husband, even if the wife earns more than the husband (Steil & Weltman, 1991). Similarly, in most dual-career marriages, the couple sees the wife's career as secondary to the husband's (Steil, 2001). Finally, it may be difficult for the family to adjust to new roles and expectations when the stay-at-home mother returns to work or school.

These first two patterns have many advantages in the family domain, but significant disadvantages in the work domain. The next two patterns have disadvantages in the family domain, but advantages in the work domain.

The Career Woman (Married or Unmarried) without Children

Women may choose not to have children or may be childless through circumstances beyond their control. Women may choose to remain childless in order to pursue educational or career goals (Landa, 1990) and/or because they value their autonomy and independence (Houseknecht, 1979). There are clear economic advantages to this model. Women without children now earn almost 90 percent of men's wages (Waldfogle, 1998). Further, childless marriages often are happier than marriages with children (MacDermid, Huston, & McHale, 1990). There is little evidence to suggest that the psychological well-being of childless women is lower than that of mothers (Muller & Yoder, 1997). Even women who are childless by circumstances beyond their control rather than by choice are no more likely than mothers to suffer decreased psychological well-being (Baruch, Barnett, & Rivers, 1983).

Nor are single women necessarily unhappy. Many single women do not regret being childless or single and report enjoying the freedom to live their lives as they please. They often derive satisfaction from a sense of self-sufficiency and competence. Many never-married women report having active and fulfilling lives (Paradise, 1993). For example, Loewenstein, Block, Campion, Epstein, Gale et al. (1981) found that 75 percent of childless single women expressed no regret at not having had children. There are, of course, disadvantages to both childlessness and being single. Women who are childless often are evaluated harshly by society (Baruch et al., 1983), and much of our social structure is organized around couples. However, single women often develop social support networks with friends and family and do not necessarily feel lonely (Burnley & Kurth, 1994).

The Married Career Woman Wants a Baby

The married career woman who decides to have a baby later in life enjoys many of the advantages of the childless woman. She has been able to devote herself to her education and career during her twenties and early thirties. Further, she and her husband are likely to enjoy a level of financial security, professional accomplishment, and emotional security that will make the transition to parenthood somewhat less stressful. Couples may also have grown accustomed to sharing household responsibilities and are more likely to share parenting duties (Gilbert, 1993). However, postponing childbearing until the mid-thirties may be problematic if fertility becomes an issue (Schwartz & Mayaux, 1982).

The Career Mother Becomes a Stay-at-Home Mom

If the career mother decides to stay at home, she will avoid the guilt and role strain that her working counterparts often experience. However, she may find that she has lost status with her colleagues (Crittenden, 2001) and is at higher risk of depression (Crosby, 1991; Ferree, 1984; Lennon, 1998; Nolen-Hoeksema, 1990; Shehan, 1984). Further, she will certainly lose the income that she earned and the advantages that come with that income. If she returns to work later, her career may never be as successful as it was previously (Crittenden, 2001).

Double-Duty Mom: Begin Family and Career Simultaneously

In many ways, the double-duty mom is the new norm. She has some of the advantages of both the stay-at-home mother and the career mother. She has less trouble finding a partner and is less likely to experience fertility problems. However, she may find that she is "mommy tracked" as she struggles to balance her family responsibilities with her career goals. In regard to her career, she will be seen as less ambitious and be given fewer opportunities for advancement. Moreover, in terms of her mother role, a great deal of flexibility is required on the part of both partners and is often accompanied by role strain for both partners (Kossek & Ozeki, 1998).

Single Mothers

The single mother who chooses this pattern often feels that it expresses her need for a child, but not for a partner (Bock, 2000), and single mothers are as satisfied with being parents as are married mothers.

Even mothers who find themselves single through widowhood or divorce often are proud of their ability to survive and handle a difficult job (Smith, 1997). The obvious disadvantages of this pattern include financial stress and the necessity of managing a household and children alone. Families headed by women are much more likely to be poor than other families (Steil, 2001). Finding good childcare is crucial for all working mothers, and single mothers are particularly vulnerable to the lack of quality care for their children (Polakow, 1993).

DISCUSSION AND IMPLICATIONS

In sum, there are several conclusions that can be drawn from this chapter. First, despite our movement forward in equality for women, working mothers are perceived negatively by society, and there still are negative perceptions of mothers as compared to fathers. Mothers often are stereotyped as either housewives or career women (Riedle, 1991). These subgroups of mothers are strongly held and prevent changes in overall stereotypes of mothers (Richards & Hewstone, 2001). Given that stereotypes can affect how people behave (Olson et al., 1996), research needs to explore how to change these negative stereotypes. For example, Herrera and Del Campo (1995) noted the need to change the stereotype of Latina women as submissive. This stereotype is outdated and disempowers Latina women.

Second, the research from this chapter has demonstrated that working mothers are struggling with their multiple roles. Mothers often do not admit that they struggle with balancing work and family life because they worry about being deemed bad mothers (Nicolson, 1998). Mothers also are hesitant to admit that they enjoy other aspects of their lives, such as their careers. Feeling isolated and overworked are understandable responses to work–family conflict. It is healthy to deal with stress by acknowledging tensions between work and family with statements such as "I wouldn't be without [my child], but . . ." (Woollett & Marshall, 2001, p. 172). This statement acknowledges the positive aspects of being a mother while admitting that there are negative components.

Third, organizations cannot afford to ignore work–family conflict. Research indicates that employees with high levels of work–family conflict are more likely to perform poorly, be absent or tardy, leave the job, and have less organizational commitment than employees with little or no work–family conflict (Baltes, Briggs, Huff, Wright, &

Neumann, 1999; Krausz, Sage, & Sidemen, 2000; Ralston & Flanagan, 1985). In response to problems of work–family conflict, organizations have implemented "family friendly" policies such as alternative work schedules, or flextime, family care leave, and childcare services. However, the effectiveness of these policies in the reduction of work–family conflict is minimal. Other variables, such as ability to manage multiple roles, marital status, spouses' attitudes, perceptions of spousal support, and perceptions of organizational support, may be related to whether organizational policies will be effective (Kossek & Ozeki, 1998).

Coping with the Challenges of Being a Working Mother

Based on the conclusions drawn from this literature review, there are many resources for coping and overcoming these challenges. It should come as little surprise that working mothers often rely on several coping strategies for reducing their role strain (DeMeis & Perkins, 1996). After all, working mothers often are intensely devoted to both their families and careers. Women have been found to utilize several strategies for coping with multiple roles, ranging from trying to do everything more efficiently to adjusting their attitudes about their multiple responsibilities (Elman & Gilbert, 1984).

Fortunately, coping strategies generally help working women deal with their role stress (McLaughlin, Cormier, & Cormier, 1988). However, researchers have noted the tendency of working mothers to hold themselves personally responsible for reducing work–family conflict rather than consider the structural, institutional, and societal changes that could help them balance their work and family lives. For example, the most commonly used coping strategy of working women is increased role behavior, a strategy whereby women attempt to do everything more efficiently (Elman & Gilbert, 1984). Working mothers should not only rely on themselves to reduce role strain but also on external resources such as "flextime, paternity leave and quality daycare in close proximity to one's place of employment" (Elman & Gilbert, p. 326).

Some mothers who can afford to do so choose to work part-time and report satisfaction with fulfilling their desire to work and also enjoy their mothering role. At first glance, it seems as if women benefit from working part-time. After all, women who work part-time experience numerous benefits, ranging from increased satisfaction with their home environments, personal efficiency, and life overall. However, there is a complex relationship between working part-time and experiences with role strain. For example, researchers have found that working part-time does not necessarily benefit employed women equally, as nonprofessional women typically have more to gain from part-time work than professional women, and professional women continue to experience work–family conflict, even if they work part-time. Although professional women recognize certain benefits of working part-time, they also report considerable negative consequences such as feeling less included in their work environments, worrying that their opportunities for growth and enhancement at work have been jeopardized, and feeling stigmatized by their coworkers for choosing to work less than full-time (Barker, 1993). Interestingly, Barker found that role strain for working women was reduced not by working part-time but by working in an environment where the majority of workers were women. Overall, the role of part-time employment in reducing role strain for women remains unclear, but the research on this topic is promising. As noted by Higgins, Duxbury, and Johnson (2000), "In order to truly make a difference in the quality of life for women with children, part-time work also must be made desirable and rewarding" (p. 29).

Perceived spousal support and help with the housework often have been associated with less role strain and work–family conflict (Herrera & Del Campo, 1995; Krause & Markides, 1985). In a relationship, the experiences of one partner often influence the experiences and well-being of the other partner (Parasuraman, Greenhaus, & Granrose, 1992). If a husband supports his wife's career, then positive psychological outcomes become more likely. However, if he is not supportive, the opposite holds true, and negative psychological outcomes are more likely.

How Can Policy Changes Reduce Work–Family Conflict?

As of 1999, around 60 percent of employers offered flexible work schedules to at least some of their employees. While employees value flextime, little research has identified the conditions under which flextime will be most effective at reducing or preventing work–family conflict. Most of the research examining the impact of flextime has been focused on organizational benefits of using alternative schedules. It has been demonstrated by a vast amount of research on the availability of alternative work schedules that flextime is the most

Toolbox for Change

For	Images/perceptions	Strategies for change
Individuals	Mothers expected to be primary caretakers and men primary financial providers.	Promote egalitarian division of family work, such as shared household tasks, shared childcare.
	Working mothers viewed as more masculine, stay-at-home moms viewed as feminine, but less competent; stay-at-home and part-time employed fathers viewed as feminine.	Recognize and promote nontraditional roles in self and others, which will help change stereotypes.
		Seek spousal and family support.
	Conflict of traditional gender roles or cultural beliefs with need to work.	Redefine gender roles, including perceptions of motherhood and fatherhood, to match your current situation.
	Trouble with fertility.	Accept change as a natural part of adult development.
	Tendency of working mothers to hold themselves personally responsible for alleviating work–family conflict.	Seek fertility treatment, adopt children.
	Stigma against childlessness and remaining single.	Recognize that structural, institutional, and societal changes need to be made to alleviate work–family conflicts.
		Promote the legitimacy of childlessness and singlehood.
Community/ society	Assumptions about behavior based on stereotypes may lead to job discrimination.	Greater rewards for part-time work.
		Flexible and alternative work schedules.
	Mommy track.	On-site affordable quality daycare.
	Work–family conflict leads to dissatisfied and less-effective employees.	Reward family friendly organizations to achieve greater organizational support.

Toolbox for Change

For	Images/perceptions	Strategies for change
	Part-time work is not rewarded or desirable.	**Government policies:** Subsidized daycare for low-income families.
		Improved family care leave legislation, such as extended paid family leave time, paid paternal leave.
		Stricter laws to prevent discrimination against working parents.
Practitioners	Mothers may not admit that motherhood has negative aspects.	Promote strategies to reduce stress among mothers and fathers.
	Mothers may not admit their struggles with an unrealistic ideal of "the good mother."	Acknowledge the positive aspects of being a mother while admitting there are negative components.
	Fathers may have unrealistic expectations about being a good provider.	Promote egalitarian division of labor, such as legitimacy of female primary financial providers and male primary caretakers.
	Stereotypic assumptions of mothers' and fathers' roles, traits, and behavior	Recognize and promote nontraditional roles in others, which will help change stereotypes.

beneficial schedule to employers, with the prime benefits of reduced absenteeism and tardiness (Baltes et al., 1999).

Another policy to improve work–family conflict is on-site daycare facilities. Few organizations provide on-site, high-quality daycare, which is a much-needed resource for many working mothers (Scarr, Phillips, & McCartney, 1989).

However, even before the organizational policies are implemented within work settings, changes need to be made with family care leave policies. The mandated twelve weeks of unpaid parental leave (Family and Medical Leave Act [FMLA] of 1993) are not sufficient for most working mothers because they only allows twelve weeks of *unpaid* parental leave, which many women cannot afford to take (Marks, 1997). Organizations concerned about the impact of work–family conflict, such as employee productivity and absenteeism, as well as organizations with genuine concerns for employees' well-being, should augment the mandated policy with at least partial paid leave. The United States is the only nation, among 100 countries, that does not provide paid, job-protected maternal leave (Kamerman, 1989). Sweden offers mothers and fathers nine months of job-protected leave at 90 percent pay, with the option of extending the leave by three months with less pay (Scarr et al., 1989). The FMLA policy needs to extend the time limit and provide some wage replacement.

CONCLUSION

Based on what we have provided within this chapter, we believe that there is not only a need for organizational change but also a need for more empirical research. Areas that need to be further explored are (1) multi-method research using both qualitative and quantitative instruments; (2) interdisciplinary research that forges the links between psychology, sociology, economics, and politics; (3) the intersection of race, ethnicity, social class, and sexual orientation on work–family conflict; (4) person perception research with non-student samples such as adults from the community; (5) research that includes both employees and employers; (6) moderators and mediators of negative perceptions and reality of working mothers; (7) how stereotypes affect actual experiences, such as discrimination, and ways to change these stereotypes; and (8) research directly addressing issues relevant to mothers' experiences as distinct from issues relevant to women in general.

REFERENCES

Amaro, H., Russo, N., & Johnson, J. (1987). Family and work predictors of psychological well-being among Hispanic women professionals. *Psychology of Women Quarterly, 11*, 505–521.

Baltes, B. B., Briggs, T. E., Huff, J. W., Wright, J. A., & Neumann, G. A. (1999). Flexible and compressed workweek schedules: A meta-analysis of their effects on work-related criteria. *Journal of Applied Psychology, 84*, 496–513.

Barker, K. (1993). Changing assumptions and contingent solutions: The costs and benefits of women working full- and part-time. *Sex Roles, 28*, 47–71.

Barnett, R. C., & Hyde, J. S. (2001). Women, men, work, and family: An expansionist theory. *American Psychologist, 56*, 781–796.

Barnett, R. C., & Marshall, N. L. (1993). Men, family-role quality, job-role quality, and physical health. *Health Psychology, 12*, 48–55.

Bart, P. B. (1971). Depression in middle age. In V. G. Gornick & B. K. Moran (Eds.), *Women in sexist society*. New York: Basic Books.

Baruch, G. K., Barnett, R. C., & Rivers, C. (1983). *Lifeprints: New patterns of love and work for today's women*. New York: New American Library.

Benin, M., & Keith, V. (1995). The social support of employed African American and Anglo mothers. *Journal of Family Issues, 16*, 275–297.

Bernard, J. (1972). *The future of marriage*. New York: World Publishing.

Bernard, J. (1981). The good provider role: Its rise and fall. *American Psychologist, 36*, 1–12.

Bock, J. D. (2000). Doing the right thing? Single mothers by choice and the struggle for legitimacy. *Gender and Society, 14*, 62–89.

Booth, R. (2002). Age and beauty: Stereotypes as factors in women's careers. In L. Diamante & J. A. Lee (Eds.), *The psychology of sex, gender, and jobs: Issues and solutions* (pp. 47–68). Westport, CT: Praeger.

Bridges, J. S., & Etaugh, C. (1995). College students' perceptions of mothers: Effects of maternal employment-childrearing pattern and motive for employment. *Sex Roles, 32*, 735–751.

Bridges, J. S., & Orza, A. M. (1992). The effects of employment role and motive for employment on the perceptions of mothers. *Sex Roles, 27*, 331–343.

Bridges, J. S., & Orza, A. M. (1996). Black and white employed mother's role experiences. *Sex Roles, 35*, 377–385.

Broman, C. L. (1988). Household work and family life satisfaction of blacks. *Journal of Marriage and the Family, 50*, 743–748.

Broman, C. L. (1991). Gender, work-family roles, and psychological well-being of blacks. *Journal of Marriage and the Family, 53*, 509–519.

Burnley, C. A., & Kurth, S. B. (1994). Never married: Alone and lonely? *Humbolt Journal of Social Relations, 18*, 57–83.

Byars, A. M., & McCubbin, L. D. (2001). Trends in career development research with racial/ethnic minorities: Prospects and challenges. In J. G. Ponterotto, J. M. Casas, L. A. Suzuki, & C. M. Alexander (Eds.), *Handbook of multicultural counseling* (2nd ed., pp. 633–654). Thousand Oaks, CA: Sage Publications.

Cook, E. P. (1993). The gendered context of life: Implications for women's and men's career-life plans. *Career Development Quarterly, 41*, 227–237.

Crittenden, A. (2001). *The price of motherhood*. New York: Henry Holt.

Crosby, F. J. (1991). *Juggling: The unexpected advantage of balancing career and home for women and their families.* New York: Free Press.

DeCherney, A. J., & Berkowitz, G. S. (1982). Female fertility and age. *The New England Journal of Medicine, 306,* 424–426.

DeMeis, D., & Perkins, H. (1996). "Supermoms" of the nineties: Homemaker and employed mothers' performance and perceptions of the motherhood role. *Journal of Family Issues, 17,* 777–792.

Doherty, K. T. (1998). A mind of her own: Effects of need for closure and gender on reactions to nonconformity. *Sex Roles, 38,* 801–819.

Eagly, A. H., & Steffen, V. J. (1984). Gender stereotypes stem from the distribution of women and men into social roles. *Journal of Personality and Social Psychology, 46,* 735–754.

Eagly, A. H., Wood, W., & Diekman, A. (2000). Social role theory of sex differences and similarities. In T. Eckes & H. M. Trautner (Eds.), *The developmental social psychology of gender* (pp. 123–174). Mahway, NJ: Erlbaum.

Elman, M., & Gilbert, L. (1984). Coping strategies for role conflict in married professional women with children. *Family Relations, 33,* 317–327.

Engel, J. (1988). Japanese and American housewives' attitudes toward employment of women. *Journal of Social Behavior and Personality, 3,* 363–371.

Erel, O., Oberman, Y., & Yirmiya, N. (2000). Maternal versus nonmaternal care and seven domains of children's development. *Psychological Bulletin, 126,* 727–747.

Espiritu, Y. (1999). Gender and labor in Asian immigrant families. *American Behavioral Scientist, 42,* 628–647.

Etaugh, C., & Folger, D. (1998). Perceptions of parents whose work and parenting behaviors deviate from role expectations. *Sex Roles, 39,* 215–223.

Faludi, S. (1991). *Backlash: The undeclared war against American women.* New York: Doubleday.

Ferree, M. M. (1984). Class, housework, and happiness: Women's work and life satisfaction. *Sex Roles, 11,* 1057–1074.

Fiske, S. T., Bersoff, D. N., Borgida, E., Deaux, K., & Heilman, M. E. (1991). Social science research on trial: The use of sex stereotyping research in *Price Waterhouse vs. Hopkins. American Psychologist, 46,* 1049–1060.

Friedman, S. D., & Greenhaus, J. H. (2000). *Work and family—Allies or enemies? What happens when business professionals confront life choices.* New York: Oxford University Press.

Furr, S. R. (2002). Men and women in cross-gender careers. In L. Diamante & J. A. Lee (Eds.), *The psychology of sex, gender, and jobs: Issues and solutions* (pp. 69–80). Westport, CT: Praeger.

Ganong, L. H., & Coleman, M. (1995). The content of mother stereotypes. *Sex Roles, 32*, 495–512.

Gilbert, L.A. (1993). *Two careers/one family.* Newbury Park, CA: Sage Publications.

Gilbert, L. A., & Rader, J. (2001). Current perspectives on women's adult roles: Work, family, and life. In R. K. Unger (Ed.), *Handbook of the psychology of women and gender* (pp. 156–182). New York: Wiley.

Golding, J. M. (1989). Role occupancy and role-specific stress and social support as predictors of depression. *Basic and Applied Social Psychology, 10*, 173–195.

Gore, S., & Mangione, T. W. (1983). Social roles, sex roles, and psychological distress: Additive and interactive models of sex differences. *Journal of Health and Social Behavior, 24*, 300–312.

Granrose, C. S., & Cunningham, E. A. (1988). Post-partum work intentions among black and white college women. *The Career Development Quarterly, 37*, 149–164.

Greenhaus, J. H., Parasuraman, S., Granrose, C. S., Rabinowitz, S., & Beutell, N. J. (1989). Sources of work-family conflict among two-career couples. *Journal of Vocational Behavior, 34*, 133–153.

Harris, M. J. (1991). Controversy and cumulation: Meta-analysis and research on interpersonal expectancy effects. *Personality and Social Psychology Bulletin, 17*, 316–322.

Herrera, R., & Del Campo, R. (1995). Beyond the superwoman syndrome: Work satisfaction and family functioning among working-class, Mexican American women. *Hispanic Journal of Behavioral Sciences, 17*, 49–60.

Higgins, C., Duxbury, L., & Johnson, K. (2000). Part-time work for women: Does it really help balance work and family? *Human Resource Management, 39*, 17–32.

Hochschild, A. R. (1989). *The second shift: Working parents and the revolution at home.* New York: Basic Books.

Hondagneu-Sotelo, P., & Avila, E. (1997). "I'm here, but I'm there": The meanings of transnational motherhood. *Gender and Society, 11*, 548–571.

Hossain, Z., & Roopnarine, J. L. (1993). Division of household labor and childcare in dual-earner African American families with infants. *Sex Roles, 29*, 571–583.

Houseknecht, S. K. (1979). Timing of the decision to remain voluntarily childless: Evidence for continuous socialization. *Psychology of Women Quarterly, 4*, 81–96.

Jost, J. T. (1997). An experimental replication of the depressed-entitlement effect among women. *Psychology of Women Quarterly, 21*, 387–393.

Kamerman, S. (1989). Childcare, women, work and the family: An international overview of childcare services and related policies. In J. Lande,

S. Scarr, & N. Gunzenhauser (Eds.), *The future of childcare in the United States* (pp. 93–110). Hillsdale, NJ: Erlbaum.

Kossek, E. E., & Ozeki, C. (1998). Work-family conflict, policies, and the job-life satisfaction relationship: A review and directions for organizational behavior-human resources. *Journal of Applied Psychology, 83*(2), 139–149.

Krause, N., & Markides, K. (1985). Employment and psychological well-being in Mexican American women. *Journal of Health and Social Behavior, 26,* 15–26.

Krausz, M., Sage, A., & Sidemen, Y. (2000). Actual and preferred work schedules and scheduling control as determinants of job related attitudes. *Journal of Vocational Behavior, 56,* 1–11.

Landa, A. (1990). No accident: The voices of voluntarily childless women: An essay on the social construction of fertility choices. In J. P. Knowles & E. Cole (Eds.), *Motherhood: A feminist perspective* (pp. 139–158). New York: Haworth.

LeMaster, J., Marcus-Newhall, A., Casad, B. J., & Silverman, N. (In press). Perceptions of working mothers and fathers: Interacting effects of passion, job prestige, and gender. Manuscript submitted for publication.

Lennon, M. C. (1998). Domestic arrangements and depressive symptoms: An examination of household conditions. In B. P. Dohrenwend (Ed.), *Adversity, stress, and psychopathology* (pp. 409–442). New York: Oxford University Press.

Loewenstein, S. F., Block, N. E., Campion, J., Epstein, J. S., Gale, P., & Salvatore, M. (1981). A study of satisfactions and stresses of single women in midlife. *Sex Roles, 7,* 1127–1141.

MacDermid, S. M., Huston, T. L., & McHale, S. M. (1990). Changes in marriage associated with the transition to parenthood: Individual differences as a function of sex-role attitudes and changes in the division of labor. *Journal of Marriage and the Family, 52,* 475–486.

Malson, M. R. (1983). Black women's sex roles: The social context for a new ideology. *Journal of Social Issues, 39,* 101–113.

Marcus-Newhall, A., LeMaster, J., Casad, B. J., & Shaked, N. (In press). Between a rock and a hard place: Attitudes toward working and stay-at-home mothers. Manuscript submitted for publication.

Marks, M. R. (1997). Party politics and family policy: The case of the Family and Medical Leave Act. *Journal of Family Issues, 18,* 55–70.

Matthews, K. A., Raikkonen, K., Everson, S. A., Flory, J. D., Marco, C. A., Owens, J. F., et al. (2000). Do the daily experiences of healthy men and women vary according to occupational prestige and work strain? *Psychosomatic Medicine, 62,* 346–353.

McHugh, M. C., Frieze, I. H., & Browne, A. (1993) Research on battered women and their assailants. In F. L. Denmark & M. A. Paludi (Eds.),

Psychology of women: A handbook of issues and theories (pp. 513–552). Westport, CT: Greenwood Press.

McLaughlin, M., Cormier, L. S., & Cormier, W. H. (1988). Relation between coping strategies and distress, stress, and marital adjustment of multiple-role women. *Journal of Counseling Psychology, 35*, 187–193.

Min, P. (2001). Changes in Korean immigrants' gender role and social status, and their marital conflicts. *Sociological Forum, 16*, 301–320.

Muller, K. A., & Yoder, J. D. (1997). Gendered norms for family size, employment, and occupations: Are there personal costs for violating them? *Sex Roles, 36*, 207–220.

Myers, L. W. (1989) Affect or consequential? *The Western Journal of Black Studies, 13*, 173–178.

Napholz, L. (1995). Mental health and Native American women's multiple roles. *American Indian and Alaska Native Mental Health Research, 6*, 57–75.

Napholz, L. (2000). Balancing multiple roles among a group of urban midlife American Indian working women. *Health Care for Women International, 21*, 255–266.

Nicolson, P. (1998). *Post-natal depression: Psychology, science, and the transition to motherhood.* London: Routledge.

Nolen-Hoeksema, S. (1990). *Sex differences in depression.* Stanford, CA: Stanford University Press.

Oakley, A. (1974). *The sociology of housework.* New York: Pantheon Books.

Olson, J. M., Roese, N. J., & Zanna, M. P. (1996). Expectancies. In E. T. Higgins & A. W. Kruglanski (Eds.), *Social psychology: Handbook of basic principles* (pp. 211–238). New York: Guilford Press.

Orbuch, T. L., & Custer, L. (1995). The social context of married women's work and its impact on black husbands and white husbands. *Journal of Marriage and the Family, 57*, 333–345.

Paradise, S. A. (1993). Older never married women: A cross-cultural investigation. *Women and Therapy, 14*, 129–139.

Parasuraman, S., Greenhaus, J. H., & Granrose, C. S. (1992). Role stressors, social support, and well-being among two-career couples. *Journal of Organizational Behavior, 13*, 339–356.

Parents of baby killed in au pair's case want millions in damages. (1998, November 2). Retrieved November 2, 2003 from http://www.cnn.com/US/9811/02/woodward.money/index.html

Peplau, L. A., & Gordon, S. L. (1985). Women and men in love: Gender differences in close heterosexual relationships. In V. E. O'Leary, R. K. Unger, & B. S. Wallston (Eds.), *Women, gender, and social psychology* (pp. 257–292). Hillsdale, NJ: Erlbaum.

Phillips, S. D., & Imhoff, A. R. (1997). Women and career development: A decade of research. *Annual Review of Psychology, 48*, 31–59.

Pleck, J. (1992). Work–family policies in the United States. In H. Kahne & J. Giele (Eds.), *Women's lives and women's work: Parallels and contrasts in modernizing and industrial countries.* Boulder, CO: Westview.

Polakow, V. (1993). *Lives on the edge: Single mothers and their children in the other America.* Chicago: University of Chicago Press.

Prentice, D. A., & Carranza, E. (2002). What women and men should be, shouldn't be, are allowed to be, and don't have to be: The contents of prescriptive gender stereotypes. *Psychology of Women Quarterly, 26,* 269–281.

Price, S. J., & McKenry, P. C. (1988). *Divorce.* Beverly Hills, CA: Sage Publications.

Ralston, D. A., & Flanagan, M. F. (1985). The effect of flextime on absenteeism and turnover for male and female employees. *Journal of Vocational Behavior, 26,* 206–217.

Richards, Z., & Hewstone, M. (2001). Subtyping and subgrouping: Processes for the prevention and promotion of stereotype change. *Personality and Social Psychology Review, 5,* 52–73.

Riedle, J. E. (1991). Exploring subcategories of stereotypes: Not all mothers are the same. *Sex Roles, 24,* 711–723.

Rivera, R., Torres, M., & Carre, F. (1997). Role burdens: The impact of employment and family responsibilities on the health status of Latino women. *Journal of Health Care for the Poor and Underserved, 8,* 99–113.

Rushing, B., & Schwabe, A. (1995). The health effects of work and family role characteristics: Gender and race comparisons. *Sex Roles, 33,* 59–75.

Russo, N. F. (1976). The motherhood mandate. *Journal of Social Issues, 5,* 143–153.

Scarr, S., Phillips, D., & McCartney, K. (1989). Working mothers and their families. *American Psychologist, 44,* 1402–1409.

Schindehette, S., Carswell, S., Sheff, V., & Micheli, R. (1990, August 20). Waking up late to the biological clock. *People Weekly, 34,* 74–77.

Schwartz, D., & Mayaux, M. J. (1982). Female fecundity as a function of age. *The New England Journal of Medicine, 306,* 404–406.

Schwartz, F. N. (1989, January/February). Management women and the new facts of life. *Harvard Business Review, 67,* 65–76.

Shehan, C. L. (1984). Wives' work and psychological well-being: An extension of Gove's social role theory of depression. *Sex Roles, 11,* 881–894.

Smith, M. (1997). Psychology's undervaluation of single motherhood. *Feminism and Psychology, 7,* 529–532.

Snyder, M., & Cantor, N. (1979). Testing hypotheses about other people: The use of historical knowledge. *Journal of Experimental Social Psychology, 15,* 330–342.

Steil, J. M. (2001). Family forms and member well-being: A research agenda for the decade of behavior. *Psychology of Women Quarterly, 25,* 344–363.

Steil, J. M., & Weltman, K. (1991). Marital inequality: The importance of resources, personal attributes, and social norms on career valuing and the allocation of domestic responsibilities. *Sex Roles, 24,* 161–179.

Thompson, L., & Walker, A. J. (1989). Gender in families: Women and men in marriage, work, and parenthood. *Journal of Marriage and the Family, 51,* 845–871.

U.S. Department of Labor, Bureau of Labor Statistics. (2003). Labor force statistics from the Current Population Survey: Employed persons by occupation, sex, and age. Retrieved August 11, 2003, from http://www.bls.gov/cps/ - nempstat_m

Waldfogel, J. (1998) Understanding the "family gap" in pay for women with children. *Journal of Economic Perspectives, 12,* 137–156.

White, L., & Rogers, S. J. (2000). Economic circumstances and family outcomes: A review of the 1990s. *Journal of Marriage and the Family, 62,* 1035–1051.

Woollett, A., & Marshall, H. (2001). Motherhood and mothering. In R. K. Unger (Ed.), *Handbook of the psychology of women and gender* (pp. 170–182). New York: Wiley.

Zambrana, R., & Frith, S. (1988). Mexican-American professional women: Role satisfaction differences in single and multiple role lifestyles. *Journal of Social Behavior and Personality, 3,* 347–361.

CHAPTER 4

Running into the Wind: The Experience of Discrimination in an Academic Workplace

Michelle Kaminski

What does it feel like to be the target of discrimination at work? At first, you feel isolated and definitely not valued. After a while, you think it's your fault, that you are somehow not good enough. Later, you start to notice that some groups of people are treated differently by the boss. Some are treated better, for example by being given more support to get their job done, or more rewards for the same level of performance. Others are treated worse—denied access to resources, for example. You notice that those who are treated worse look like you and those who are treated better don't look like you. You start to get angry. Maybe you make efforts to improve things. But at some point you come to a choice: stay and fight, or go somewhere else where you believe it will be better.

That briefly captures the emotional process I went through on my last job as a university faculty member. I have two goals in using this narrative form to describe my personal experience with discrimination there. First, I hope to identify specific behaviors by organizational leaders and members that contribute either to a feeling of inclusion or exclusion. I will do this by describing my interactions with other faculty members, as well as by identifying some general patterns that might occur in other organizations. Although sexism and racism are institutional problems and require change at organizational and institutional levels, it is still *individuals* within those organizations who must make those changes. By focusing on specific behaviors, we can identify concrete steps that individuals can take to promote change.

Second, I want to describe the emotional impact of working in an environment that systematically undervalues women. This is important because so many people believe that issues of discrimination have been solved, that it's just not a problem in today's workplace. Others believe that managers actually favor women and minorities because they are so afraid of lawsuits. My experience is quite the contrary. On my previous job, I saw systematic ways in which men (all white men, as it happens) were given more resources, higher pay, and better evaluations than the women who were as good as—or even better—than their male counterparts. And that bias has a cost, both to the organization, which loses the talents of some of its members, and to the individual who may suffer both a psychological and an economic impact (Belle & Doucet, 2003; Cortina & Magley, 2003).

Kathy Germann, a diversity trainer and consultant, suggested this metaphor for working and living in a discriminatory environment: it's like running into the wind. It might be a small breeze or a stiff headwind, but you feel it. It slows you down. You have to work harder to succeed. I'd like to expand on that a little bit. In work organizations, some people are running with the wind at their back; they get extra help and so it's not surprising that they achieve their goals quickly. Others are running into the wind, so even with the same levels of effort and ability, it's going to take them longer to achieve the same goal. How much difference does it make? Well, to extend the track example, a race time is declared "wind-aided" (and therefore not comparable to other times) if there is a tail wind of only two meters per second, or about 4.5 miles per hour. That's not very much. It's difficult to quantify the extra help that a member of a dominant group might get in a discriminatory work organization, or the extent of the resistance faced by women and minorities in the same settings. But even a small pattern of differences can have a large cumulative effect.

MY EXPERIENCE

At my previous job, I was working as a faculty member at one of the top public universities in the United States. I believe I experienced gender discrimination on that job. "Discrimination" has a specific legal definition. But I am not a lawyer, and the sense in which I am using it may or may not meet the legal definition. What I mean is that male and female faculty members of the same rank were treated differently, and the men were given significantly more advantages than the women.

Here is some background information about my former department. About 60 percent of the students were women. During the four years I was there, the faculty composition was approximately as follows: ten senior male faculty, one senior female faculty (who retired during this period), five junior male faculty (two of whom became tenured during this time), and three junior female faculty. The department had not granted tenure to a female faculty member since the mid-1980s, about fifteen years before I got there. Several women faculty had come and gone since that time. Some were denied tenure, and some, like me, were so frustrated with the atmosphere there that they left for other jobs before going up for tenure.

When I began that job, I was, like most people, eager to succeed and confident in my abilities. I had just co-authored a book I was proud of (Kaminski, Bertelli, Moye, & Yudken, 1996) and looked forward to conducting additional research. But the warning signs came early. Even in my interview for the job, a retired male faculty member took me aside and said that I should be careful because women had a hard time getting tenure there. One of the women faculty members was quite candid about the issue. Naively, perhaps, I believed that although it would be challenging, I could still succeed in that environment. Ultimately, my decision to leave had less to do with my level of success and more to do with my psychological well-being.

Again, let me emphasize that I started the job with confidence and hope. And so I would like to describe the events that changed my feelings to frustration and futility. Academic readers will understand that, at many universities, research publications are by far the most significant factor in career advancement, including becoming tenured. While I had my own research plans, shortly after I arrived one of the senior faculty members (I'll call him "A") asked whether I was interested in working on a case study about a very controversial event in our field. Of course I said yes. About a month later, he told me that he was going to offer the work to a graduate student instead of me, because the (male) student needed the money. I said fine, I had plenty of other projects in mind. Privately, I thought it was odd. I had been trained in case study methodology and had published several case studies before. To my knowledge, neither "A" nor the student had the methodological and interviewing skills that I did. So,

I thought it was odd to exclude me. In addition, while the student would be paid to work on the project, as a faculty member, I would have done it as part of my normal workload. I did not have to be paid extra. All *three* of us could have worked on it. I didn't make much of being excluded at the time, but it turns out that that was the first and last time in my four years there that any senior faculty member would offer to work with me.

So, I went ahead with my own research agenda. One of the things that help faculty members accomplish their research is having a graduate student work with them. In our department, graduate students were given positions as research assistants (which include a tuition waiver and a modest salary) and assigned to work with certain faculty members. The students were paid out of the department's budget, and all faculty were entitled to one research assistant who worked for ten hours per week. I was given a research assistant, but only for five hours per week. When I asked the department head for the same amount of research assistant hours as the other faculty, he said that it was not up to him. This seemed disingenuous, since he was the boss. He said that it was up to one of the administrative staff members. While the staff person handled the paperwork and indeed exercised some discretion about which student was a good match for which professor, the head of the department outranked her considerably. If he had told her to give me a research assistant for ten hours, she would have been required to do so. I've noticed over the years that management always has some reason why women and minorities deserve less. But the reason often is not a logical one. Similarly, Moss and Tilly (2001) describe a complex mix of fact and fiction in what employers say about hiring decisions and race.

About this time, I was beginning to compare the research support the department gave me to what it gave the male junior faculty. While not all the men received favorable treatment, some did. One man in particular ("B") received an extraordinary level of support from one of the most powerful senior members ("C"). Junior faculty member B was excused from a number of his duties as a faculty member so he could put more time into his research and therefore increase his chances of being tenured. Whenever B was assigned to serve on an administrative committee, C would tell the department head that B could not serve on the committee because he needed time to focus on his research. (Committee work, while necessary to the functioning of the university, is generally both unglamorous and unrewarded.) The department head would agree and release B from any committee assignment. In fact, the department head repeatedly said that he would protect junior faculty from having to do too much committee work. But in my case, it didn't work that way. I was required to serve on the executive committee, which was one of the more burdensome committees in terms of number of hours required. I also served on two search committees, a strategic planning committee, and was the faculty liaison to the alumni board. I did not mind doing the committee work. But in hindsight I see what an advantage it was to B not to have to spend much time doing this kind of work.

C helped B out in an even larger way. He taught one of his classes for him. Technically, the class was jointly taught by B and C, but the students reported that B did almost nothing and didn't come to the class very often.

To understand what impact this had on B's tenure prospects, consider this: Faculty have three components to their jobs: teaching, research, and service (such as committee work). In terms of getting tenure, research is the top priority, teaching matters a little, and service does not count at all. C removed all of B's service obligation, and some of his teaching load, leaving B more time than his peers to focus on his research—and therefore increasing the likelihood he would receive tenure.

There was something else about B and C that might seem unimportant at first: every day they went to lunch together. Sometimes other male faculty members, including the department head, joined them. Every day they walked by my office door on their way to lunch. In the four years I worked there, they did not invite me to join them even once. Admittedly, lunch is not the most important thing about work. But being excluded both in work and social events can have a double impact on one's psyche. The social ease that comes with sharing meals, or the lack of it, can make a difference in how people treat each other at work.

When one of the other women confronted them and asked why they never invited the women to lunch, their response was quite interesting. They said that they just talked about sports, and the women wouldn't enjoy it. Well, that might be true for some women, but not in my case. I've played a number of recreational sports—softball, skiing, swimming, basketball, volleyball, and a little bit of street hockey. I'm also a fan. I have attended, in person, a World Series, a Super Bowl, a Stanley Cup final, and regular season events in those and other sports, from basketball to lacrosse. I watch sports on television. B and C knew I was a sports fan. I beat them in their football pool one year, and they helped me get basketball season tickets. So, it's just not true that they didn't invite me to lunch *because* I wouldn't want to talk about sports. Again, there is always a reason that more powerful people use to justify why they exclude some people but not others. But the reasons frequently do not withstand even the most basic level of scrutiny.

The lunches would not have mattered if other aspects of the department were not so systematically biased. A real turning point in my awareness of this bias was the time I served on the executive committee. Among other duties, the executive committee assists the department head in evaluating the faculty's performance at the end of every year. By this time, I had been in the department for three years and had heard the department head and others talk about what constituted good performance. I thought I had a pretty good understanding of it. But it absolutely did *not* match the performance ratings and raises given out. (As a junior faculty member with no security, I did not feel comfortable criticizing my senior colleague's pay raises, and I'm not proud to admit that I just went along with what the department head said, even though I thought some of his decisions were clearly biased.)

What I learned was that good performance seemed to hinge on having a male name at the top of the annual activity report. In some cases, men with no publications were given higher ratings than women with publications. Publications by women were often discounted. One year, I had a publication in the same outlet as the department head. My publication, however, did not "count." Regarding another journal, one of the very few publications focused on my area. I was *repeatedly* told by the department head not to publish there because it was considered too low-quality. (They accept approximately 20 percent of the manuscripts they receive.) I was told it would not count in my performance evaluation. This disappointed me because my work was an especially good fit with that journal, and it would have been easier for me to publish there than elsewhere. So, I was very surprised when one of my male colleagues (D) had two publications there and it was considered outstanding performance.

At this point I felt misled at best, and flat-out lied to at worst. But I also felt betrayed. Anytime B was in danger of receiving poor performance reviews, C intervened and explained that while B's work was low in quantity (in spite of all that extra time he had when he was not teaching or serving on committees), it was extremely high in quality; and it might not be published this year, but when it finally was, it would be great. I'm glad B got that kind of support. But I felt betrayed because my own supervisor did not support me in this way. To my knowledge, he never said, "Why would a publication in the same journal count for D, but not for Michelle?" This was a supervisor who said he was on my side and said he wanted me to get tenure. But he would simply not do what C did for B. He would not argue a case in my favor. As a junior faculty member, it's hard to make these arguments for yourself. You might be intimidated. You might fear retaliation. But even if you're not concerned about that, there's a pretty good chance that you don't have access to the information that goes into the performance review process or on who is getting extra money for what from the department head. It was only because I was on the executive committee—which junior faculty are normally excluded from—that I saw this behavior. My overall impression of the performance review process there was that if you changed the names at the top of the annual report, the ratings would change dramatically as well.

My supervisor played a role in another incident. He assigned me to host a women's conference. This conference is an annual event in our field, and it is rotated among a group of universities in the region. I was both excited and overwhelmed at the prospect of hosting it. I was excited because I had taught at the conference before when it was at other schools, and I knew what a powerful experience it was for the participants. But I was also overwhelmed because it was a huge amount of work. The coordinator had to organize about fifteen instructors, seventy-five to 100 participants, food, lodging, and evening activities, and do it on a shoestring budget. (Participants paid about $475 each, which covered five nights' lodging, six days of meals, and five days of instruction.)

But in addition to my concern about pulling the conference together, I faced another problem. Senior faculty member E argued in an executive committee meeting and later sent me a series of email messages claiming that we should not host it. His argument was that we should not host a women's conference of any sort because it would be biased against men. He said that neither the department nor the university could sponsor a women's conference. I pointed out that the university hosted its own working women's conference every year, and our department had hosted this regional conference at least twice before. But this did not change E's mind. He continued to send me email messages a few times a day. I estimate that I spent two hours a day for two weeks reading and responding to E's emails. And I stewed about it every night when I went home, and woke up feeling angry every morning. I was furious at E both for the position he took, and for the process he followed. Why was he attacking me for something I was *assigned* to do by my supervisor? Why didn't he take it up with my supervisor? My supervisor tried to handle this as though it were a personal dispute between E and me, which it was not. He told me that E was really a nice guy, and that over the years he had been one of the senior faculty who was most helpful to women. (The latter point might be true. In fact, after this incident he was noticeably more helpful to me.)

The point was not whether E and I got along. I was assigned to do this work by my supervisor, and E should have directed his concerns toward my supervisor. My supervisor should have said that it was his decision and he stood by it. But that's not what happened. Instead, I was forced to spend a considerable amount of time defending myself—time that could have been better spent doing other things. Furthermore, I could not imagine anyone attacking any of the male junior faculty for teaching a course they were assigned to teach. And if anyone attacked B, C was certain to defend him. In contrast, I was largely left alone to battle an unwarranted attack from a person who, if I had stayed there, would have voted on whether or not I got to keep my job.

Before I talk about my responses to these events, I would like to mention one more story. It's about one of the other women who worked in this department, but who also left without becoming tenured. She lived several hours from campus, because her husband could not find work in the small university town and instead worked in a larger city. This issue was discussed when she was hired. She kept an apartment in town and was on campus three days a week. At one point, one student complained that he couldn't find her. The department head told her she had to be more accessible. So, she started coming to campus Monday through Thursday. This is the story as she told me, and I observed that she was indeed in the office four days a week.

But immediately after she left, faculty and staff started saying that she had been in the office only one day a week, and that was why she never got tenure there. I came to realize that this was part of a pattern of telling public stories that, first, did not match the actual events and, second, explained why the woman left or would soon leave.

THE EMOTIONAL TOLL

In the introduction, I said that one of my goals in writing this was to describe the psychological impact that working in this environment had on me. But I find that it is difficult, and somewhat painful, to do so. I glanced at some of the notes I kept during that period, and in doing so, I felt like I was reliving the same emotions again—the pain of knowing you are not valued, the frustration at trying to make improvements and making no progress whatsoever, and the deep disappointment in some whom I believed to be genuinely well-meaning but unwilling to admit there was a problem. But it is also difficult because someone who is professionally competent is not supposed to admit that he/she was in this situation. They are supposed to say that everything is fine and they will do a good job no matter what. There is a stigma associated with saying you have been harmed because of discrimination. In this way, it is somewhat like what happens to women who are subject to sexual harassment at work, who are raped, or who are the victims of domestic violence. You don't really want to admit it in public. Because if you do, there are plenty of folks who will think it is your fault. Although workplace discrimination is clearly not as violent or traumatic as those experiences, it is another example of blaming the victim.

In this case, I want to talk about it. In part, this is because many people believe that there is no more discrimination in the workplace. Yet, women earn about 78 percent of what men do in the United States (Bureau of Labor Statistics, 2003) and are significantly underrepresented in leadership positions (Estrich, 2000). But a more important reason to mention it is that if we don't talk about it, it won't change. In fact, I feel an obligation to speak out about it. Why? Because in other work settings in which I was treated well, I was reaping the benefit of battles that other women before me had fought. And the only way to repay that debt is to fight for the women and others who will come after me.

In this particular case, I can state unequivocally that this job damaged my psychological well-being. I began to doubt my skills and abilities. I knew things were not quite right. But I didn't know exactly what was wrong. Whatever it was, I thought it was my fault. Some describe this as internalized oppression (Weber, 2001). My sleep suffered, and so did my self-esteem. When B talked to me about what a great place he thought it was, I even felt shame. If it was such a great place, why was I so unhappy? After a time, I didn't even want to run into some of the senior faculty in the halls. I felt that they had judged me as unworthy of sharing a workplace with them. I had accumulated too much negative affect and did not want to risk any interactions that would lead to more.

But a few key events changed my emotional perspective. The battle about the women's school was one of them. Serving on the executive committee was an even more important one. There, I learned that discretionary funds controlled by the department head, which I didn't even know existed, were generally used to support the activities of male faculty members. If the women didn't even know the money was there, how were they supposed to know to ask for it? But it was witnessing the performance evaluations that really made me angry. There was a significant discrepancy between the public stories about who published how much and what actually showed up in the annual reports and resumes.

Seeing these things, I started to get angry. I sought support from the other junior women in my department, from my husband, and from women faculty in my field at other universities. The women in my department provided social support. The women from other universities, who were senior and had seen these kinds of issues before, confirmed my views about the institutional nature of the problem (that is, that it wasn't my fault) and helped me think about strategies to address them. My husband provided both kinds of support.

I also noticed a discrepancy between internal and external evaluations of my research and teaching skills. Within my department, some of my colleagues did not seem to think that well of my work. But I consistently got very positive feedback from people outside my department, which helped restore my confidence.

FIGHTING BACK

Without the support of people outside my university, I would have remained very unsure of my assessment that much of what I was experiencing was a work environment that was hostile to women. But within the university, a report was published that offered me an opportunity to raise the issue in my department. This report assessed the status of women faculty at the university, including the percentage of women faculty and the salary gap between men and women faculty in each unit. Our unit was the only one that showed a significant decline in the percentage of women faculty during the period reported (1993–1998). In addition, the salary gap in our unit was among the largest on campus. Surely, I thought, this would call attention to the plight of women faculty in my unit.

I was wrong.

I tried to use the report to raise the issue of support for women faculty at an executive committee meeting. I was told there was no problem with the department. If there was an issue, it was my problem. I tried to raise it again at our annual faculty retreat at the start of the next semester. Among the points I made (most of which are discussed above) were the following:

- Currently, there are no women with tenure in the department.
- The last time tenure was granted to a woman was in the mid-1980s. That faculty member since retired.
- When she retired, at the start of my third year, I became the longest-serving female faculty member in the department.
- I got less research support in the form of graduate student assistants than my male colleagues.
- I was burdened with far more committee assignments than the male junior faculty.
- Some men were mentored, and some men weren't. No women were mentored.

The department head, in planning for the meeting, collected some data. He reported that of the fifteen faculty who had been hired in the previous ten years, four had already left. All four were women.

The topic was discussed considerably. Some of the senior males denied there was a problem. C played an especially central role. He said that all four women who left did so for personal reasons. I said that some of them had told me otherwise. They told me that they were treated badly because they were women, and that was why they left. But, needing letters of recommendation, and not wanting to burn their bridges, all of them did give a plausible personal reason as the public explanation for their departure. Admittedly, that did not help my cause. But, in this meeting, I asked the faculty directly, "How many women is it going to take? How many have to leave here before you admit there's a problem?" There was no answer.

Ironically perhaps, E, the faculty member with whom I had had the conflict about the women's conference, took one of the more constructive approaches in this meeting. E suggested that we as a department needed to look at how we treated *all* junior faculty, male and female, and how much support we provide them. While this may seem to skirt the question of discrimination, I thought it was potentially a helpful approach. First, I believed that if we really examined how all the junior faculty were treated, we would find a noticeable gender difference. Second, and more importantly, this approach had the potential to solve the problem. If we committed to providing support to all junior faculty, and actually acted on it, then both the women and the men would get support, which is what I wanted to accomplish.

One of the aspects of support we discussed was mentoring. C claimed that "Everybody knows that women and minorities need mentors," implying that white men did not. My view is that everyone needs mentors, but that in this particular workplace, men had more access to them. Surprisingly, C denied that he served as a mentor to B. He said he did all these things because he and B were friends. Indeed, they were friends. But he definitely provided professional support to B in a way that fits with most definitions of mentoring.

So, in the end, what was the result of my efforts? The faculty as a whole would not yet acknowledge that there was a problem. Therefore, they saw no need to try to fix it. The resolution for me was a personal one. I found a new job at another university, at a higher salary.

But I also left feeling more positive about myself. Standing up to those who had power over me, even though I did not see any real change, gave me confidence. I can't change that workplace—in fact at least one more woman has left. But perhaps I can provide support to others who find themselves in similar situations by helping them recognize some of the signs that they are working in a discriminatory environment. They are not crazy. It is not their fault. They are running into the wind.

WHAT CAN BE DONE ABOUT DISCRIMINATION IN TODAY'S WORKPLACE?

Although we have had laws in the United States that prohibit employment discrimination because of sex, race, color, religion, or national origin since the 1964 Civil Rights Act, the laws tend to address the most egregious forms of discrimination. And in many ways, discrimination against what I will call disadvantaged groups (e.g., women, racial and ethnic minorities, gays and lesbians, people with disabilities) takes more of a subtle form today than in the past. As a result, it can be even harder to fight. Gaertner and Dovidio (1986) describe a parallel bias based on race as "aversive racism," and McPhail (2003) argues that the concept should be extended to include aversive sexism.

Below, I've listed a set of behaviors that I believe can combat discrimination in today's workplace. But first, I also list some behaviors that I see as warning signs that a workplace has significant diversity issues.

Warning Signs

1. **Stories that justify unfavorable actions toward members of disadvantaged groups.** My experience was that there was always some reason why the women were treated badly, and in each case it was an idiosyncratic reason. In other settings, there might be one common explanation, such as having children. But the theme was that the woman was always an exception to the rule, and it was always her fault (or her choice). But the rules aren't made for women; they are made for men. So it's not surprising that women's lives don't fit them as well. If almost every member of a disadvantaged group is viewed by dominant group as not so successful, there is likely a problem. But the problem may well lie with the organization and its leaders rather than in the members of the disadvantaged groups. Similarly, if the only women to be thought successful had behaved "just like men," that would not be evidence that a workplace was free from discrimination. Indeed, it supports the view that only people who are "like men" can succeed there, and people who behave "like women" are not welcome.

2. **Leaders who are aware of the problem but unwilling to speak out.** Although I did not dwell on it above, one of the department leaders told me privately that he agreed that there really was a problem with the way women faculty were treated. But he added that, when in front of other faculty members, he would claim that there was no problem. Although he may have meant well, thinking he was making me feel better, that kind of behavior is not helpful. It only makes it harder to solve the problem because it can't be acknowledged.

3. **Denying the experience of the disadvantaged group.** We all want to succeed at work. I believe people generally don't want to admit that they have been the targets of discrimination. I think that in many cases, by the time someone comes to the point of saying they feel discriminated against, they have gone through some difficult experiences and have entertained a variety of explanations that include self-doubt and self-blame among them. They likely have quite a bit of evidence before they cite discrimination as the cause.

Often, when someone in a disadvantaged group complains, or even when a group of them get together and formally complain, the immediate response from the leadership is to deny it. But I argue that by the time the individual or group of people gets to the point of making an official complaint, they usually have very solid grounds. Whether the experience meets the legal definition of discrimination or not, those in power do not have the right to deny what the members of the disadvantaged group have experienced.

Constructive Behaviors

In contrast to the warning signs described above, I believe that the positive behaviors described below can help to create an environment in which *everyone* feels included.

1. **Transparency in decision-making.** This can prevent discrimination as well as other kinds of ethical problems. Also, it is consistent with democratic beliefs. Decision-making processes should include input from those whom the decisions affect. Both the process and the results should be made known to the entire group. Information about resource distribution (what resources are available and who gets them) should be available to all, so that potential biases can be revealed.

2. **Fairness in performance evaluation.** At first glance, it might seem that fairness is easy to achieve. Most workplaces have some numeric measure to assess performance in different jobs-annual sales, number of goods produced per day, number of defects per 1,000 parts. At research universities, the number is publications. But in real life, sales staff can be given better or worse territories; production workers can be stationed at newer, more efficient machines or at older ones that break down frequently. This analogy from a track and field official is instructive: "If an athlete runs 10.6 in still air, and another athlete in the next town runs 10.6 with a 20 mile-per-hour wind at his back, it would be unfair to say their performances are equal" (Hollobaugh, 2003). Similarly, the employees with the twenty-mile-per-hour wind at their backs typically run faster (achieve more), in part because they are given more resources, are mentored, and sometimes are simply outright favored because of bias. When the employees who are running *into* a twenty-mile-per-hour wind run a little slower (achieve less), it doesn't necessarily mean they are worse athletes. It simply means they are running in different environments and their performances cannot be directly compared.

   However, the same information about what kinds of performance matter should be given to all. Imagine a track coach who told the men on the team that they would be considered top performers if they won the 100, 200, or 1500 meter races or the marathon. If this same coach told the women that the only way for them to perform was in the 100 meters, and that no other race counted, there would only be a certain type of female athlete who could fit in. It would be a substantially less-well balanced team, with fewer chances of winning. Most organizations need a variety of skills to prosper in the long term.

3. **Tracking resource distributions.** To make high performance equally likely, give the same resources and support to both men and women. How do you know you are doing this? Monitor it. Keep track. Count up the graduate assistant hours, the travel funds, and everything else you can. Measure the wind speed—whatever elements make performance easier in your work environment. Then compare the environment for each group. Track the salaries as well. A group of senior women faculty at the Massachusetts Institute of Technology (Committee, 1999) measured a variety of items and surprised themselves and much of academia with the results. But the disparity in numbers (such as lab space and other resources) was hard to dispute and was fixable.

From my point of view, it is not the case that we want everyone to be competing with no support (or at zero wind). We want *all* of our organizational members to succeed. We want them to have the wind at their backs to the extent possible. What we don't want is for only the group with the most power to have the wind at its back, and the rest to be running into the wind.

4. **Inclusivity.** Discrimination is about one group exercising power over another (Connell, 1987; Weber, 2001). While some of the items above address the issue of power, the issue of group identity is important as well. I'm disappointed to say that some of my male colleagues simply could not see women as peers. Rather than seeing us all as part of the same profession, they seemed to see me and the other women faculty as "*the other.*" In a very basic, simple, and human sense, we need to find common ground, so that everyone in the workplace and beyond can find ways in which people of other demographic groups are nevertheless identified as "*like me.*" (See Gaertner & Dovidio, 2000, for a description of the Common Ingroup Identity Model.) I believe that it is much harder to discriminate against someone we identify as "*like me*" than someone we view as "*not like me.*" We all need to have a broad and accepting view of who is "like me."

5. **Labor unions.** Although many professional workers find unions distasteful, unions have been a significant force for equality in our society. In many workplaces—hospitals, manufacturing plants, government offices—people receive the same pay for the same job regardless of their race, gender, age, religion, or disability status because that is what unions have negotiated. In workplaces that base pay on merit, unions can still play a role. Unions represent professional athletes, journalists, and faculty using contracts that set a minimum pay for each job classification, with the possibility of being paid more for better performance. But more importantly, unions establish a form of procedural

justice in the workplace. Delaney and Lundy (1996) discuss the advantages and limitations of unions in promoting diversity in the workplace.

If there had been a faculty union at my old university, I could have taken my complaint to them, and they would have helped me to confront management. I would not have had to battle alone. And I would have had the power of the collective group behind me. I might have had the wind at my back instead of blowing hard against me.

Additional Suggestions

Both the warning signs and the constructive behaviors described above are categorized in the Toolbox for Change. My focus thus far has been on individual and organizational factors. In order to be consistent with other chapters in this book, I will add a few comments about what practitioners and educators can do to combat prejudice and discrimination.

First, practitioners (that is, clinicians) may need to recognize that low self-esteem, depression, and avoidance behaviors may be symptoms of discrimination. Clearly, these are also symptoms of a variety of other mental health problems, and do not, in and of themselves, lead to a diagnosis that involves the experience of discrimination. However, they can be the result of discrimination.

Second, many people do not want to admit that their work problems involve discrimination. Someone who experienced the types of things described in this narrative, but who did not have enough information to make the comparisons to how other people in similar jobs were treated, might not even know they were being treated differently. A practitioner could raise questions about how other employees, particularly those in the same job category, are treated. For example, are they given more resources?

Third, educators can develop programs (either conferences or courses) that are targeted at members of disadvantaged groups. Those who come to these programs will likely learn a great deal from each other, as well as from the instructor. It will help them analyze whether their issues involve discrimination or whether they involve more general problems faced by all workers (communication issues, work demands that are too high, supervision that is ineffective, etc.). But if their particular experience does involve discrimination, other program participants will likely have suggestions about specific strategies to handle it.

Toolbox for Change

For	Images/perceptions	Strategies for change
Individuals	Don't deny what members of disadvantaged groups describe as their experience. Don't blame the victim. View all people as "like me."	Powerful individuals must speak out, just as the disadvantaged must. Be inclusive.
Community/ society	Don't create, accept, or transmit an organizational mythology about why members of certain (disadvantaged) groups "inevitably" fail.	Implement transparency in decision-making. Implement a fair performance evaluation system. Monitor the distribution of resources. Form a labor union.
Practitioners	Recognize that low self-esteem, depression, and avoidance behaviors may be symptoms of discrimination.	Ask how members of dominant versus disadvantaged groups are treated at work or in the relevant environment. Teach classes targeted at the needs of disadvantaged groups.

EPILOGUE

Although this is likely obvious to the reader, I would like to point out that I have described things from my own perspective—how I observed and experienced them. I suspect that my male colleagues would describe the situation differently. I should also add that there were other men, including senior men, in this workplace who did not behave in exclusionary ways. But the proportion was a problem. In the four years I worked in this department, there were about a dozen senior male faculty members, and I have described issues with six of them above. Another problem, insurmountable without support from higher up within the university, was a leadership that was quite tolerant of the existing situation. While I was willing to fight about these issues for a time, I ultimately lost hope that anything would improve. So I chose to leave. I found a similar job with my current employer, Michigan State University. In my few short years here, I have felt more productive and more satisfied with my work.

But I have the luxury of geographic mobility and portable skills. Not everyone can afford to leave a job, or is willing to move to another state. In a tough economy, new jobs can be hard to find. Pension and health insurance rules sometimes handcuff people to jobs they would otherwise leave. I believe that we should not be forced to choose between a job and our psychological well-being. So we must all work to make our organizations more inclusive. We can start by taking the newcomers to lunch.

ACKNOWLEDGMENTS

Thanks to Elaine Yakura and Dan Hamilton for their thoughtful comments on this chapter and to John Siebs for technical input.

REFERENCES

Belle, D., & Doucet, J. (2003). Poverty, inequality, and discrimination as sources of depression among U.S. women. *Psychology of Women Quarterly, 27,* 101–113.

Bureau of Labor Statistics. (2003). *Highlights of women's earnings in 2002.* U.S. Department of Labor Report No. 972.

Committee on the Status of Women Faculty, Massachusetts Institute of Technology (MIT). (1999). A study on the status of women faculty in science at MIT [internal report].

Connell, R. W. (1987). *Gender and power: Society, the person, and sexual politics.* Stanford, CA: Stanford University Press.

Cortina, L. M., & Magley, V. J. (2003) Raising voice, risking retaliation: Events following interpersonal mistreatment in the workplace. *Journal of Occupational Health Psychology, 8,* 247–265.

Delaney, J. T., & Lundy, M. C. (1996). Unions, collective bargaining, and the diversity paradox. In E. E. Kossek & S. A. Lobel (Eds.), *Managing diversity: Human resource strategies for transforming the workplace* (pp. 245–272). Cambridge, MA: Blackwell Publishers, Ltd.

Estrich, S. (2000). *Sex & power.* New York: Riverhead Books.

Gaertner, S. L., & Dovidio, J. F. (1986). The aversive form of racism. In J. F. Dovidio & S. L. Gaertner (Eds.), *Prejudice, Discrimination, and Racism* (pp. 61–89). San Diego, CA: Academic Press.

Gaertner, S. L., & Dovidio, J. F. (2000). *Reducing intergroup bias: The common ingroup identity model.* Philadelphia, PA: Psychology Press.

Hollobaugh, J. (2003). Frequently asked questions. Retrieved October 27, 2003, from www.michtrack.org/FAQ/faq2.htm

Kaminski, M., Bertelli, D., Moye, M., & Yudken, J. (1996). *Making change happen: Six cases of unions and companies transforming their workplaces*. Washington, DC: Work and Technology Institute.

McPhail, T. L. (2003). Selection and race: A test of the aversive racism theory. *Dissertation Abstracts International: Section B: The Sciences and Engineering, 64*(1-B), 452.

Moss, P. I., & Tilly, C. (2001). *Stories employers tell: Race, skill, and hiring in America*. New York: Russell Sage Foundation.

Weber, L. (2001). *Understanding race, class, gender, and sexuality: A conceptual framework*. New York: McGraw-Hill.

CHAPTER 5

Internalized Oppression among Black Women

Anita Jones Thomas
Suzette L. Speight
Karen M. Witherspoon

Toni, a thirty-two-year-old black university professor, is waiting in line to make some last-minute copies before her class begins. A white woman quickly approaches Toni, saying, "Be a dear and add this to your stack. When you finish, bring it to room 405." She disappears as quickly as she appeared, leaving Toni stunned and overwhelmed.

Rhonda is a twenty-four-year-old black woman who recently started a new position as an administrative assistant. Many of the men in her department make suggestive joking comments to her, and she finds herself uncomfortable when alone with them. She befriends Tina, a white woman, who indicates that the men never make comments to her. Tina says, "Maybe they think you're okay with it."

Linda is a fifty-four-year-old corporate executive who has been with the same company for twenty years. Her immediate supervisor, Anthony, is a recent MBA who started with the company just over six months ago. Whenever Linda makes suggestions in team meetings, Anthony ignores her, but her ideas are always presented to the board as if they were originally Anthony's. Linda's friends and family encourage her to confront Anthony or the board about this, but Linda is reluctant as she is unsure whether she will be able to control her temper.

There are a number of alternatives that the three women can ponder before responding to their scenarios. The women can consider how their race influences the reactions that others have to them. After all, blacks frequently experience racism and discrimination, especially in the workplace (Jackson & Sears, 1992; Landrine & Klonoff, 1996). Or they can consider how their roles as women influence the scenarios. Women often experience sexual harassment and discrimination and are characterized as overly aggressive in the workplace. But, more than likely, these women are going to process their experiences through both their race and gender, as black women. Toni will assume that she was asked to make the copies because her colleague assumed that she was a secretary instead of a professor. She may believe that her colleagues assume that she is helpful and happy, almost eager to serve. Rhonda will assume that her male colleagues see her as sexually desirable and available, as black women are thought to be more sexualized than white women. And while Linda may be aware that many corporate women are seen as aggressive instead of assertive, she may also fear that her colleagues will respond to her as "that angry black woman" and easily dismiss her concerns. It is also likely that all three women will attempt to cope with experiences such as these by improving their performance, watching their language, and controlling their emotions (Jones & Shorter-Gooden, 2003). They are likely to believe that any negative reaction to their experiences, any sign that they are not strong, competent, under control, and capable of handling everything, may be a failure to themselves, their families, and their community.

This is often the fate of black women who must negotiate and develop an identity in an oppressive society, overcoming barriers in their lives from experiences of the unique combination of racism and sexism. Black women experience the "'double jeopardy' condition of having to deal with both racism and sexism but also the commonplace condition of unique combinations of the two. . . . This real-world blending often makes it difficult to know the separate contributions of each element in particular situations that involve both racial and gender barriers to social mobility and personal achievement" (St. Jean & Feagin, 1998, p. 16). In addition to navigating oppressive experiences, black women have to develop a self-concept that incorporates both gender and racial identity. Theory and research exploring racial and gender identity have treated them as separate processes, concluding that for black women, racial identity may occur before womanist or gender identity (Carter & Parks, 1996; Parks, Carter, & Gushue, 1996). It is as if women must explore the two as parallel processes without considering their interaction and interactions. The phrase "women and minorities" highlights the dilemma; society forces black women to choose gender or race. But for many, it can be difficult to separate the two intertwined components of identity, as they see themselves simultaneously as black and female. Their gender is raced, and their race is gendered (Omi & Winant, 1994).

This chapter will explore the influence of multiple oppressions on identity and both healthy and unhealthy responses to internalized oppression on black women. It will present the three prevalent stereotypes of black women based on images and myths from slavery, along with the more recently occurring image of the "superwoman." The implications for psychological functioning and the influence of the stereotypes on interpersonal relationships will also be included. The chapter will conclude with recommendations to alleviate distress from internalized oppression, including the development of critical consciousness and an authentic self.

STEREOTYPES OF BLACK WOMEN: HOW DO OTHERS SEE ME?

Society has unique perspectives on black women due to the legacy of slavery. Societal images of black women differ from those of white women. The images of black women include that they are dominant, hostile, sexually promiscuous, defiant, rude, and loud (Bell, 1992; Fordham, 1993; Greene, 1994, 1997; Jackson & Sears, 1992; McNair, 1992). There are three stereotypes of black women that derive from slavery: Mammy, Sapphire, and Jezebel (Abdullah, 1998; Mitchell & Herring, 1998; West, 1995).

Mammy

Mammy is characterized as an obese, dark-skinned woman with broad features who, during slavery, worked in the master's house, often serving as nanny, housekeeper, and cook. She was allowed in the slave owners' household because her physical characteristics were deemed asexual and unattractive, making her non-threatening to the slave owners. Mammy was expected to take care of the needs of others, a task that she was believed to delight in, even to the neglect of her own needs. Mammy never complained and was viewed as amiable and a deferential problem solver. The image of Mammy has led to black women being perceived as nurturing, good caretakers, strong, supportive, and selfless (Mitchell & Herring, 1998). Media images that reflect this stereotype include the pancake icons Aunt Jemima and Mrs. Butterworth, Louise from the television show *The*

Jeffersons, and Florida from *Good Times*. Black women who internalize this stereotype may feel the need to be nurturing and supportive of others, often at their own expense, leading to lower self-concept and self-confidence (Abdullah, 1998; Gainor, 1992; Greene, 1994; West, 1995). Many black women feel guilty if they cannot help others and may set aside personal needs to give to others. One of the authors of this chapter strongly identifies with the Mammy image. She was elected to serve as chair of the department at each university where she was employed as an assistant professor before receiving tenure. While she does have organizational skills and leadership abilities, it may be that her candidacy was a reflection of the Mammy image. Her choice to serve as chair despite the negative consequences for her own scholarly productivity also stems from her desire to be seen as helpful and supportive, the internalization of the Mammy stereotype.

Sapphire

Sapphire was a character from the 1940s and 1950s *Amos and Andy* radio and television show and was seen as callous, crude, loud, argumentative, full of verbal assaults, and a woman who took pleasure in emasculating men. The perceptions of black women from the Sapphire image include that they are arrogant, controlling, loud, hostile, obnoxious, and never satisfied (Bell, 1990, 1992; Mitchell & Herring, 1998; West, 1995). Since the days of *Amos and Andy*, Sapphire has been popularized in the media through various characters on television. Florence, the maid from the television series *The Jeffersons*, is a good example of Sapphire's characteristics through her constant "playing the dozens" with her employer, George Jefferson. Aunt Esther from *Sanford and Son* is remembered for the constant berating of brother-in-law Fred Sanford and even going so far as to strike him with her purse during her humorous, yet debasing assaults. We are bombarded with these "tough girl" images in videos. Sapphire is the woman on the corner rolling her neck, with both hands on her hips, telling off the person who has just offended her.

The internalization of this image may cause women to have difficulty expressing their needs or displaying anger comfortably. They may assume that the only way to be heard is to be full of rage, aggressive, or loud (Mitchell & Herring, 1998). Black women may have difficulty with assertiveness and may restrict their assertiveness to protect others for fear of overwhelming others (Adams, 2000). They may also fear being verbally expressive, restrict their anger, or may use anger to hide their vulnerability (West, 1995). They may also fear that signs of assertiveness or anger label them as manipulative, hostile, and controlling (Bell, 1992). Smith (1999) recounts her own challenges with the Sapphire image as a law professor at a predominately white university. Peers and students frequently perceive her as loud, aggressive, argumentative, bitchy, and quick-tempered. Students' perceptions of her clothing and hair were used to solidify their image of her as threatening, intimidating, and angry. White students have come to her office to say that they were upset because she unfairly interrupted them while they were talking in class. Others came to office hours to say that she had a personal problem with them either because she looked at them in class and did not call on them or because she did not give praise for their answers. Professor Smith reports that she cannot stand too close to a student without that person later reporting that they felt oppressed and should she correct a student's error of law, then she is "picking on them." If Professor Smith uses supplemental handouts to the reading, then she is overloading them. If she does not, then she is not adequately educating them. She is trapped by the Sapphire image.

Jezebel

Jezebel, another image from the legacy of slavery, is perceived as seductive, manipulative, and unable to control her sex drive (Mitchell & Herring, 1998). The sexual exploitation and victimization of black women was often justified by the notion that black women were highly sexualized and animalistic in their desires for men and sex. The Jezebel image served several functions during slavery. Sexualizing African women justified the widespread sexual assaults of white plantation owners, their sons, and friends against enslaved women. Second, it raised expectations of high fertility among black women, which justified increasing their property value. Finally, it served as a controlling image against white women, by reinforcing oppositional characteristics and the gender hierarchy held in place by a racist, classist, and sexist system (Collins, 1990). A modern-day variety of the Jezebel image is the welfare queen stereotype who is promiscuous, loose, immoral, and lacking sexual restraint (Bell, 1992; Daniel, 2000; Greene, 1994, 1997). The character Jackee from the show *227* is an excellent example of a sex-crazed black woman who uses her body to get what she wants. The Jezebel image has implications for how sexual victimization is experienced by black women (Wilson, 1993; Wyatt,

1997). Women may fear reporting rape because of victim-blaming (West, 1998). Internalizing this stereotype may lead women to perceive sexuality as one of their few assets or may cause them to repress sexual feelings (West, 1995). Rochelle is a poor, fifteen-year-old black who was molested by her uncle as a pre-teen. Rochelle sees herself as unattractive but thinks that she can use her body to get things she wants from boys. She is willing to do sexual favors in exchange for money. Having boyfriends makes her feel powerful and popular.

These stereotypes are not the only images of black women that exist, but are the ones that are written about and studied the most. Black women have also been seen as over-recipients of affirmative action, as welfare queens, and as tragic mulattos. More successful black women can be seen as raceless, or perceived as being somehow "different" from other black women (Daniel, 1995; West, 1995).

CONSEQUENCES OF OPPRESSION: WHERE DOES IT HURT?

Internalizing the stereotypes of Mammy, Sapphire, and Jezebel may influence mental health and psychological functioning of black women. The stereotypes are dangerous because they tell black women that they can take anything anyone throws their way, that they need little nurturing or support, and that they must not have problems. Strong identification with the stereotypes may also influence interpersonal relationships, as they convey messages that others are not to be trusted, sex can get you what you want, there is only one right way to be black, and that loving, gentle communication does not get black women anywhere (Mitchell & Herring, 1998). Greene (1994) states that women often fear that their behavior is associated with the stereotypes, leading them to inhibition, to emotional restriction, and to avoid rather than acting out the characteristics of the stereotypes. Other women may distance themselves from other blacks, or may feel like impostors or frauds despite their success. Facing the stereotypes of Mammy, Sapphire, and Jezebel may cause black women to exert tremendous psychological energy each day.

Perhaps the most overwhelming message from the stereotypes is the notion that black women should feel guilty when they put others' needs before their own. Many black women will develop a façade of strength and may have difficulty admitting to problems or asking for support (McNair, 1992). Many black women are socialized to view themselves as the "superwoman" who is capable of accomplishing multiple tasks successfully (Mitchell & Herring, 1998). Historically rooted in slavery, there was a notion that black women were incapable of being over-worked. It is this illusion that causes black women in our society to be thought of as born with extraordinary strengths and an ability to with-stand an extreme level of work and stress (Scherenzel, 2002). Black women have witnessed their grandmothers and mothers raising chil-dren, extended family members, and communities while balancing work outside the home without complaint and with apparent little diffi-culty. This image of the superwoman, the strong, independently func-tioning woman, leads many to feel weak and like failures if they are not successful or need to ask for help (Greene, 1994; Thompson, 2000). "'Strong black woman' is a mantra for so much a part of U.S. culture that it is seldom realized how great a toll it has taken on the emotional well-being of the black woman. As much as it may give her the illusion of control, it [strength] keeps her from identifying what she needs and reaching out for help" (Romero, 2000, p. 225). Claire Huxtable, the mother on *The Cosby Show*, is an example of the super-woman, as she took care of her family, worked as a lawyer, took in extended family members, and volunteered at community agencies, seamlessly and without exhaustion or a hair out of place.

The desire to portray an image of endurance and strength often prevents women from expressing their inner desires and needs, psy-chological distress, depressive or anxiety symptoms, or from seeking therapy (Boyd, 1993; Gainor, 1992; Greene, 1994; West, 1995). In-ternalizing the superwoman can lead to a façade of high self-esteem while women hide feelings of anger, fear, shame, pride, and loneli-ness. When the façade is cracked, it may reveal anxiety and low self-esteem (Jordan, 1997; Neal-Barnett & Crowther, 2000). For exam-ple, Marva has accomplished more in a day than most of her family members have accomplished all week. She rose early this morning and went to the office to prepare for her agency's important meeting with one of their largest contributors. Her day was intense, and she only took a break once during the day, and that was to call her mother and remind her to take her diabetes medication. After work, she at-tended a training session for mentors in the volunteer program from her church. At twenty-seven, she was one of the youngest volunteers. She stayed after the training to help clean up and graciously accepted leftovers that she later gave to her neighbor down the hall, who was struggling to feed her family. After dutifully returning phone calls to family members and completing a few chores around the house, Marva settled down for the evening by rereading her chapters in the marketing course she attended twice a week to obtain her master's degree in business. This seemed like a typical day for Marva, and as usual, she found herself exhausted with difficulty falling asleep.

SELF-CONCEPT: WHO AM I?

Oppression has the adverse side effect of causing its victims to engage in psychological "armoring," the process of finding ways to protect their self-concept and self-esteem while facing and confronting discrimination (Edmondson-Bell & Nkomo, 1998). Recipients of oppression often spend a great deal of time and exert much psychological energy coping with their experiences. For example, if a black woman is ignored while trying to make a purchase, she will have to process whether the slight occurred because she is black, a woman, or a black woman. She is likely to think about the incident for some time after it occurs and to seek out others to confirm or validate her experience.

Repeated acts of oppression can influence the psychological and behavioral functioning of individuals and the development of the self-concept. The processing of oppression influences two components of identity: public and private regard (Sellers, Smith, Shelton, Rowley, & Chavous, 1998). Members of ethnic minority groups come to understand that members of the majority have particular perceptions of them. Sellers and colleagues define "public regard" as the extent to which one feels that others view blacks positively or negatively. Private regard is defined as how the person feels about blacks and being black. The internalization of oppression can lead individuals to adopt personas that match the stereotypes, based on their feelings of public and private regard. Individuals who feel that others have low regard for their group may intentionally act in an opposite fashion, to prove that they are better than the perceptions or stereotypes of their group. If these individuals also have low private regard and feel negative about being a member of their group, then their self-esteem will be low, and they may react more negatively to oppressive acts. Members may also internalize oppressive stereotypes and act them out. Others may fear negative public regard and attempt to overcome it but fail by acting out the stereotypes. For example, if a person is regarded as hostile, she may lose her temper due to the frustration of being treated as if she were hostile. Blowing up confirms the stereotype, which will lead the individual to experience a sense of guilt and shame for confirming the stereotype.

The images of black women are inconsistent with the stereotypic image of white women, who are seen as submissive, docile, and feminine. The message black women often receive is that they cannot be feminine in the "right" way, like white women are. Internalizing this message may lead to a sense of self-hatred and inferiority (Gainor, 1992).

In addition to differences in psychological characteristics, black women also face white physical standards of beauty, such as skin color, facial features, hair color and texture, and body size and shape. Commercials for hair care products, cosmetics, and fashion magazines usually feature women with long, flowing blonde hair and blue eyes. The black women featured tend to have long straight hair and more Caucasian or fine features. When model Alek Wek, a Sudanese woman, became famous, many were surprised at her very strong traditional African features. Although research has suggested that black girls and women have better body images (Kempa & Thomas, 2000), some of them develop a sense of low self-esteem because they do not meet the ideal standards for beauty. Many black women go to great lengths to straighten and lighten their hair and have issues with skin color (Abdullah, 1998; Adams, 2000; Gainor, 1992; Greene, 1994; Neal, 1989). Our initial research examining the stereotypes and self-esteem found that women who endorsed the Mammy and Sapphire images were more likely to have lower self-esteem (Thomas, Witherspoon, & Speight, 2004).

DEPRESSION AND ANXIETY: SICK AND TIRED

There is some evidence that internalizing the stereotypes may lead to psychological symptoms, including depression and anxiety (Jones & Shorter-Gooden, 2003; Neal-Barnett & Crowther, 2000). As previously discussed, adapting to the Mammy image may lead women to become overly nurturing, sometimes to the neglect of self. When women feel overly burdened by the demands, they may become anxious about their ability to handle life's demands, and may feel depressed about their inability to maintain control. The "superwoman" image in particular may be linked to the denial of psychological problems, such as depression. The National Mental Health Association conducted a survey of black attitudes toward depression and found that blacks were confused about the definition, causes, and symptoms of depression (Mitchell & Herring, 1998). For example, 63 percent of blacks believed that depression was a personal weakness, suggesting that it is unlikely that a black woman will admit to experiencing depressive symptoms, even when they are noticeable to others. Only 31 percent of blacks in the study believed that depression was a health problem. About 40 percent of the participants indicated that they would not seek treatment because of denial—that is, trouble admitting that it is happening—and 38 percent would not seek treatment because of shame or embarrassment (NMHA, 1996). In a qualitative study of twelve West-Indian Canadian women, Schreiber, Stern, and Wilson (2000) found that the women attempted to "manage their depression with grace and to live up to the cultural imperative to be strong" (p. 4). The women thought that suffering was a normal part of life and that one endured personal misery privately in isolation. The women attempted to divert themselves, turning to spiritual support, getting involved in activities, and thinking positively. Less than half of the women sought professional help.

One reason black women do not get treated for depression is that they often expect to feel sad, tired, and unable to think straight. There are some spiritual and religious proverbs, such as "God won't give you any more than you can bear," that support the notion that women should continue to function, often past the point of exhaustion (Thomas, 2001). Therapists must start challenging this notion and empower black women to engage in better self-care and to seek out and accept support from others.

Neal-Barnett and Crowther (2000) summarized the literature on anxiety (post-traumatic stress, panic, generalized anxiety, obsessive-compulsive disorder, and phobias) for black women, who are more likely to experience anxiety than white women are, due to combined racism and sexism. Victimization, most commonly associated with post-traumatic stress disorder, may be an underlying factor in the development of other anxiety disorders (Bell, Hildreth, Jenkins, & Levi, 1988). Higher levels of violence and sexual trauma are associated with severe agoraphobia (Michelson, June, Vives, Testa, & Marchione, 1998). Data from the National Institute of Mental Health (NIMH) suggest that blacks report more simple phobias than other groups do (Brown, Eaton, & Susman, 1990).

Black women are unlikely to seek help for anxiety-related symptoms but more often seek services for relationship problems or bereavement. Black women often do not seek treatment because they interpret the anxiety as a normal part of their lives as black women: "We have to keep on keeping on." This is the internalized stereotype of the super-woman, the strong black woman who bears all. They may also fear that once they disclose the source of their anxiety, they will become flooded by other negative emotions (Neal-Barnett & Crowther, 2000). Our initial research examining the stereotypes and psychological functioning found that women who endorsed the superwoman and Sapphire images were positively related to paranoia, interpersonal insensitivity, hostility, and depression symptoms (Witherspoon, Thomas, & Speight, unpublished).

RELATIONSHIPS: CAN I CONNECT?

One of the unfortunate byproducts of oppression in its racist and sexist forms is the creating of interpersonal difficulties between groups as well as within groups. Oppression can influence relationships with whites at work. Many black women experience discrimination in the workplace. Although they may often be preferred for hiring over black men, they often may not be accepted in a warm and inviting way into their places of employment. Many black women have the challenge of overcoming stereotypes while concentrating on their professional roles. The need to appear competent and successful often causes women to take on too many responsibilities at work and to become overburdened (Romero, 2000). Women report experiences with gendered racism on the job (St. Jean & Feagin, 1998). Women may suffer from anger and feelings of powerlessness due to gender and race-related stress. They also report feeling social isolation and exclusion. Black women often report that they find it difficult to be their true selves in the workplace (Bell, 1990; Jones & Shorter-Gooden, 2003). The pressure to perform well and be a good representative of the black race can add psychological stress and ultimately influence physical health of women. Finally, women may try to decrease the discomfort that whites often feel from interracial contact (Greene, 1994), thus preventing them from speaking up about discrimination. This "taking care of others" might feel familiar for women with the internalized superwoman and Mammy images, but it also takes an emotional toll on them that remains hidden.

Internalized oppression can contribute to a sense of divisiveness among black women. Controversy exists regarding skin color, as women with light and dark complexions wrestle with issues of attractiveness. Historically, skin color was used to determine social status and standing, with lighter complexions preferred (Hall, 1995). There is often some judgment among black women about hairstyles, from relaxed hair to natural styles, and the presence of Caucasian features (Neal, 1989). Conflict can also occur with black women from different social class status. As women gain more education and work in professional settings, they often become more bicultural, able to function effectively in the mainstream and the home culture. Being bicultural often comes at a cost, as women feel isolated or are accused of being "uppity and too good" for their black peers (Jones & Shorter-Gooden, 2003).

Internalization of the stereotypes can also lead to problems with intimacy and romantic heterosexual relationships. Relationships with men and women have also been negatively impacted by the presence of gendered racism (St. Jean & Feagin, 1998). A recent *Newsweek* article highlighted the difficulties that may occur due to the "gender gap" between black women and men. Black women are educated at higher levels and are more likely to be hired in managerial or professional roles than black men, which may strain relationships. Black women may often downplay their education or success in order to maintain relationships (Jones & Shorter-Gooden, 2003). Many women fear remaining single due to the shortage of available black men (Cose, 2003). Some women prefer to take on men who need to be fixed or molded from personal and professional problems rather than be alone (Romero, 2000). Another byproduct of oppression is black women's victimization from domestic violence, rape, and sexual assault. Many are not able to report sexual harassment or victimization against black men because of pressures to "protect" the race (Bell, 1992), as evidenced by the Anita Hill and Clarence Thomas controversy.

Finally, the most damaging influence of internalized oppression on black women, and the superwoman image in particular, is the difficulty women face in being vulnerable (Adams, 2000; Romero, 2000). The need to be strong may prevent women from confiding in others and may place distance in interpersonal relationships. Relationships with other black women and intimate relationships with black men have been influenced by internalization of the stereotypes. The most costly influence has been the inability of many black women to fully connect with others, as the fear of vulnerability in relationships often feels overwhelming. Black women may suffer silently, finding some relief in church services or through prayer but denying themselves the benefits of social support and comfort from family and friends.

COPING/HELP-SEEKING BEHAVIORS: I DON'T NEED HELP, DO I?

Although many black women recognize symptoms from the stress of discrimination and oppression, they continue to function and often do not seek mental health services. There are a number of reasons why women do not pursue treatment. Many women seek family members or friends to discuss their issues or seek advice from spiritual and religious leaders (Jones & Shorter-Gooden, 2003). Unfortunately, many are reluctant to seek services from social service professionals due to suspicion and lack of familiarity with professional mental health services. Mental health professionals are also mandated reporters of abuse, suicide, and homicide, and women often fear having children removed from their household by child protective services. Oppression has also led many blacks to be protective of family members, leading them to avoid treatment altogether or withhold information once in treatment. Black women carrying their shield of strength in front of them will view any need for assistance as an admission of failure or weakness, thus evoking feelings of shame. This shame often proves counterproductive because black women may deny issues like child abuse, incest, domestic violence, and alcohol and drug addiction.

Other women seek to cope with oppression and oppression-related stress through negative behaviors. One popular form of self-medicating in black women is overeating. Much of the research focuses on the formal *Diagnostic and Statistical Manual IV-TR* (American Psychiatric Association, 2000) criteria for anorexia or bulimia, suggesting that these eating disorders are less prevalent in black women (Kempa & Thomas, 2000). Research has also suggested that black women have fewer distortions and dissatisfaction with body image (Hall, 1995; Makkar & Strube, 1995). While black women may not meet the criteria for bulimia, they often display symptoms of binge eating, or eating for comfort. Other women may cope by abusing alcohol and drugs. It may be easy for a woman to relieve stress from discrimination and pressures at work by using substances to relax. Rather than discuss emotional problems and risk vulnerability, black women may mask symptoms with substance abuse or other medical conditions (NMHA, 1996).

CRITICAL CONSCIOUSNESS AND THE DEVELOPMENT OF THE AUTHENTIC SELF: WHO AM I, REALLY?

Although experiences with oppression can be exhausting and overwhelming, there are ways to cope with these adverse experiences, and ways to develop and protect positive self-esteem. This process has been called *psychological armoring* (Edmondson-Bell & Nkomo, 1998). There are two primary ways for black women to address and overcome oppression: by developing critical consciousness and creating an authentic sense of self. In order to survive and resist oppression, it is important to understand the nature of oppressive systems and the broader sociopolitical context. Individuals need to be able to assess their experiences in light of the context and to separate their personal response from societal expectations. Individuals need to be able to identify oppressive systems and question why oppression occurs; this is the process of developing critical consciousness (Watts & Abdul-Adil, 1997). Watts and Abdul-Adil developed a program to develop critical consciousness for black boys. Participants were encouraged to critically examine and interpret situations as a means to externalize oppressive experiences and to inspect them in a depersonalized fashion. The program is grounded in Freire's (1990) notion of *praxis*, "reflection and action on the world in order to transform it" (p. 33). In order to liberate oneself from oppression, one must first recognize the external constraints that oppression places on self-development and self-determination (Young, 1990).

Again, women struggle with the internalization of the Mammy, Jezebel, Sapphire, and superwoman images. Internalizing oppression manifests in various ways. Attempts to distance oneself from the stereotypes can cause a woman to develop a façade of strength, to repress feelings, to restrict anger, or to be uncomfortable with sexuality. Women may feel the need to be giving and nurturing to others, often to the sacrifice of themselves. In short, black women may often feel compelled to be, act, behave, and feel in ways that make others comfortable, or in ways that match the expectations of others. Many women discuss feeling like impostors and/or feeling uncomfortable with themselves, and they fear letting others down. Instead of being defined by others, black women need to develop an authentic sense of self, a self that is internally defined. Women who have self-determination are able to develop their identities, make choices, and behave in ways consistent with their own standards, values, and ideals. This is both an internal and external struggle. One must combat the oppressor "within" and the oppressor "without" (Freire, 1990).

The development of an authentic sense of self involves the following steps: see it, name it, question it, resist it, and transform it (Isom, 2002). First, women need to develop an awareness of the pervasiveness of oppression; they need to see it. This includes understanding the reality of racism and sexism, understanding the history of the stereotypes and the sociopolitical context within which they operate, and recognizing individual acts of oppression as well as the institutional structures that support and maintain oppression. The second step is to name it, to define the true nature of oppression as it occurs. This step is critical to the development of an authentic sense of self. It is the process of separating societal influences, allowing the person to correctly label her experiences. The next step involves questioning one's experiences. Am I responsible for this image? Did I cause the person to respond to me in a particular way? Interrogating allows the woman to critically explore and scrutinize her experiences, to further separate societal images, systematic oppression, and internalization of oppression. The fourth step is to resist it. Resistance includes being assertive and defending the self. Resistance may also mean confronting an oppressor, letting the person know that their comments or behaviors have been hurtful. These steps allow women to overcome oppression by transforming it and becoming fully self-defined women of African descent. Transforming oppression ends up transforming society through transforming the self. As black women begin to define themselves on their own terms, the negative historical images from slavery will lose their hold on the women's psyches and the society within which they live. Seeing, acknowledging, naming, questioning, and resisting oppression and societal images will empower black women to be more fully human— willingly, boldly, and unapologetically able to create their own truths and realities.

The model can be seen through the examples presented at the beginning of the chapter. Toni can see and acknowledge that the professor assumed she was a secretary, as black women are often seen in clerical or service roles more easily than in professional roles. She can name the experience of oppression. She can begin to question the motives of the professor who left the copies and explore her role and possible response to the actions. She can resist the temptation to respond to the stereotype. Toni may feel guilty for feeling angry, or she may feel uncomfortable in not making the copies and then choose to go late to her own class. Or she can resist and simply correct the professor in mistaking her for a secretary. Acknowledging that she has the right to be treated respectfully will help her to transform the incident. Rhonda can engage in a similar process. She can see and name the sexual harassment for what it is: a response to the Jezebel image of her as a black woman. She can question the motives of the male co-workers and question her role in the harassment. After the critical examination of the harassment, she can resist it by insisting that the harassment stop. She can tell her co-workers about her discomfort, and if necessary, report them to human resources. Taking a stand against harassment will help her to respect herself, transforming the

Toolbox for Change

For	Images/perceptions	Strategies for change
Individuals	Mammy Jezebel Sapphire Superwoman	Developing an authentic self: resisting and transforming oppression Seeking social support Seeking mental health treatment for stress, depression, and anxiety
Community/ society	Mammy Jezebel Sapphire Superwoman	Policies that promote equity and fairness Sexual harassment policies Child care support for families Mission statements that promote gender and racial equity
Practitioners	Mammy Jezebel Sapphire Superwoman	Recognizing social injustice and power inequities in relationships with clients/ students Resisting oppressive practices in classroom settings Diversity and sensitivity training

oppression. Finally, Linda can see and name her supervisor's abuse of power. She can question his motives and examine her role in allowing him to take credit for her ideas. She can also begin to determine whether her anger is justified and resist the oppression by finding acceptable forms of expression of her anger. Standing up for herself and her ideas, and claiming them, can help her to transform the oppressive images of black women.

The development of the authentic sense of self needs to occur both within communities and within the sisterhood of other black women. Black women need to socialize young girls to develop self-concepts that transform negative images. Black women can have divisive relationships due to differences in skin color, hair texture, social class, and educational levels. One of the ways that the oppressor works to maintain the system is by creating and highlighting intragroup differences, so that those who are oppressed engage in in-group fighting instead of fighting the oppressor. Black women can benefit from supporting each other in developing an authentic self. They can uniquely embrace the reflected beauty of one another. By encouraging one another, caring for one another, and connecting with one another, black women can inspire, sustain, and buttress their sisters as they struggle to resist their individual and collective oppression. Black women supporting and empowering each other provide the ultimate method of transforming society and liberating the self.

CONCLUSION

Black women face the unique interaction of discrimination and prejudice and are perceived and evaluated according to the stereotypes of Mammy, Sapphire, and Jezebel. Many women adopt the "superwoman" image, the need to do it all, without help or assistance. The internalization of these images has led to psychological symptoms, particularly depression and anxiety, interpersonal difficulties, and problems at work. Black women need to develop critical consciousness, the ability to sort and evaluate negative messages and oppressive images. They also need to develop an authentic self, to find their own voice, and to support each other in the struggle for liberation.

REFERENCES

Abdullah, A. S. (1998). Mammy-ism: A diagnosis of psychological misorientation for women of African descent. *Journal of Black Psychology, 24,* 196–210.

Adams, J. A. (2000). Individual and group psychotherapy with African American women: Understanding the identity and context of the therapeutic patient. In L. C. Jackson & B. Greene, (Eds.), *Psychotherapy with African American women: Innovations in psychodynamic perspectives and practices* (pp. 33–61). New York: Guilford Press.

American Psychiatric Association. (2000). *Diagnostic and Statistical Manual of Mental Disorders IV-TR*. New York: Author.

Bell, C. C., Hildreth, C. J., Jenkins, E. J., & Levi, D. (1988). The need for victimization screening in a poor outpatient medical population. *Journal of the National Medical Association, 80,* 853–860.

Bell, E. L. (1990). The bicultural life experience of career-oriented black women. *Journal of Organizational Behavior, 11,* 459–477.

Bell, E. L. (1992). Myths, stereotypes, and realities of black women: A personal reflection. *The Journal of Applied Behavioral Science, 28,* 363–376.

Boyd, J. A. (1993). *In the company of my sisters: Black women and self-esteem.* New York: Dutton.

Brown, D., Eaton, W. W., & Susman, L. (1990). Racial differences in prevalence of phobic disorders. *Journal of Nervous and Marital Diseases, 178,* 434–441.

Carter, R. T., & Parks, E. E. (1996). Womanist identity and mental health. *Journal of Counseling and Development, 74,* 484–489.

Collins, P. H. (1990). *Black feminist thought: Knowledge, consciousness, and the politics of empowerment.* Cambridge, MA: Unwin Hyman.

Cose, E. (2003, March 3). From schools to jobs, black women are rising much faster than black men. What it means for work, family and race relations. *Newsweek.*

Daniel, J. H. (1995). The discourse on *Thomas vs. Hill*: A resource for perspectives on the black woman and sexual trauma. *Journal of Feminist Family Therapy, 7,* 103–117.

Daniel, J. H. (2000). The courage to hear: African American women's memories of racial trauma. In L. C. Jackson & B. Greene, (Eds.), *Psychotherapy with African American women: Innovations in psychodynamic perspectives and practices* (pp. 126–149). New York: Guilford Press.

Edmondson-Bell, E. L. J., & Nkomo, S. M. (1998). Armoring: Learning to withstand racial oppression. *Journal of Comparative Family Studies, 29,* 285–295.

Fordham, S. (1993). "Those loud black girls": (Black) women, silence, and gender "passing" in the academy. *Anthropology and Education Quarterly, 24,* 3–32.

Freire, P. (1990). *Pedagogy of the oppressed.* New York, NY: Continuum.

Gainor, K. A. (1992). Internalized oppression as a barrier to effective group work with black women. *The Journal for Specialists in Group Work, 17,* 235–242.

Greene, B. (1994). African American women. In L. Comas-Diaz & B. Greene (Eds.), *Women of color: Integrating ethnic and gender identities in psychotherapy* (pp. 10–29). New York: Guilford Press.

Greene, B. (1997). Psychotherapy with African American women: Integrating feminist and psychodynamic models. *Smith College Studies in Social Work, 67,* 299–322.

Hall, C. C. I. (1995). Beauty is in the soul of the beholder: Psychological implications of beauty and African American women. *Cultural Diversity & Mental Health, 1,* 125–138.

Isom, D. (2002). *Me, I got many parts: An exploration of racialized gender with African American youth.* Unpublished dissertation.

Jackson, A. P., & Sears, S. J. (1992). Implications of an Afrocentric worldview in reducing stress for African American women. *Journal of Counseling and Development, 71,* 184–190.

Jones, C., & Shorter-Gooden, K. (2003). *Shifting: The double lives of black women in America.* New York: Harper Collins.

Jordan, J. M. (1997). Counseling African American women from a cultural sensitivity perspective. In C. Lee (Ed.), *Multicultural issues in counseling: New approaches to diversity* (pp. 109–121). Alexandria, VA: American Counseling Association.

Kempa, M., & Thomas, A. J. (2000). Culturally sensitive assessment and treatment of eating disorders. *Eating Disorders: The Journal of Treatment and Prevention, 8,* 17–30.

Landrine, H., & Klonoff, E. (1996). The schedule of racist events: A measure of racial discrimination and a study of its negative physical and mental health consequences. *Journal of Black Psychology, 22,* 144–168.

Makkar, J. K., & Strube, M. J. (1995). Black women's self-perceptions of attractiveness following exposure to white versus black beauty standards: The moderating role of racial identity and self-esteem. *Journal of Applied Social Psychology, 25,* 1547–1566.

McNair, L. D. (1992). African American women in therapy: An Afrocentric and feminist synthesis. *Women and Therapy, 12,* 5–19.

Michelson, L., June, K., Vives, A., Testa, S., & Marchione, N. (1998). The role of trauma and dissociation in cognitive-behavioral psychotherapy outcome and maintenance for panic disorder with agoraphobia. *Behavior Research & Therapy, 36,* 1011–1050.

Mitchell, A., & Herring, K. (1998). *What the blues is: Black women overcoming stress and depression.* New York: Perigee.

National Mental Health Association (NMHA). (1996). Clinical depression and African Americans. Retrieved November 19, 2003, from www.nmha.org/ccd/support/africanamericanfact.cfm

Neal, A. M. (1989). The role of skin color and features in the black community: Implications for black women and therapy. *Clinical Psychology Review, 9,* 323–333.

Neal-Barnett, A., & Crowther, J. H. (2000). To be female, middle class, anxious, and black. *Psychology of Women Quarterly, 24,* 129–136.

Omi, M., & Winant, H. (1994). *Racial formation in the United States* (2nd ed.). New York: Routledge.

Parks, E. E., Carter, R. T., & Gushue, G. V. (1996). At the crossroads: Racial and womanist identity development in black and white women. *Journal of Counseling and Development, 74,* 624–631.

Romero, R. E. (2000). The icon of the strong black woman: The paradox of strength. In L. C. Jackson & B. Greene (Eds.), *Psychotherapy with African American women: Innovations in psychodynamic perspectives and practices* (pp. 225–238). New York: Guilford Press.

Scherenzel, M. S. (2002). Debunking the myth of the black superwoman. *Black Entertainment Television.* Retrieved September 26, 2003, from www.bet.com

Schreiber, R., Stern, P. N., & Wilson, C. (2000). Being strong: How black West-Indian Canadian women manage depression and its stigma. *Journal of Nursing Scholarship, 32*, 39–45.

Sellers, R. M., Smith, M. A., Shelton, J. N., Rowley, S. A. J., & Chavous, T. M. (1998). Multidimensional model of racial identity: A reconceptualization of African American racial identity. *Personality and Social Psychology Review, 2*, 18–39.

Smith, P. J. (1999). Teaching the retrenchment generation: When Sapphire meets Socrates at the intersection of race, gender, and authority. *William and Mary Journal of Women and the Law, 6*, 53–214.

St. Jean, Y., & Feagin, J. R. (1998). *Double burden: Black women and everyday racism.* Armonk, NY: M. E. Sharpe.

Thomas, A. J. (2001). African American women's spiritual beliefs: A guide for treatment. *Women and Therapy, 23*(4), 1–12.

Thomas, A. J., Witherspoon, K. M., & Speight, S. L. (2004). Toward the development of the Stereotypic Roles for Black Women scale. *Journal of Black Psychology, 30*, 426–442.

Thompson, C. L. (2000). African American women and moral masochism: When there is too much of a good thing. In L. C. Jackson & B. Greene (Eds.), *Psychotherapy with African American women: Innovations in psychodynamic perspectives and practices* (pp. 238–250). New York: Guilford Press.

Watts, R. J., & Abdul-Adil, J. K. (1997). Promoting critical consciousness in young, African-American men. *Journal of Prevention and Intervention in the Community, 16*, 63–86.

West, C. M. (1995). Mammy, Sapphire, and Jezebel: Historical images of black women and their implications for psychotherapy. *Psychotherapy, 32*, 458–466.

West, C. M. (1998). The connection between historical images of black women and domestic violence. In *Assembling the pieces: Leadership in addressing domestic violence in the African American community.* Conference proceedings of the Institute on Domestic Violence in the African American Community. Washington, DC: U.S. Department of Health and Human Services.

Wilson, M. (1993). *Crossing the boundary: Black women survive incest.* Seattle, WA: Seal Press.

Witherspoon, K. M., Thomas, A. J., & Speight, S. L. Psychological functioning of African American women: The role of stereotypical images. Unpublished manuscript.

Wyatt, G. E. (1997). *Stolen women: Reclaiming our sexuality, taking back our lives.* New York: John Wiley & Sons.

Young, I. M. (1990). *Justice and the politics of difference.* Princeton, NJ: Princeton University Press.

CHAPTER 6

Black Women Coping with Stress in Academia

Lena Wright Myers

Alll women in America have experienced some form of oppression in their lifetimes. In a world of unjust and cruel experiences perpetrated by "others" who consider themselves holders of power and privilege, expressions of gender differences appear to be the order of the day.

A quick window of opportunity is clearly seen in our daily lives as we go about our business in the workplace. However, for women of color in general and black women specifically, there is something more than just gender differences.

You may ask, "Don't all women understand their oppression?" Of course we all do. But the liabilities of intersecting the *female* sex and the *black* race make a distinct gender for black women. Let me give an example of this.

A few years ago, I served as an invited distinguished scholar in residence for a week at a very elitist all-female college in the Midwest. My responsibilities included delivering a keynote address for a public forum, as well as three classroom lectures focusing on gender and multiculturalism in academia. I welcomed the opportunity!

The experience was emotionally rewarding, until I gave my final classroom lecture on women in the work force, in which I related my experiences as a black woman in the academy. Twenty minutes after the start of my lecture, the professor interrupted and asked, "Are you saying that you have experienced more racism than sexism in your academic career?" before she abruptly concluded, "That's not what you are to talk about."

With as much civility as I could possibly maintain, I politely replied, "I am coming to an explanation of that in my next statements." I completed my lecture and entertained students' interesting and thought-provoking questions, none of which suggested I should make a distinction between racism and sexism. The events of that classroom lecture engendered a two-page letter from a white male professor who had accompanied me to the classroom and remained to hear my lecture. His letter questioned the other professor's rationale for unethically interrupting my presentation, and he sent copies to high-level administrators. The following evening at a pre-planned reception in my honor, the professor tearfully apologized to me for her behavior in the classroom, saying, "I had some problem with your emphasizing racism more than sexism to the girls . . . and I'm sorry for what I said to you, because I really don't know your experiences." I accepted her apology and enjoyed the rest of the reception.

It is interesting to note that neither the content of the course nor my lecture intended to assign effectual weight to racism or sexism. Instead, it was about gender, multiculturalism, and my experiences. That situation replayed itself in my mind with heightened clarity as I considered possible motivations for the professor's comments. It is a good example of how some white women, who have not been victims of racism, lack a full understanding of the impact racism has on women of color. In an effort to raise social consciousness, the events of that classroom lecture led me to question the necessity of choosing whether racism or sexism holds greater significance in the lives and careers of black women. Clearly, both "-isms" and most other forms of "-isms" are an injustice to human beings. People are products of their experiences; determining the repercussions of "-isms" should be an assessment process unique to individuals.

The classroom lecture experience also illustrates the idea that some people have little difficulty assessing their own victimization within American society systems of oppression—be they racism, sexism, ageism, heterosexism, or another "-ism." However, at the same time, people typically fail to comprehend ways in which their thoughts and actions can ultimately reinforce and uphold another's subordination.

After my experience as an invited distinguished scholar in residence, I was presented with an important decision. I could attempt to systematically divide the effects of racism and sexism; however, I felt that in doing so I would compromise my perception of my experiences as a black woman. Therefore, writing this chapter is very important to me in addressing our experiences in the workplace and how we deal with stress resulting from our experiences.

WHERE WE STAND TODAY

We live in a world that devalues both the female sex and the black race. Within this world, black women have been stereotyped as

> nurturing, scheming, lewd, and unintelligent. In ways parallel to many of the obstacles Black men face, they are assigned personally limiting occupational roles—servant laborer, mammy, prostitute, church lady, matriarch, etc. Black women who become professionals, entrepreneurs, or even successful entertainers are often viewed as "strong" black women or else are perceived to be emotionally cold, selfish, and aggressive in unwomanly ways. Missing from the traditional occupational roles for black women, to this day, is a wide-scale recognition of their intellectual competence. (Zack, 1998, p. 123)

Until recently, we were excluded from professional positions in traditionally white colleges and universities. Just before World War II, we, as faculty and/or administrators were deliberately excluded by law or tradition from predominantly white institutions of higher learning (Benjamin, 1991, p. 123).

However, even with present-day opportunities for greater inclusion, many of us have found life inside white academia to be fraught with numerous contradictions and dilemmas. Some scholars describe this experience very well:

> It is difficult to talk about being Black in a White space, even though in the United States such is usually the case. The difficulty to speak, to name, without appearing to whine, is a near impossibility, since African American women are not expected to speak at all. It is particularly difficult to be heard since despite reality, the myth still prevails that African American women are making great professional strides. Enmeshed within this myth is the belief that even when African American women are suffering, obstacles are faced stoically and handled with a prayer, and a smile. In other words we always overcome. We African American women are reluctant to dispel this myth for it is one of the positive stereotypes afforded us. (Farmer & James, 1993, p. 205)

In addition to the previous statements, we are very much aware of what is going on in our lives as we work within the walls of white academia. As Carthy (1992) puts it,

> Black women have been more than victims; they have been actors, conscious builders of relations from which they benefit, and though confined certainly to a very limited sphere of the white patriarchal world, their position affords them clear understanding of their oppression. (pp. 43–44)

Nationally, 2.2 percent of faculty in higher education are black females. Once we accept a job in academia, we inevitably face obstacles that other faculty members are able to avoid. Black women hold 6 percent of the full professional rank compared to 1.6 percent for black men, 9.9 percent for white women, and 88.2 percent for white men. Most of us are typically found among non-tenure-track lecturers, instructors, and assistant professors, and we also earn less than our white colleagues at these institutions.

THE RESEARCH

I collected data from sixty-two black women who worked at traditionally white-collared universities throughout the country. The sample included black faculty and administrators from both private and public four-year colleges and universities and community colleges. The women were from various disciplines, from the ranks of instructor to full professor. There were two recent retirees who had "spent almost a lifetime" at very reputable research universities from which they retired. Data were collected by email and regular mail. Fifty-three of the women responded by email, and nine responded by regular postal mail. The women wrote their own narratives in answers to five general issues/questions:

1. Their early experiences of how persons with whom they worked perceived their ability to fulfill their responsibilities as faculty/administrators.
2. Their experiences of racism from their assumed superiors, such as chairpersons, deans, students, etc.
3. Their experiences of sexism from their assumed superiors, such as chairpersons, deans, students, etc.
4. Which of the two practices (racism or sexism) would you say had the greater effect on you? Please explain why you chose this practice.

5. What is your present rank at the college/university where you are/ were employed?

Our Experiences as We See Them

My reflections for this chapter complement what Powell (1983) so poignantly stated:

> Historically, the Civil Rights and Black Power Movements were transforming for all kinds of people—black, white, male and female. These movements were the political training grounds for thousands who would later be active in anti-war, anti-nuclear, women's and continuing Black community organizing. It was a time of open resistance and defiance, when many of us tested the limits set by our oppression to see how far they would give. (p. 285)

With those movements came several social and political benefits for some oppressed groups. However, the omnipresence of oppression remains in the lives of many black women in academia as we approach the twenty-first century. The following discussion is the scenario that is frequently enacted in our everyday lives.

I grew up in Mississippi, and at sixteen years old as an accelerated student, began my freshmen year at a historically black private college during the height of the civil rights movement. I had a real sense of my experiences of racism—experiences by which any individual undoubtedly would have been affected. My birth circumstances let me know what racism was about while growing up at a time before the profound period of consciousness-raising about sexism had fully developed. But, it was very clear to me during my early years that to be denied the opportunity to drink from a water fountain marked "white only" was not because I was a woman. The fact that I could not enter any white-owned and/or operated restaurant and be served food was not based on the fact that I was female. All of my early education was restricted to an all-black school—not because I was female, but because I was black. When I began college, I lived fewer than eight blocks from the one traditionally white four-year coeducational state university in Hattiesburg, Mississippi. I could not attend that college— not because I was female, but because I was black. The preceding chronology of my early experiences brings me to where I have been in academia for the past several years.

An earlier experience at traditionally white institutions that stands out in my mind was a statement on one of my student evaluations.

It read, "I was told by one of my [other] professors not to expect to learn much in this class—but I learned a lot." I read the comment but did not think much about it until the next term when a white female student stopped by my office to discuss a project about violence against women during the following term. She asked me, "Did you see the comment that I made on your teaching evaluation?" I realized that students remained anonymous on evaluations, so I asked her, "What was the comment?" With a seemingly noticeable level of naivete, she continued, "Professor _____ (white male) told me to go ahead and take your class, but not to expect to learn very much, but I learned a lot." Wow! Was that one for the books?! I believed her. I realized that this was a case of a white male perceiving me as lacking in knowledge of social psychology—a specialty in which I am very well prepared. He expressed this to a young white female, who later told me she was encountering a black female in her classroom for the first time in her life. The fact remains that as black women, these questions are often raised about our expertise and knowledge, despite the fact that we come from the same universities and academic backgrounds. Some of us were even trained in universities that outranked the ones from which some white women and men graduated.

A few years later, I chose to teach a graduate seminar, which I had taught in previous years at the same university. Through some unexplainable decision in the graduate committee meeting, I was denied the opportunity to teach the course that term. It was assigned to an untenured, white female assistant professor.

Being aware of the fact that a proposed system of rotating among the faculty who had earned PhDs in that specialty was made earlier, I inquired about why it was decided that I could not teach the course. After discussing this with a few colleagues, I got responses ranging from a shrugging of shoulders to "you know . . . I really don't remember how they came up with that decision."

I have kept written documentation that the same white male mentioned earlier, who had told the student not to expect to learn anything in my class, also stated, "As long as I am in my present position, Lena Wright Myers will never teach another graduate course." Well, how wrong was he? I taught the course later. This is a prime example of racism that totally contradicts his façade of staunchly supporting women's rights and racial equality. Even in the face of a traditionally irrefutable, excellent record in grantsmanship and publishing, I can document comments made by certain white male colleagues when referring to the work of some specific black women. Statements such as the following are made: "She is a prolific writer and researcher who is known nationally—*but* her works are mostly about blacks, and are lightweight."

Even though black women in academia do speak the English language, there is the tendency for some whites to interpret what *they* think *we* mean. On numerous occasions, I have served on committees and advisory boards in traditionally white university settings. As I begin to make statements about the issue being discussed, invariably some personally assumed authoritative figure says, "Professor Myers means that you should think about the issue *this* way." That person—typically a white male—continues to explain to the group what he thinks I meant, until I ask him not to speak for me. Clearly this person's behavior suggests that we black women in academia need an interpreter and are not capable of saying what *we* mean. This type of behavior also suggests the serious need to exude a level of domination, or rather to exhibit control.

At the same university, I was giving a final exam. Students were given their term papers as they turned in their exams. As a white female student received her term paper, she looked at me and shouted, "How can you give me a D+ on this paper?" Before I could explain the reason for the grade, as was already noted on her paper, she walked a few steps away from the desk where I was seated, then turned around and threw the paper at me and shouted, "You don't like me, anyway! I'm going to tell the dean on you, black bitch!" She then stormed out of the classroom, kicked over a wastebasket near the door, and continued to shout from the hallway, "Fuck you, black bitch!" It took all the emotional guts I had to avoid stooping to her level, and at that moment, I was determined to take every measure possible to ensure that she would never again call me a black bitch.

After she left, six students remained in the classroom, still taking their exams; all of them gave testimony to her conduct in a judiciary council. She was given disciplinary probation for the duration of her undergraduate education at the university. Although it has been a few years since that incident, my reminiscence of that experience brings to mind another very recent incident—harassment by a young white male student.

Hence, black women are not only victims of demeaning acts of male dominance, but some of us have to deal with harassment as well. An example of this follows.

Recently, I encountered an unusual interaction with a white male student enrolled in one of my classes. On two consecutive days, as

I sat in my office with the door closed and working with my graduate assistant, the student opened the door, walked directly to me, and standing less than eighteen inches from me, asked, "Where is my exam paper?" He was referring to exam papers that had been returned to the students sometime earlier, during his absence from class. When I attempted to go over to a table to get his paper, he moved with me. In other words, each time I moved away from him, he moved toward me. When I requested, "Please don't stand so closely as we talk," he replied, "I'm not doing anything." He finally left my office. I closed the door behind him and resumed work with my graduate assistant, who remained in the office during both encounters. Within less than two minutes, there was a loud knock on my door, at which time I asked, "Who is there, please?" Then came the voice saying, "Me." I opened my door, and there he stood, saying, "You don't like me, do you?" I responded, saying, "I like all of the fifty-eight students in that class—and I don't want to continue a verbal confrontation with you." Again, he left the office, but the next day, much of the same behavior continued; plus, he left a threatening message on my office answering machine. Through the assistance of the judiciary council director and the campus police, the problem was finally solved—at least I hope so—at the writing of this chapter.

I had another experience in which I was accused of tampering with my student evaluations. At the end of spring term, I had gone home for the summer as I traditionally do. I received a letter from one of my white male colleagues encouraging me to hurry and sign my contract for the next year. At the end of the letter was the statement "By the way, I want you to give me the names of students who delivered your evaluations to the department office last spring." Considering the fact that I had not been asked such a question during my career in academia, and since I could not recall the names of students, I asked other colleagues what this was about and whether they had received such a request. They informed me that they had no knowledge of such a request. I had been experiencing health problems during the latter part of that spring quarter, so I decided to concentrate on my health as opposed to worrying about such a request. I was not contacted again about the evaluations, so I assumed it must not have been that important.

However, when the budget and merit committee met later that fall, I received a response to my appeal from the same colleague who had requested the names of students. It read, "I wrote to you last summer

asking you for information about problems with your student evaluation forms and did not receive any responses . . . our concern about the
way you handled student evaluation forms, without any input from
you, led this fall to a series of changes that everyone must now follow."
(The change was to seal the envelope and have both student and
professor sign their names across the seal.) When I asked for a one-
on-one conversation about the reason for such a request, he nervously
stated, "We just want you to give us the names of students."

After that, my written response to the committee and him was, "If
the budget and merit committee is basing my teaching evaluations
on their assumption that I have mishandled student evaluations in
some way, they must be able to back up such an allegation with
documentation. Therefore, I am requesting that you and the committee either formally charge me in writing along with documentation to
back up such an allegation, or drop the matter entirely." I never heard
anything more from the colleague or the committee.

That experience is sad on one hand, yet laughable on the other.
Why? Because in the twenty-six years I have been a tenured full
professor at several colleges and universities, including that university,
I had never heard of such a ridiculous thing. It is important to note
that I was actively recruited by that same university based strictly on
my "national reputation as a sociologist" per media coverage. Since
that white male could not come up with a better reason to demean
and label me as "incompetent," he was fishing for something that was
utterly preposterous. What a serious waste of his energy because of
his intimidation of my mere presence.

Some experiences can be devastating, to say the least. Thus far, I
have discussed some of my experiences in academia. Examples of the
experiences of other black women are included in this chapter. Our
lives in academia may result in different expressions of our experiences.
The accounts and commentaries of black women are very important
because we have realistic, first-hand knowledge of every aspect of our
lives, and specifically, experiences in white academic environments.
Therefore, we are better judges of our experiences than any nonblack
outside observers.

There are very real differences between us in terms of race, sex, age,
class, and other characteristics that make people different. But it is not
those differences between us that are separating us. It is rather our
refusal to recognize those differences and to examine the distortions
that result from them or from misnaming them and their effects upon
human behavior and expectation (Lorde, 1998). Therefore, fair but

general definitions of racism and sexism for this chapter are as follows: *Racism* is the belief in the inherent superiority and dominance of one race over all others, and thereby the right to dominance. *Sexism* is the belief in the inherent superiority and dominance of one sex over the other, and thereby the right to dominance.

The preceding discussion should provide the reader with subsequent common themes identified by other black women faculty/administrators in predominantly white institutions. Common themes such as patronizing, disrespect for knowledge, unethical behavior, structural impediments, and numerous other examples indicate the impact of racism, as well as the intersection between racism and sexism.

While space will not permit detailed narratives of the sample, the results show that numerous black women of the sample reported that their qualifications were continuously challenged in their academic environments. Some noted that often their ideas were only viewed as legitimate when white colleagues stated them as their own. Frequently noted by most of the respondents was that their colleagues subjected them to magnified and extreme evaluations. In addition, a large number of the women stated that they felt pressured to outperform other (white) colleagues just to maintain perceived equal performance status with them.

Several of the black faculty members also noted that research topics that focused on race were not considered of much importance, especially in the tenure and promotion process. It was shown that even when their research was published in journals dedicated to such a focus, the journals were not considered prestigious or reputable enough.

A number of the respondents addressed faculty–student interaction as an issue in the academic environment. This included harsh judgment of teaching style and disrespect for course content, especially when race was discussed. Some even noted outright verbal and nonverbal attacks by some of the students. The majority of the women noted that racial experiences were typically far more overwhelming sources of oppression than gender experiences.

COPING WITH THE STRESSFUL EXPERIENCES

Over the past several years (1973 to the present), I have researched and written about *self-esteem* and *coping* among blacks in general and black women specifically. I define coping as alternative ways of dealing with the pressures of society. Hence, coping helps us to provide some explanation of resources used by black women in adjusting to the various social pressures we experience in every day life. This is to say that there is a *causal* relationship between what we think of ourselves and how we cope. It is to suggest that feelings of self-worth lead to a greater ability to cope (Myers, 1991, 1998, 2002).

If we know who we are and what we are about, we should know fairly well how we would deal with unpleasant experiences. This simply means "tapping our inner resources." After this, we develop and maintain an image of ourselves, despite adverse experiences (Myers, 1991, p. 22). It has been proven that numerous black women at various levels of employment appear to retain a remarkable sense of self-worth (Dill, 1988; Rollins, 1985). It is through the power of self-definition that we as black women intellectuals have long explored this private, hidden space of our consciousness that allows black women to cope with and, in most cases, transcend the confines of race, class, and gender oppression (Collins, 1989, pp. 92–93).

I chose not to include any questions about *self-esteem* and *coping* for this chapter. However, it is very interesting that several of the respondents addressed how they dealt with experiences of adversity in academia. For example, one woman wrote,

> It is believed that my general outlook on life not only colors my perceptions of my experiences in the workplace but also colors how my superiors and colleagues think of and relate to me. I am told that I approach life as "a detached onlooker" rather than as "an active participant," meaning that I have the ability to be involved and yet maintain a certain distance. In all probability, this attitude (approach) towards life and work was developed as a result of my beliefs about living in a society that presumed me to be inferior by reason of race. To this extent, it appears that I developed an "inner-directed" philosophy of life to regulate and control my behaviors, which enables me to have a positive sense of self. Therefore, I approach my work as a job more so than as a career. This attitude allows me to focus on doing the best work that I can do without a great deal of "self-esteem" investment.

Another respondent expressed her feelings in dealing with her experiences. According to her,

> My experiences have made me tremble with anger, heightened my distrust, and tested my perseverance. But I never allowed the situation to destroy my hope and alter my dreams. Why? Simply because I know who I am and what I am about, and I will never allow any acts of racism, sexism, or any other -isms to destroy my sense of who I am or destroy my level of competence in academia.

One respondent discusses her personal experiences and how they have helped her cope with the experience of racism:

> I really believe that having gone to a historically Black college for my undergraduate degree contributed greatly to my ability to deal with my experiences of racism in traditionally white institutions where I received my Ph.D. and where I am presently employed. Why do I say this? Simply because my sense of who I am was reaffirmed in that early environment prior to going into traditionally white environments.

In her narrative, titled *Trying to Fit In*, one of the black respondents gives her take on our experiences as follows:

> Alienation, social dislocation, political and psychological bankruptcy are descriptors of what I felt while teaching at two predominantly white colleges. While the outcomes were different, the experiences were as psychologically damaging. This made healing a slow process, which for some African American women is never complete, while for others we slowly regain our center.

Truer words were never spoken! Yes, we do regain "our center." If we were not able to regain our center, the few of us would not have remained in traditionally white institutions throughout the nation. For years it has been my belief that our key to coping with racism and sexism as black women is to get an image of ourselves based on how well we do whatever we are doing and how *others* whose opinions matter to us view our successes.

My previous research shows that our *social support systems* provide the primary function for our developing and maintaining a positive level of self-esteem. One of the black women's narratives complements the notion of special support systems. She writes,

> My family experiences provided the strength to compete in a white racist academic environment. My father always told me that I could be anything I wanted to be. However, he admonished that whites would try to block my progress. In addition, a strong church participation helped to buffer the effects of racism. I was raised in a close knit church that encouraged my intellectual pursuits.

We may observe that some of the women made specific reference to their early socialization in terms of a sense of "self." What do I mean by *social support systems*? I define social support systems as those helping

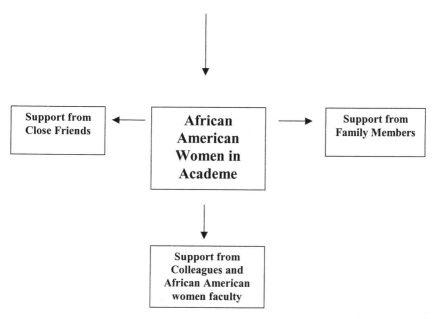

Figure 6.1 Social support systems in development and maintenance of self-esteem

agents or individuals within their environment whom black women identify as providing social support and feedback in solving problems or during periods of crisis.

We can observe from Figure 6.1 that close friends and family are of equal importance for black women. I can certainly relate to this! I often find myself touching base with my significant others through whatever forms of communication necessary. It has been proven that close friends are more supportive of emotional feelings, values, and beliefs. In society at large, some people tend to discuss problems only with personal friends rather than family members. This, again, is a way of coping with otherwise unbearable life situations (Myers, 1991, p. 28).

Our self-worth and self-reliance must be internally generated and support networks established in and out of the academic settings. This process is forever present as we interact with our significant others throughout life. We tend to maintain a steady pace by holding on to external and internal support systems in the face of adversity. It may not be so obvious, but it is equally true that, as black women separated in space but belonging to the same social category (race, sex, class, and in some cases, age), we have come to recognize our common fate.

Thus, we may deal with efforts of racism and sexism in a somewhat uniform manner (Myers, 1991). As one scholar puts it,

> No other woman on earth could have emerged from the hell of force and temptation which once engulfed and still surrounds Black women in American with half the modesty and womanliness they retain. (Du Bois, 1969)

The preceding statements are not to imply that black women in traditionally white institutions are "superwomen" in terms of physical strength. Coping is not to be interpreted as being hardened to the effects of adversity. We certainly are vulnerable to being moved by such things as sorrow, loneliness, neglect, unhappiness, and even happiness. But we are also capable of finding the means and alternatives for developing and maintaining our emotional stability in terms of a positive sense of self. However, our positive sense of self does not erase the negative effects of racism and sexism that we experience in our everyday lives in traditionally white colleges and universities. It only makes it a little bit easier to deal with.

In a truly just society, both racism and sexism as well as other types of "isms" should be eradicated. Moving toward the successful inclusion of women and minorities involves commitment and action by institutional leadership. Institutional leaders can show commitment to the advancement of black women in many ways. Possibilities include highlighting the excellent work of individual black women faculty, placing the participation and success of minority women high on the list of critical issues to the institution, and recruiting qualified black women for significant positions within the administration. Other faculty should be educated about the needs of black faculty and be committed to making noticeable change. It is not enough to simply tolerate diversity. Instead, it should be accepted and embraced. In the journey toward tenure or other promotions, as well as long-term job satisfaction, it is most important that black women maintain self-confidence . . . because this is what will help transform predominantly white institutions.

The stories have been told, and undoubtedly their tellers have known a range of human experiences unknown by most. The frustration of reaching endlessly can be exhausting to the black woman who captures victory after victory—only to tell herself to push harder. She knows that the respect she so desperately seeks, as a black *and* as a woman, is not likely to find its way past the rigidity of an environment defined by someone else.

Toolbox for Change

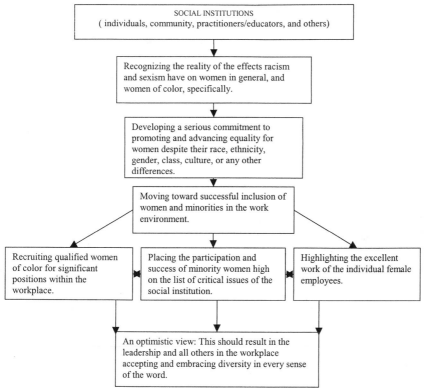

Many women experience differential treatment not only because of race but because of gender as well. For black women, this subordinate status twice defined is very pronounced in academia for its victims.

The sample of black women in traditionally white colleges and universities reported general experiences that were significantly influenced by racism and sexism. In many ways, black women were not given credit for outstanding work efforts and achievements. Whether it is through exclusion, through behavior based on prevailing stereotypes, or a blatant skepticism of their professional ability, colleagues directly and indirectly acted to undermine the success of the black women used in the research for this chapter.

Such influence is by no means undetected in the everyday struggles of black women in academia. However, of one thing nearly all respondents are certain: the *racism* and *sexism* that work to hinder black women are largely unnoticed by others. The continual fight for change is a lonely battle for many, at times fueled only by an incredible fortitude. Such profound inner strength rests at the heart and soul of women who refuse to wear labels—especially the label that calls them *victim*.

> Perhaps in the future the realities of African American women in academia will be significantly brighter. It will be through joint efforts of academic institutions as a whole and through the dedication of determined individuals that today's realities will be replaced by new revolutions in thought and action. Reality is not infinite and unchangeable; rather, it has the potential to be shaped by a society that embraces diversity. In the end, reality will be what we want it to be. And for African American women in academia, this reality will be a promising indicator of our outstanding accomplishments—past, present, and future. (Myers, 2000, p. 22)

We recognize stress imposed upon us by the stressors, and we deal with it in social psychological ways that work for us.

REFERENCES

Benjamin, L. (1991). *The black elite: Facing the color line in the twilight of the twentieth century.* Chicago: Nelson-Hall.

Carthy, L. (1992). Black women in academia: A statement from the periphery. In H. Bannerji et al. (Eds.), *Unsettling relations: The university as a site of feminist struggles.* Boston: South End Press.

Collins, P. (1989). *Black feminist thought: Knowledge, consciousness, and the politics of empowerment.* New York: Routledge.

Dill, B. T. (1988). Making your job good yourself: Domestic service and the construction of personal dignity. In A. Bookman & S. Morgen (Eds.), *Women and the politics of empowerment* (pp. 33–52). Philadelphia: Temple University Press.

Du Bois, W. E. B. (1969). *The souls of black folks.* Greenwich, CT: Fawcett.

Farmer, R., & James, J. (Eds.). (1993). *Spirit, space, and survival: African American women in (white) academe.* New York: Routledge.

Lorde, A. (1998). Age, race, class, and sex: Women redefining difference. In P. S. Rothenberg (Ed.), *Race, class, and gender in the United States: An integrated study.* New York: St. Martin Press.

Myers, L. W. (1991). *Black women, do they cope better?* (Rev. ed.). Englewood Cliffs, NJ: Prentice-Hall. (Original work published 1980)

Myers, L. W. (1998). *Black male socialization: Revisited in the minds of respondents.* Stamford, CT: JAI Press.

Myers, L. W. (2000). Realities in academe for African American women. *The Journal of Women in Higher Education, 9*(4), 21–22.

Myers, L. W. (2002). *A broken silence: Voices of African American women in the academy.* Westport, CT: Greenwood Publishing Group.

Powell, L. C. (1983). Macho and black feminism. In B. Smith (Ed.), *Home-girls: A black feminist anthology.* New York: Kitchen Table-Women of Color Press.

Rollins, J. (1985). *Between women: Domestics and their employers.* Philadelphia, PA: Temple University Press.

Zack, N. (1998). *Race, class, gender and sexuality: The big questions.* Malden, MA: Blackwell.

CHAPTER 7

Sexually Underrepresented Youth: Understanding Gay, Lesbian, Bisexual, Transgendered, and Questioning (GLBT-Q) Youth

Shannon D. Smith

My son, Matthew, was a bright star poised to take on the future. He had such hopes and potential. He was an enthusiastic student, an articulate speaker, and he was honestly gay. His life was crushed by the hatred of others. I believe that my son was killed because somehow, somewhere, his killers learned that the lives of gay people are not as worthy of respect, dignity and honor as the lives of other people. I ask you to ensure that students in your school never learn that dangerous lesson.

(Judy Shepard, 1999)

Just imagine that you were the author of these words about *your* son—how would you feel? How would you respond to the killers? What would you say to them? How might the course of your life be altered if your child became the victim of a hate crime?

Unless you were to experience such a tragic event, you could only speculate about the distressing possibilities. Unfortunately, Judy Shepard has no need to speculate about this possibility. These are her words in an open letter addressed to school administrators, urging them to take steps to stop acts of violence toward sexually underrepresented youth. Young people oppressed due to nontraditional sexual orientations and gender identity and expression can include any young person who identifies as gay, lesbian, bisexual, transgendered, and/or questioning (GLBT-Q). They are deemed "underrepresented" because they are a minority population within the dominant culture and larger group of heterosexual-oriented people.

Many people may not be familiar with the names Judy and Dennis Shepard, but most people are familiar with the name Matthew Shepard. Across the nation, in mid-October 1998, the headlines reported the brutal beating and cruel murder of this twenty-one-year-old human being. This crime of hate was provoked in response to the nature of Matthew's sexual orientation. That is, he was gay. And for being gay, he was brutally murdered. Matthew was physically assaulted by two men, tied to a fence alongside a desolate road in Wyoming, and left to die in the dark cold of the night on October 12, 1998.

As if the murder of their son were not enough pain and grief to endure, Reverend Fred Phelps arrived at Matthew Shepard's funeral to tell Mr. and Mrs. Shepard that their son "got what he deserved." This is a prime example of how cruel people can act based upon heterosexist notions about human sexuality. Heterosexism (the belief that heterosexuality is superior to homosexuality), transgenderism (the fear and hatred of transgendered persons), biphobia (the fear and hatred of bisexual persons), and homophobia (the fear and hatred of homosexuality) ultimately lead to prejudicial notions, discrimination, violence, and anti-gay hate crimes toward the sexually underrepresented. Sexism, the belief in the inherent superiority of one sex type over another type and thereby the right of dominance, is the major form of oppression that supports heterosexist notions.

This murder was tragic, and it is even more tragic and difficult to comprehend that this type of hate crime could be carried out in our modern society. However, it demonstrates the destructive powers of fear and hatred when combined in heterosexist notions and sexual prejudice(s). Although Matthew was a young, gay, Caucasian male, such crimes are not limited by age, gender, race, culture, religion, or other social and ethnic factors. There have been many cases of blatant discrimination and hate crimes toward diverse people groups who are sexual minorities. For example, Sakia Gunn, a fifteen-year-old girl, was recently stabbed (May 11, 2003) due to her proclamation of being a lesbian after Richard McCullough, twenty-nine, approached her and her friends and propositioned sexual and lewd advances. Sakia died shortly afterward in the emergency room. Some three thousand people turned out for Sakia's funeral, many of them young, queer people of color. This tragic murder is one more among many examples of the destructive power of sexual prejudice.

To prevent more needless deaths like Sakia's and Matthew's (as well as the grief of parents and friends) due to hate crimes and other forms of prejudice, all people must have a better understanding of both the external obstacles (violence, lack of resources, societal attitudes, etc.) and the associated internal impediments (that is, internalization of sexual prejudice) of GLBT-Q youth. To understand the sexual development crises that GLBT-Q youth face, it is necessary to understand basic sex terminology, theories of sexual development, the risks of certain sex behaviors, and the societal prejudices against people of nontraditional sexual orientations and gender identity and expression. Finally, we must all be aware of the consequences of the physical and emotional violence often perpetrated by family, friends, and strangers against GLBT-Q youth.

First, I provide an overview of key terminology related to prejudice and discrimination of the sexually underrepresented. Then, the discussion continues with a brief outline of sexual development, including its biological components, and a review of sexual orientation and identity development. This backdrop will provide the reader with accurate information and understanding regarding GLBT sexual development across the lifespan. Once this outline is complete, the discussion focuses on specific ways in which GLBT-Q youth experience discrimination and prejudice. Five major areas of focus are reviewed: (1) anti-gay hate crimes, (2) disclosure of sexual orientation, or "coming out," (3) family discrimination, (4) discrimination at school, and (5) medical discrimination and health care needs. Finally, practical tools and methods of advocating for GLBT-Q youth are presented.

DEFINING SEXUAL PREJUDICE AND DISCRIMINATION

The term *homophobia* was initially coined in 1967 to signify an irrationally negative attitude toward gay or lesbian people (Weinberg, 1972). The definition included dread of being in close quarters with gay men and lesbian women, and an irrational fear, hatred, and intolerance by heterosexuals. In the United States, two particularly prominent historical influences fostering anti-GLBT-Q attitudes have been heterosexism, the belief in the moral superiority of institutions and practices associated with heterosexuality (Greenberg, 1988), and religious fundamentalism. Recently, the focus on negative attitudes toward GLBT-Q persons has expanded to include traditional ideologies of family, gender, and personal and social relationships/constructs (Herek, 1988; Zea, Reisen, & Diaz, 2003). Homophobic attitudes have been found to be associated with an acceptance of traditional gender roles, involvement in religious fundamentalism (Herek, 1984a, 1984b), and the belief in a psychological cause of homosexuality (Matchinsky & Iverson, 1996).

Some people make a distinction between homophobia and heterosexism. Homophobia has been defined at the individual level as a person-centered negative emotional response to homosexuality, whereas heterosexism has been defined in ecological terms. In other words, it is a systematic process of privilege toward heterosexuality relative to homosexuality based upon the notion that heterosexuality is normal and ideal. Therefore, the foundation of heterosexuality is one of power and privilege. Herek (1993) defines heterosexism as the "ideological system that denies, denigrates, and stigmatizes any non-heterosexual form of behavior, identity, relationship, or community" (p. 90). It is also important to differentiate between homonegativity and homophobia. Homonegativity is a multidimensional construct that includes anti-gay attitudes, beliefs, and judgments.

Additional views of homophobia include a unidimensional construct that comprises several emotional responses (such as fear, anger, disgust) that persons experience while interacting with GLBT people (Hudson & Ricketts, 1980). A three-dimensional view of homophobia consisting of negative attitudes, culture-bound commitments to traditional sex roles, and personality traits has been proposed (Fyfe, 1983). O'Donohue and Caselles (1993) outlined an interactive model of cognitive, behavioral, and emotional components with situational determinants in producing homophobia-driven aggression. Finally, others have suggested that homophobia is a construct that consists of negative attitudes, affective regulation, and malevolence toward gay men and lesbians (Adams, Wright, & Lohr, 1997; Hagga, 1991). Throughout this chapter, I intend to use this term in its broadest sense.

Other terms have emerged recently to capture more specific prejudicial attitudes toward homosexuality, including the term *biphobia*, which is the fear or dislike of people who do not identify or behave as either gay, lesbian, or heterosexual (Hutchins & Kaahumanu, 1991). *Transgenderism* is prejudice multiplied by power that is used by traditionally gendered people toward nontraditionally gendered people (transgendered, transsexual, cross-dressers, intersexuals, drag queens, and drag kings) to restrict access to resources (Chen-Hayes, 2000) or to deny resources altogether.

There have been many terms used to describe prejudicial attitudes and behaviors toward the sexually underrepresented. Herek (2000) proposed the use of the term *sexual prejudice* for the scientific analysis of all negative attitudes based upon sexual orientation, including heterosexuality, bisexuality, transsexuality, and homosexuality. For the purpose of this chapter, *sexual prejudice* will refer to negative attitudes and acts of violence toward gay, lesbian, bisexual, transgendered, and questioning (GLBT-Q) persons, perceived or otherwise, same-sex behaviors, and GLBT-Q communities. Occasionally, I will use previously mentioned terminology when it is appropriate for purposes of readability and to maintain consistency with the original cited authorship when referring to the literature.

AN OVERVIEW OF SEXUAL ORIENTATION AND SEXUAL IDENTITY

The term *sexual orientation* is one that conjures up many different ideas due to the various definitions that have emerged from the literature in recent years. Although a comprehensive discussion of the nature of sexual orientation is beyond the scope of this chapter, an operational definition of sexual orientation is supplied for the reader. For an in-depth discussion of sexual orientation, the reader is referred to Broido (2000).

The construct of sexual orientation has been redefined over the past several decades. It has been thought of as a consistent pattern of sexual arousal toward persons of the same and/or opposite gender (Spitzer, 1981) and tends to encompass the elements of fantasy, conscious attractions, emotional and romantic feelings, sexual behaviors, and other potential components (Friedman, Green, & Spitzer, 1976; Remafedi, 1985). Numerous variations of sexual orientation (GLBT) are not only plausible but are also probable in most populations (Gonsiorek, Sell, & Weinrich, 1995). In recent years, sexual identity has adopted the component of self-identification, as homosexual, bisexual, gay, lesbian, heterosexual, or questioning (Klein, Sepekoff, & Wolf, 1985; Chung & Katayama, 1996.). Therefore, *sexual orientation* is defined here as a multidimensional construct that encompasses several interconnected dimensions of sexual attraction, behavior, and fantasies, as well as emotional, social, and lifestyle preferences including the use of a sexual identity self-label (Smith & Chen-Hayes, 2003).

Sexual orientation should not be confused with sexual identity. For the purpose of this discussion, it is important to distinguish between sexual orientation and sexual identity. While they may be interrelated, they are not similar in meaning. Sexual identity is an organized set of beliefs that a person holds to be true about the meaning of sexual attractions, desires, and related affections. These are perceptions of how attractions, desires, and affections correlate to a sense of self and one's chosen identity. This self-identification may be classified using socially established categories including heterosexuality and homosexuality, and more specifically those of gay, lesbian, bisexual, transgendered, and questioning (GLBT-Q). Sexual identity is conceptualized in historic and culturally specific notions, it is changeable over the life course, and it may or may not be congruent with one's sexual orientation (Savin-Williams, 1998). For example, some youth who engage in same-sex sex behavior may not identify as lesbian, gay, or bisexual. Other youth who do identify as GLB have not, as of yet, engaged in same-sex sexual activity. Therefore, sexual behavior is not the determining factor of sexual orientation, but sexual identity may dictate how one engages in sexual activity/behaviors.

The nature of sexual orientation can be a confusing matter for developing children and adolescents, and it is often confounded by sexual prejudice (homophobia and heterosexism). Adolescence is a confusing time for young people as their bodies undergo numerous physical and hormonal changes, especially during puberty. Added confusion occurs for many youth as they try to make sense of their immature affections and attractions to others, including members of the same sex. Sexual experimentation with the opposite and same-sex partners is often a part of the experiences that assist young people toward learning about sex behaviors and developing an understanding of their own sexuality, including sexual orientation and sexual identity. Young people begin to engage in various sexual activities during adolescence, including same-sex behaviors, for a variety of reasons. Although young people often provide numerous explanations for their sexual behaviors, such rationales generally can be grouped into three main categories: experimentation, sexual attraction, and social and cultural factors.

Experimentation is one major reason for pre-adult sexual activity. Young people engage in child and adolescent sexual experimentation with either the same or opposite sex/gender partners or both, primarily as means to "try out" their sexual abilities. The motivation for sexual experimentation can originate from many sources, such as curiosity, peer pressure, or as is often the case with children, acting out some behaviors that they have observed at home (such as television) or elsewhere.

Sexual attraction is another major reason that young people engage in sex activities. Sexual attraction may include the physical, emotional, or social attractions and fantasies that cause one to feel romantic or erotic toward the same or opposite-sex gender, or both.

Finally, social and cultural factors have a major influence upon young people's sexual behaviors. Examples include age of sexual engagement, marital rituals, and family lifestyle practices.

Once again, it is important to note that same-sex behavior does not necessarily dictate a gay, lesbian, bisexual, or transgendered orientation. For many children and youth, this type of sexual activity is a normal part of sexual development. Same-gender/sex activity via experimentation is one way that young people learn about sex behaviors. For example, a thirteen-year-old boy once said to me that he couldn't wait to kiss his new girlfriend, saying, "I finally got enough practice with my friend Mark." It was obvious to me that this boy was learning about sexual behaviors with a member of his peer group, but indeed he was not of a gay orientation.

Same-gender/sex behavior can also help young people to sort through some of the confusion associated with their sexuality, particularly when it comes to understanding the "true nature" of their sexual orientation. Research indicates that there is an age span ranging from early childhood to late adolescence when GLBT individuals tend to develop an awareness of their same-sex/gender feelings and attractions, with the average age range between eight and eighteen, and the average age of accepting the knowledge of one's minority sexual orientation at approximately fifteen (D'Augelli, Hershberger, & Pilkington, 1998; Elze, 2002; Floyd & Stein, 2002; Telljohann & Price, 1993). While engaging in same-sex/gender behavior, young people may confirm their sexual orientation as gay, lesbian, bisexual, transgendered (GLBT), or heterosexual. Those who are GLBT-oriented will likely find confirmation between their psycho-emotional-social-sexual attraction and feelings and their same-sex/gender behavior over time.

Although I have been discussing various behaviors, and those behaviors imply choice, I have not used terminology that implies that sexual orientation is a choice. For example, the term *sexual preference* is considered to be scientifically and politically incorrect when referring to sexual orientation because it implies that one chooses or that one can choose a specific sexual orientation (heterosexual or GLBT-Q). The notion that one has the ability to choose among the existing options of sexual orientation is not consistent with the current state of scientific knowledge and research. Many GLBT people believe that they did not choose their sexual orientation, nor did they ever have the option to choose (Chen-Hayes, 2000). In addition, many heterosexual people hold the same belief that they did not (nor could not) have the choice to be heterosexual in sex orientation. Gonsiorek and Weinrich (1991) suggest that the term *sexual preference* is misleading because it not only assumes conscious or deliberate choice but also trivializes the depth of psychological process involved in sexual development. They also recommend use of the term *sexual orientation*, indicating that homosexual feelings are a natural part of one's psyche and are established earlier than conscious choice would necessarily indicate. As mentioned above, people can make choices about how they express their sexual and gender identity and their sex/gender behavior; however, this is often confused by the use of the term *sexual preference*. Therefore, the term *sexual orientation* will be used throughout this writing.

SEXUAL IDENTITY

Sexual identity is not the same as sexual orientation. Instead, sexual identity development emerges over a lifetime, interacting in tandem with sexual orientation and sexual behavior, which are mediated by sociocultural, religious, and family influences. However, it is a unique component of both individual identity and these mediating factors. Several models of sexual identity development that have been proposed are briefly noted here; however, they will not be discussed in detail here. Cass (1979) proposed a six-stage developmental model, Coleman (1987) proposed a five-stage model, and Troiden (1989) introduced a five-stage model with several stage dimensions. Other models have been proposed (D'Augelli, 1994; Fassinger & Miller, 1996; McCarn & Fassinger, 1996; Minton & McDonald, 1984; Troiden, 1979), and they are highlighted here for the reader to reference, and to stress the fact that many aspects of sexual identity are developmental: in many respects, sexual identity is a unique, ongoing process that unfolds over the lifespan.

Although phases or stages of sexual identity have been proposed, Floyd and Stein (2002) recently identified that gay, lesbian, and bisexual youth display multiple patterns of reaching milestone experiences in their sexual identity development. Therefore, regardless of the particular model of sexual identity development that one uses to view this process, sexual identity development is a unique experience for each individual and will not always reflect proposed stage models of development. Stage models of sexual development are useful in capturing broad aspects of identity development; however, unique aspects of this process must be understood for an individual perspective.

It is also important to understand that sexual identity development is unique across variants of homosexuality for young people (Eliason, 1996b). Although there are similarities, there tend to be unique differences among underrepresented sexual groups. Research and theory have acknowledged the uniqueness of gay (McDonald, 1982), lesbian (Chapman & Brannock, 1987; Eliason, 1996a; Whitman, Cormier, & Boyd, 2000), bisexual (Weinberg, Williams, & Pryor, 1994), and transgendered (Grossman, O'Connell, & D'Augelli, 2002) identity development processes.

GLBT-Q identity can be confusing for many individuals because they may feel the need to change the presentation of their sexual identity depending on the social/environmental context. Homosexual youth will act "straight" in one setting and "gay" in another environment depending what type of behavior is socially acceptable, appropriate, and safe. Managing this double life and identity can become a preoccupation and add to the minority stress and the burden that many GLBT-Q carry. This double or even triple minority status can become difficult to manage over time and across various settings, particularly when group memberships cross over, bringing to question any inconsistencies. For example, some ethnic-minority GLBT-Q individuals feel that they have to choose between their ethnic/racial group and being homosexual, a view that is supported by many ethnic groups because a GLBT lifestyle is seen as rejection of the "ethnic heritage" or assimilation into the "white" culture (Harper, Contrearas, Correa, & Clack, 1999). Depending on the cultural context, Latino gay men have been noted to identify as gay in the context of an identified "gay" bar, but not in the context of their family (Zea, 1999); thus, it is seen as "context dependent" (Zea, Reisen, & Diaz, 2003). This form of sexual orientation environmental shifting is adopted by many GLBT-Q youth, particularly as they learn to understand their homosexuality against the backdrop of the hetero-sexist world and all of the prejudice and discrimination that it affords. Encounters with sexual prejudice and discrimination including hetero-sexism, social stigma, and anti-gay hate crimes are major determinants of how the sexual identity development process unfolds for each GLBT-Q person. Until an atmosphere of homosexuality is accepted as just as normal as heterosexuality, heterosexism will dominate social and culture norms, and sexually underrepresented groups will suffer from both subtle and blatant forms of oppression and prejudice.

THE BIOLOGY OF SEXUAL ORIENTATION

There are numerous theories about the origin of sexual orientation. However, current research indicates that sexual orientation derives from a complex interaction of environmental, psycho-emotional, and biological factors (Swaab, Gooren, & Hofman, 1995; Klein, Sepekoff, & Wolf, 1985; Weinberg, 1984). In most people, sexual orientation is shaped at an early age.

It is both scientifically and socially inappropriate to ask, "What makes you gay?" just as it is inappropriate to ask, "What makes you straight?" Questions regarding sexual orientation should not focus more intently on homosexuality any more than heterosexuality, al-though this has been the historical trend. This trend has been strongly influenced by heterosexist privilege and multiple forms of oppression, including sexual prejudice and genderism. Rather, inves-tigation into the nature of sexual orientation should focus on just that, sexual orientation—not homosexuality any more than hetero-sexuality. I find it interesting that no scientific endeavors have yet to embark on the discovery of the cause of heterosexuality.

Although the precise origin of sexual orientation is not known, there is some preliminary evidence to suggest that a biological basis is involved (Bancroft, 1990; Bancroft, 1994). There are four major areas of investigation into the biology of sexual orientation, including the role of hormones, neuropsychological functions, brain structure, and genetic factors. I will briefly highlight two areas that have received much attention recently: evidence from research on the brain structure and from genetics.

Several research studies indicate that differences in the structure of the human brain may help to account for uniqueness in sexual orien-tation. For example, morphometric analysis of the hypothalamus re-vealed that the volume of the suprachiasmatic nucleus (SCN) in gay men is 1.7 times as large as that of a reference group of male subjects and contains 2.1 times as many cells (Swaab & Hofman, 1990; Swaab, Gooren, Hofman, 1995). The sexually dimorphic nucleus (SDN) data indicate the selectivity of the enlarged SCN in gay men. The size of the third interstitial nuclei of the anterior hypothalamus (INAH) were found to be more than twice as large in the heterosexual men as in the gay men (LeVay, 1991). The anterior commissure was examined in ninety postmortem brains from gay men, heterosexual men, and women. The midsagittal plane of the anterior commissure in gay men was 18 percent larger than in heterosexual women and 34 percent larger than in heterosexual men. This finding supports the hypothesis that factors operating early in development sexually differentiate the structures and functions of the brain, including the anterior commissure and sexual orientation, in a global fashion (Allen & Gorski, 1992). However, one recent study (Lasco, Jordan, Edgar, Petito, & Byne, 2002) was not able to replicate these findings and indicated that speculation regarding the role of sex differences in hemispheric functioning must be regarded as premature.

Biology, including genetic and inborn hormonal factors and chromosomes, may play a significant role in a person's sexuality (Hu et al., 1995), although many questions remain (Banks & Gartrell, 1995). Recent studies of monozygotic twins indicate a high correlation of like sexual orientation, which suggest that a biological mechanism is involved in shaping both homosexuality and heterosexuality (Buhrich, Bailey, & Martin, 1991; Eckert, Bouchard, Bohlen, & Heston, 1986; Whitam, Diamond, & Martin, 1993). A half century ago, Kallman (1952) first noted 100 percent concordance for a sample of homosexuality in monozygotic twins and 12 percent in dizygotic pairs. Of a sample of 115 gay men who had male twins, 52 percent of identical twin brothers were also gay compared with only 22 percent of fraternal twin brothers and 11 percent of adopted brothers (Bailey & Pillard, 1991). In a comparable sample of 115 lesbians, 48 percent of identical twin sisters were also lesbians compared with only 16 percent of fraternal twin sisters and 6 percent of adopted sisters (Bailey, Pillard, Neale, & Agyei, 1993). Therefore, there appears to be a high correlation between genotype and sexual orientation.

Genetics have also provided evidence that sexual orientation may be linked to the X gene. Hamer, Hu, Magnuson, Hu, and Pattatucci (1993) investigated male sexual orientation by pedigree and linkage analyses on 114 families of gay men. They discovered increased rates of same-sex orientation in the maternal uncles and male cousins of these subjects. DNA linkage analysis of this group of forty families in which there were two gay brothers and no indication of non-maternal transmission revealed a correlation between gay orientation and the inheritance of polymorphic markers on the X chromosome in approximately 64 percent of the sibling pairs tested. The linkage to markers on Xq28, the subtelomeric region of the long arm of the sex chromosome, shows that at least one subtype of male sexual orientation is genetically influenced. In a follow-up study, linkage between the Xq28 markers and sexual orientation was detected for the gay male families but not for the lesbian families. The results corroborate the above finding of linkage between Xq28 and male homosexuality in selected kinships and suggest that this particular chromosomal region contains a locus that influences individual variations in sexual orientation in men but not necessarily in women (Hu et al., 1995). However, one recent investigation did not find evidence to support the notion that male sexual orientation was influenced by an X-linked gene (Bailey et al., 1999). Although there is no evidence for a "gay" gene as the popular media may have indicated, the evidence does suggest that genes are involved in determining sexual orientation.

It is important to recognize that there are many factors that constitute a person's sexual orientation, and these factors will vary accordingly for each individual. Human sexual orientation is complex and diversely experienced, and biologic theories and investigations do not account for all of the complexities involved. Other models have been proposed to account for the multiple complexities involved in sexual orientation. For example, a biopsychosocial model (Friedman & Downey, 1993) and an interactionist model (Byne & Parsons, 1993) have been proposed to account for the complexities not accounted for by a strictly biological approach toward understanding sexual orientation.

PREJUDICE AND DISCRIMINATION AGAINST GLBT-Q YOUTH

Prejudice and discrimination toward GLBT-Q youth are well documented. This section addresses the nature of sexual prejudice and its impact upon children and youth. The nature of anti-gay hate crimes is presented. In addition, the impact of sexual prejudice is discussed as it pertains to the process of sexual identity disclosure ("coming out"), family relationships, the school setting, and GLBT-Q health care needs.

Anti-gay (GLBT-Q) Hate Crimes

Sexual prejudice may culminate in anti-gay (GLBT-Q) hate crimes. Antigay hate crimes are violent acts perpetrated against an innocent victim either because or on presumption that the person is of a sexually underrepresented group. The National Coalition of Anti-Violence Programs makes it clear that anti-gay hate crimes are a distinct form of hate crime; anti-gay hate crimes are based on actual or perceived sexual orientation or gender identity. Unlike the origin of other forms of hate crimes (such as anti-Semitism stemming from religious hatred), anti-gay crimes—or, more technically correct, "anti-GLBT-Q" hate crimes—are precipitated in response to actual or perceived sexual orientation and gender, that is, underrepresented sexual orientation and gender identity and/or status.

In the 2000 annual Uniform Crimes Report (UCR) published by the Federal Bureau of Investigation (FBI), a hate crime is defined in the following manner: "A hate crime, also known as a bias crime, is a criminal offense committed against a person, property, or society which is motivated, in whole or in part, by the offender's bias against a race, religion, disability, sexual orientation, or ethnicity/national origin" (p. 59). Of the 8,152 hate crime incidents reported to the FBI in 2000, 54.8 percent were motivated by racial bias, 16.5 percent by religious bias, 16 percent by sexual orientation bias, 12.4 percent by ethnic/national origin bias, and 0.4 percent by disability bias (FBI, 2000). Since the FBI started tracking anti-gay hate crimes, the rate has doubled from approximately 8 percent in 1991 to 16 percent in year 2000. The 1,589 reported victims of sexual orientation hate crimes in 2000 demonstrate that sexual prejudice and discrimination are a major problem perpetrated against sexual minority populations in the form of violence, and the increasing trend indicates that anti-gay bias is becoming substantially worse.

The UCR (FBI, 2000) data include only those hate crimes that were reported to authorities; it does not document the untold number of incidents that are never reported to law enforcement agencies. For example, of the 11,690 reporting law enforcement agencies (representing forty-eight states and the District of Columbia), 83.8 percent reported that no hate crime(s) occurred in their jurisdiction, and the remaining 16.2 percent reported that at least one hate crime occurred. It appears that many anti-gay hate crimes are not reported to authorities based upon the fact that 84 percent of law enforcement agencies indicate no hate crimes in their jurisdictions. The underreporting is consistent with information from GLBT-Q persons who indicate they do not report to authorities due to fear of discrimination and retribution (Braford, Ryan, & Rothblum, 1994; Herek, Gillis, & Cogan, 1999; Herek, Cogan, & Gillis, 2002). Research indicates that large numbers of children and youth are victims of crimes that are never identified by authorities (Boney-McCoy & Finkelhor, 1995; Saunders, Villeponteaux, Lipovsky, Kilpatrick, & Veronen, 1992).

In addition to the UCR reports, the professional literature has documented the occurrence of anti-gay hate crimes and physical violence, as well as the negative effects of such perpetration against young GLBT-Q persons from sexual prejudice (D'Augelli & Dark, 1995; Dean, Wu, & Martin, 1992; Hershberger & D'Augelli, 1995). GLBT-Q youth experience verbal and physical threats and assaults simply due to the underrepresented nature of their sexual orientation, something that they are not responsible for creating or choosing. Just as heterosexual people feel and believe that they did not choose their sexual orientation, meaning that they were "born" heterosexual, so too is the feeling and belief of the sexually underrepresented. Just as it is scientifically, socially, and politically inappropriate to ask a heterosexual person, "Why did you choose be heterosexual?" so too is the question "Why did you choose to become GLBT?" inappropriate to the sexually underrepresented.

Comparing adult lesbian and gay victims of recent non-bias crimes to anti-gay hate crimes, Herek et al. (1999) indicated that recent hate crime victims displayed significantly more symptoms of depression, anger, anxiety, and post-traumatic stress. Significant differences were not noted among bisexuals. Gay and lesbian hate crime survivors manifested significantly more fear of crime, greater perceived vulnerability, less belief in the benevolence of people, a lower sense of mastery, and more attributions of their personal setbacks to sexual prejudice than did non-bias crime victims and non-victims. This association can be psychologically harmful because sexual orientation is such an important part of the self-concept, and it can be particularly disrupting to young people. Research indicates that childhood victimization can disrupt the normal course of development and can be associated with symptoms over the life span (Boney-McCoy & Finkelhor, 1995).

Prejudice derives from irrational fears and a lack of understanding and information and generally operates out of misinformation including myths, stereotypes, and stigmas. Unfortunately, many people have not been educated about sexual development and therefore do not have a correct understanding of sexual orientation and sexual identity formation. For example, many people are unaware of the biological mechanisms involved in sex formation as well as sexual orientation and development. In addition, many people continue to maintain the false belief that GLBT persons can choose their sexual orientations (Armesto & Weisman, 2001). As a result, myths, stereotypes, and stigma about homosexuality continue to perpetuate in society, causing the perpetration of sexual prejudice in the form of anti-gay hate crimes and acts of violence.

Discrimination for "Coming Out"

Research has demonstrated that GLBT-Q youth identity development is unlike heterosexual identity development in various ways (Floyd & Stein, 2002). One obvious difference is that heterosexual youth do not have to disclose or "come out" with their sexual orientation. The "heterosexual assumption" (Cain, 1991; Plummer, 1975; Ponse, 1978) is the philosophy that, unless otherwise indicated, all individuals in society are heterosexual. This assumption establishes social privilege for heterosexuals. Heterosexist privilege automatically and unquestionably assumes a heterosexual sexual orientation within the population. This is one major component of heterosexual privilege that is reflected in the dominant culture. With this pre-established privilege, GLBT-Q youth face the unique task of having to reveal their sexual orientation as something other than the assumed social norm. As a result, GLBT-Q youth face the potential for sexual prejudice and discrimination based upon this social dynamic of heterosexist privilege as reflected in the dominant culture.

One consequence of coming out in the heterosexist, dominant culture (hetero-dominance) is that the GLBT-Q youth subculture often fear revealing their homosexuality due to personal and social stressors such as fear of rejection, fear of being ostracized, fear of verbal and physical attacks, and homelessness (D'Augelli et al., 1998; Hetrick & Martin, 1987; Pilkington & D'Augelli, 1995). This *minority stress* (Meyer, 1995, 2003) is due to stigma, prejudice, and discrimination, which create a stressful environment that can lead to psychological and emotional difficulties for GLBT-Q youth. Harry (1989) reported that gay adolescents were more likely to undergo physical abuse by a parent, mainly the father, than heterosexual counterparts were. This was especially true for those adolescents who displayed effeminate behaviors and/or who were known to have engaged in same-sex sexual behavior. Russell, Franz, and Driscoll (2001) reported that youths who experienced same-sex or both-sex romantic attraction were more likely to experience extreme forms of violence than youths who indicated heterosexual attraction. Youths reporting same-sex and both-sex romantic attractions were also more likely to witness violence and were at greater risk of experiencing, witnessing, and perpetrating violence than youths who identified as heterosexual.

D'Augelli et al. (1998) examined issues related to disclosure of sexual orientation on a sample of 105 GLBT-Q youth (ages 14–21, thirty females, seventy-five males). Average age of awareness of orientation was age ten, and self-labeling occurred about four years later. First disclosure occurred at age sixteen on average ($SD = 2.2$). Therefore, subjects in this study had lived at home for about eight years while being aware of their underrepresented sexual orientation, for four years having self-identified, and for an additional two years before "coming out." First disclosure was to a friend (77 percent) for most participants. Those who disclosed to a parent (9 percent) chose their mother. Three-quarters (76 percent, $n = 80$) revealed their sexual orientation to a parent at age 17 on average; many (39 percent) were eighteen or older. Of these eighty who told parents, 65 percent revealed to mothers, 9 percent to fathers, and 25 percent to both. Only half of the mothers and siblings, and one quarter of fathers, displayed acceptance of their coming out. One quarter of fathers and 10 percent of mothers displayed active rejection. In many cases, disclosure resulted in threats, both verbal and physical, and included verbal and physical abuse.

One major strategy that homosexual youth employ to cope with sexual prejudice is to live in silence about their sexual orientation; they simply learn to hide (Martin, 1982). Unfortunately, this protection strategy distorts relationships and creates an increasing sense of isolation and loneliness. For example, of the 25 percent of subjects from the D'Augelli et al. (1998) study who chose not to disclose their sexual orientation, 12 percent reported past suicide attempts. Although more frequent attempts and thoughts of suicide were reported by those youth who had disclosed, many were victimized; whereas there were no reports of victimization from the non-disclosed group. Non-disclosure may protect GLBT-Q youth from being physically and verbally victimized, but it has a negative, internalized impact on normal homosexual development. GLBT-Q youth internalize a sense of homonegativity related to their underrepresented status. It appears that it is safe in the "closet," but the closet seems to have its own set of minefields to watch out for, such as the increased stress of needing to hide.

A pattern of disclosure seems to exist as a necessary function of identity development, with greater disclosure occurring as GLBT-Q identity solidifies. Youth who disclose tend to feel more comfortable about being GLBT-Q and establish friends and develop peer social networks more readily than those who choose not to disclose (D'Augelli et al., 1998). Those who disclose report fewer problems revealing their sexual orientation to friends and others, despite past victimization. Therefore, there is a positive correlation between sexual orientation disclosure and development of a positive self-GLBT-Q identity. Povinelli, Remafedi, and Tao (1996) reported that identification as homosexual (gay or bisexual) at a younger age, having a large network of friends who understand one's sexuality, and having had a steady male partner reflected the extent of gay and bisexual identification and acculturation.

The bottom line is that it is potentially dangerous for young people to disclose that they are GLBT-Q. Whether at home or at school, revelation of one's underrepresented sexual status can result in verbal and physical harm. However, the paradox is that non-disclosure tends to thwart normal GLBT sexual identity development.

Family Discrimination

In addition to the negative and violent responses of family members as a result of coming out, GLBT-Q youth often face other forms of sexual prejudice from family members. Family discrimination is perhaps the most difficult for young people to deal with and to understand. From a young age, children are taught heterosexual norms and lifestyle behaviors. Comments such as "When you grow up and get married . . ." or "I can't wait for you and your spouse to have children . . ." convey heterosexist norms and subsequently deny homosexuality as a viable lifestyle and behavior. By the early age of five, children have internalized a concept of marriage that often includes members of opposite genders (Broderick, 1966). Unfortunately, the presumption of heterosexuality leaves many families unprepared for a child's disclosure of homosexuality and often leads to shattered parental expectations, hopes, and dreams. As a result, GLBT-Q youth face family isolation. Many of these young people do not want to hurt their parents by shattering their heterosexual assumptions and dreams, and therefore choose to live in silence. Often, they choose not to disclose in order to isolate their family and loved ones from anticipated turmoil that they believe would occur as a result of their sexually underrepresented status (Ben-Ari, 1995). Parents and siblings of GLBT-Q youth must also undergo a type of coming-out process. Revealing their child's underrepresented status is not an easy task, as it means overcoming the loss of a heterosexual child as well as having to face sexual prejudice in society. Robinson, Walters, and Skeen (1989) reported a five-stage progression of mourning and loss in dealing with their child's sex orientation: shock, denial, guilt, anger, and acceptance. Parents may blame themselves for their child's sex orientation—believing that they were not adequate role models, they provided too much attention or affection, or they encouraged non-stereotypical play or behavior (Hunter, 1987). Parents and siblings need to seek appropriate information, seek support, and develop a positive view of their family. Unfortunately, some families would prefer their GLBT-Q child to live in silence instead of facing the challenge of family integration and overcoming sexual prejudice.

Living in silence is another way that GLBT-Q youth protect themselves against anticipated fear of rejection and harm. Whereas many other underrepresented groups (such as black and Mexican American youth) rely on family support in the face of oppression and violence, family segregation is a unique form of isolation experienced by GLBT-Q youth. Other minority groups are not always able to hide innate characteristics that receive discrimination and prejudice (Strommen, 1990), but GLBT-Q youth are able to play the role of heterosexual indefinitely, supported in part by social norms and heterosexist privilege. Thus, GLBT-Q youth experience an "invisible" minority status in the attempt to hide their underrepresented sexual orientation. Despite the great amount of energy required to maintain a heterosexual image, the risk of rejection and sexual prejudice help maintain the silence and the decision to stay in the "closet" (Wells & Kline, 1987). Being "invisible" may have some advantages, but it also brings with it the intense anxiety of being "outed" and the tremendous amount of energy it takes to maintain a heterosexual façade.

Fear of negative parental reactions is justified in many cases of GLBT-Q disclosure (Miller & Boon, 2000; Remafedi, 1987; Strommen, 1989; Oswald, 2000). Parental reactions range from mild negative reactions to extreme acts of violence and abuse. Coming out to parents is one of the most difficult decisions that GLBT-Q youth have to make (Savin-Williams, 1989). Anticipated parental response to disclosure is very often one of negativity for GLBT-Q youth (Boon &

Miller, 1999). Adolescent males who believed that their sex orientation would result in negative parental response were found to have
accurately predicted such a reaction (Cramer & Roach, 1988).
Robinson, Walters, and Skeen (1989) reported that parents of gay
and lesbian adults felt sadness, fear, regret, and depression related to
their children's sexual orientation, in addition to concerns for their
safety and well-being. D'Augelli et al. (1998) found that 51 percent
of mothers, 27 percent of fathers, and 57 percent of siblings were
fully accepting upon disclosure. About one-third of the parents
were tolerant, but not fully accepting. However, negative reactions
were twice as common for the fathers, with 26 percent expressing rejection compared to 10 percent of mothers and 15 percent of siblings. Verbal abuse toward males was reported by one-quarter of the
mothers, and over one-third toward the females. Almost 20 percent
of fathers, as well as brothers, displayed verbal abuse. Lesbians were
threatened more often with physical attacks than were gay males and
were more often actual victims of attack perpetrated by mothers.
Brothers of gay males perpetrated the most physical threats as well
as physical assaults. There were virtually no incidences of attack
among the non-disclosed group.

Gay and bisexual men from the Corliss, Cochran, and Mays (2002)
study reported higher rates (than heterosexual men) of childhood
emotional and physical maltreatment by their mother or maternal
guardian, and major physical maltreatment by their father or paternal figure. Lesbian and bisexual women also reported higher rates of
major physical maltreatment from both mothers and maternal guardians as well as their fathers or paternal guardians.

Discrimination at School

For many GLBT-Q students, school can be an unsafe place. School
environments tend to promote heterosexism, homophobia, and strict
rules about gender conformity (Chen-Hayes, 2001). Research has documented that individuals assumed to be homosexual were harassed by
teachers and peers in elementary school and that these experiences intensified in secondary school (Uribe & Harbeck, 1992). Others have
identified the classroom as one of the most homophobic of all social
institutions (Elia, 1993; Unks, 1994) and one of the most challenging environments to work in to meet the needs of GLBT-Q youth
(Smith & Chen-Hayes, 2003). GLBT-Q students report hearing
peers use derogatory words such as *dyke* or *faggot* at least once per

day, as well as by teachers once per month. However, these verbal offenses were not disciplined or addressed by teachers or administrators. As a result, these students reported increases in negative feelings such as loneliness, alienation, and rejection, which were associated with higher suicide ideation and attempts; and running away and academic deterioration (Jordan, Vaughan, & Woodworth, 1997).

Research indicates that approximately 28 percent of GLBT-Q adolescents drop out of school (Bernstein, 1995). Negative experiences at school can lead to a drop in academic performance and attendance among sexually underrepresented youth. GLBT-Q youth are more than four times as likely as their heterosexual counterparts to miss school due to feeling unsafe (GLSEN, 1999). Due to these unique stressors, many experience an increase in academic and social failure, decreased involvement in extracurricular activities, and non-completion of a high school (Durby, 1994; Remafedi, 1987).

Staff members, teachers, and administrators often believe or do not acknowledge that GLBT-Q students exist in the school setting. Many simply deny the "possibility" that such students may be their very own. Such a rigid denial system precludes them from accepting that GLBT-Q students are present in every school. Rending these youth "invisible" is one tactic utilized to avoid having to meeting their distinct needs. A recent study found that in Seattle, Washington, of 8,406 respondents in the ninth to twelfth grades, 4.5 percent of respondents described themselves as gay, lesbian, or bisexual. Ninety-one percent described themselves as heterosexual. Another 4 percent indicated that they were "not sure" of their sexual orientation (Reis & Saewyc, 1999). Population estimates of GLBT-Q persons in the United States range between 4 percent and 10 percent, the average estimate of GLBT-Q youth population being 6 percent (Ginsberg, 1998). Denial of such facts prevents school staff from effectively meeting the psychosocial needs of these students, and it further supports the "invisibility" syndrome.

Another major problem facing GLBT-Q youth is the lack of representation in the school curriculum and in classroom instruction and discussions (Fontaine, 1997; Harris, 1997). Teachers typically do not receive training or attend workshops on their own regarding sexual orientation and GLBT-Q issues/needs, and most have less than one hour of this type of training before receiving their degrees (Bliss & Harris, 1999). GLBT-Q students also lack positive role models in the school setting (Malinsky, 1997; Martin, 1982; Uribe & Harbeck,

1992). Without identified positive role models, these students often self-identify with the negative stereotypes that are portrayed in the school system. The presence of visible GLBT staff members is essential in providing support and role identification for these at-risk students. Unfortunately, many school personnel are themselves afraid to be "out" in their school workplace due to fear of discrimination and the threat of potential job loss (Anderson, 1994; Bliss & Harris, 1998).

Discrimination in the Health Care Setting: GLBT-Q Health Care Needs

Recently there has been an increased recognition of GLBT-Q adolescent health care needs and the unique issues that they face as a sexual minority group (Allen, Glicken, Beach, & Naylor, 1998; Beach et al., 1993; Perrin & Kulkin, 1996). In order to provide adequate medical and health care for GLBT-Q youth, physicians, nurses, counselors, social workers, psychologists, and other providers must have a proper knowledge and understanding of homosexual development and its unique health care needs. Often, GLBT-Q youth will not discuss their unique medical concerns due to fear of discrimination based upon sexual orientation and homosexual sex practices (such as injury from anal intercourse). In one study (Telljohann & Price, 1993) 19 percent of males and 18 percent of females indicated that they would not disclose or discuss their sexual orientation with their physicians due to fear of discrimination. Gay males tend to choose health care providers based upon the providers' like sexual orientation, and lesbians tend to choose female providers (Paroski, 1987).

Allen et al. (1998) reported that two thirds of their GLB subjects ($n = 102$, ages 18–23) stated that they never discussed sexual orientation with their medical providers during their youth (ages 14–18), but reported the desire to do so. Sixty percent of subjects ($n = 81$) reported not feeling safe discussing sexual orientation with their providers. Fewer than half of the subjects remembered being informed about medical confidentiality. Those who were informed of such were three times more likely to discuss their minority sexual orientation. Over 70 percent of the subjects who reported not being informed about medical confidentiality indicated that they would have been more likely to discuss their sexual orientation under this blanket of security. A total of thirteen subjects had disclosed their sexual orientation to the heath care provider(s), and half of those males were given information on HIV prevention. Two of the thirteen subjects reported that their health care providers seemed to take offense at their sexual orientation, and two indicated that the information was discussed with their parents without consent. One respondent stated that her medical provider made note of her sexual orientation on the medical record against her permission to do so. None of these thirteen subjects were referred to a support group for GLBT-Q teens, even though this has been a professional recommendation for this population for over fifteen years (Gonsiorek, 1988).

The research regarding discrimination of GLBT-Q youth in the medical setting is limited. However, the investigations conducted on adult homosexuals illuminates the severity of sexual prejudice within the medical community. GLBT-Q families have also experienced sexual prejudice with the health care system. These include issues concerning conception choices and family constellation; issues of disclosure ("coming out"); family breakdown or separation; issues of custody and legal rights, particularly for non-biological parents; lack of social acceptance; overt social disapproval for GLBT-Q families; and the impact of this on children (Clay, 1990; Deevey, 1989; Eliason, 1996a; Gentry, 1992; Gold, Perrin, Futterman, & Friedman, 1994; Kenney & Tash, 1992; Nelson, 1997; Perrin & Kulkin, 1996). Research on adult GLBT persons indicates that the health care system has not always met their health-related needs and concerns, and a significant proportion of health care providers still hold prejudiced views and condemnatory attitudes toward homosexuals (Eliason & Randall, 1991; James, Harding, & Corbett, 1994; Rose, 1994; Schwanberg, 1996). Homophobia, stereotyping, and stigmatization by health professionals are crucial factors in the health care experiences of many GLBT-Q persons (Baker, 1993; Grossman, 1994; Morrissey, 1996). When their sexual orientation is known, gay men and lesbians have reported embarrassment by care providers, fear, ostracism, refusal to treat, demeaning jokes, avoidance of physical contact, rough physical handling, rejection of partners and friends, invasion of privacy, breaches of confidentiality, and feeling at risk of harm (Harvey, Carr, & Berrnheine, 1990; Mackereth, 1994; Stevens, 1994). For lesbians, these negative experiences have impacted readiness to seek medical care, causing delays in obtaining treatment, fear of disclosure of sexual orientation, feelings of anxiety and vulnerability, and fears of discrimination (Trippet & Bain, 1992).

Sex Behavior Risks and Discrimination

Certain sexual behaviors, not sexual orientation, pose medical risks for GLBT-Q youth. The notion of GLBT sexual orientation as a deviant form of sexual expression and identity can lead to unsafe sexual practices among sexually underrepresented youth. These youth engage in high-risk behaviors—including high-risk sex activity—due to negativity, rejection, violence, and other acts of prejudice and discrimination based upon underrepresented sexual orientation. Runaway and homeless GLBT-Q youth have been identified as practicing high-risk sex behaviors (Johnson, Aschkenasy, Herbers, & Gillenwater, 1996; Rotheram-Borus, Koopman, & Ehrhardt, 1991; Rotheram-Borus, Mahler, Koopman, & Langabeer, 1996), including prostitution and survivor sex (Greene, Ennett, & Ringwalt, 1997, 1999; Yates, MacKenzie, Pennbridge, & Swofford, 1991).

Examples of unsafe sex behavior include the high rate of not using a condom during anal intercourse among gay men or multiple sex partners. A common injury that occurs during rectal intercourse is damage of the epithelial surface of the rectal mucosa, thus allowing the transmission of pathogens. The most common pathogens transmitted through rectal intercourse are hepatitis B, cytomegalovirus, and HIV (Remafedi, 1990). Unprotected oral-anal and digital-anal sex contact can also transmit hepatitis A virus (Allard, Beauchemin, Bedard, Dion, Tremblay et al., 2001; Henning, Bell, Braun, & Barker, 1995). Unprotected oral-genital sex can lead to oropharyngeal disease as well as gonococcal and nongonococcal urethritis for the insertive partner (Lafferty, Hughes, & Handsfield, 1997). Bacterial vaginosis is a noted pathogen transferred in lesbians (Rich, Buck, Tuomala, & Kazanjian, 1993).

Despite the threat of HIV/AIDS and other sexually transmitted infections (STIs), high-risk sexual behavior continues among GLBT-Q youth. The Centers for Disease Control and Prevention (CDC, 1999) report that sexual exposure accounts for most adolescent AIDS cases and HIV infections. Of the 14 million people worldwide who were HIV-infected by 1993, roughly half were adolescents (Goldsmith, 1993). In the United States, estimates of HIV-infected youth range from 110,000 to 250,000 (Rotheram-Borus, O'Keefe, Kracker, & Foo, 2000). The age of infection has been rapidly declining, with one in four new infections occurring in youth ages 21 or younger (Gourevitch, 1996; Rosenberg, Biggar, & Goedert, 1994). Recent data suggest that approximately half of the new infections are among youth (CDC, 1998a). Ninety-two percent of seropositive youth acquired HIV via sex transmission, and 8 percent through drug injection (CDC, 1998b). AIDS has recently taken seventh place among the leading causes of adolescent deaths for ages 15 to 24 (Hoyert, Kochanek, & Murphy, 1999). A cumulative total of 9,507 AIDS deaths of adolescents aged 15 to 24 were reported from 1998 through 2002. The rate of AIDS diagnosis has been increasing each year from 1998 through 2002, from 1,591 to 1,833 for this same age group (CDC, 2002). Many young people tend to be well informed about HIV/AIDS and hold relatively positive attitudes about HIV/AIDS prevention; however, many do not perceive themselves to be at risk of HIV infection (Reitman, St. Lawrence, Jefferson, Alleyne, Brasfield et al., 1996; Remafedi, 1994; Sikand, Fisher, & Friedman, 1996).

Mental Health Risks and Discrimination

Unfortunately, many GLBT-Q youth do not escape the social stigma that is often associated with HIV/AIDS and other STIs. They do not seek appropriate medical, psychological, or other health care treatment due to the social prejudice that is associated with HIV/AIDS and STIs (Allen et al., 1998; D'Augelli & Hershberger, 1993; Grossman, 1994; Harper & Schneider, 2003; Robinson, Walters, & Skeen, 1989). In addition, GLBT-Q youth feel the burden that their sex orientation automatically puts them at risk for a potentially lethal infection (D'Augelli, 1998), which compounds the negative effects of their experience with minority stress (Meyer, 1995, 2003).

In addition to HIV/AIDS and STIs, depression and suicide are major health care needs facing GLBT-Q youth. Rates of suicide ideation range from 50 percent to 70 percent, and actual suicide attempts among sexually underrepresented youth are consistently higher than those of the general population of adolescents, ranging from 20 percent to 42 percent across studies (Remafedi, French, Story, Resnick, & Blum, 1998), a rate that is three times higher than that of heterosexual youth. Several researchers have suggested that bisexual and questioning youth may be at an even higher risk of suicide than self-identified gay or lesbian youth due to the lack of positive self-esteem and role identification (D'Augelli & Hershberger, 1993; D'Augelli, Hershberger, & Pilkington, 1998, 2001, 2002). Retrospective studies have identified risk factors associated with GLBT-Q suicide, including age of first awareness (Remafedi, 1987), rejection based on sex orientation (Schneider, Farberow, & Kurks, 1989), substance use/abuse, gender atypicality, and family conflict related to identity assumption (heterosexuality) (Remafedi, Farrow, & Deisher, 1991). The overall severity of GLBT-Q suicide attempts is comparable to that of their heterosexual counterparts. Some studies suggest that sexually underrepresented youth who are depressed may consider suicide as an escape, not necessarily related to their sexual orientation/identity, but as a direct result of social discrimination and sexual prejudice (D'Augelli & Hershberger, 1995; Rotheram-Borus, Hunter, & Rosario, 1994; Savin-Williams, 1994).

ADVOCACY FOR SEXUAL UNDERREPRESENTED (GLBT-Q) YOUTH

As seen in the above overview, sexually underrepresented youth face myriad acts of prejudice and discrimination, including multiple forms of oppression resulting in sexual prejudice. The developmental challenges are innumerable in the face of such opposition. However, there is hope. Progress toward reducing sexual prejudice and heterosexism is being made, and the GLBT-Q community and its advocates are experiencing increasing normalization of homosexuality, bisexuality, transsexuality, and diverse forms of gender expression. Although much progress still remains, GLBT-Q youth have greater support networks, agencies, and programs to assist them in normal GLBT development than ever before in history. Members of the hetero-dominant group must become allies for the sexually underrepresented.

GLBT-Q Advocacy

Advocating for GLBT-Q youth is paramount for ending sexual prejudice and halting acts of violence and anti-gay hate crimes. Heterosexual people have a major responsibility to advocate for members of the sexual minority. An ally is a member of the dominant majority culture—in this case, heterosexuals who work to end oppression through support of and as advocates for the oppressed population (that is, GLBT-Q persons).

Suggestions on how to have an effective counseling relationship with GLBT-Q clients include the following:

- Learn to self-reflect and examine your own heterosexism and transgenderism.

- Professional counselors must become knowledgeable of GLBT-Q issues.

- Use inclusive language (*partner*, *significant other* instead of *spouse*, etc.), and do not assume anyone's sexual orientation or gender identity/expression.

- Distinguish between heterosexual and traditional gender identity privilege.

- Clients should be accepted by the counselor without sex prejudice, regardless of their sexual orientation. Unconditional acceptance must be displayed toward clients at all times, even when clients are confused about their orientation, or even when they change their minds as to their gender identity expression.

- Counselors need to assist clients in understanding their feelings about sexuality.

- Provide accurate information about GLBT-Q issues, both in scholarly and literature writings to help do away with stereotypes.

- The counselor should be able to suggest peer support groups in the local and regional area to the GLBT-Q client.

- Aid the client toward developing personal coping skills to deal with negative and hurtful social stereotypes and stigmas.

- Counselors need to be cautious of suicidal tendencies, substance abuse, and other psychosocial risk factors of GLBT-Q youth.

- Counselors have to deal not only with the clients, but with the families as well.

- Assist clients with making their own decision about coming out, and the appropriate timing.

- Counselors must protect and advocate for GLBT-Q youth across situations and people.

- Use general counseling strategies, such as confidentiality and maintaining boundaries with clients.

Basically, in order to provide GLBT-Q youth with the warmth and understanding they want and deserve, a mental health counselor must be gay-affirming. A gay-affirming professional is one who has evaluated his/her own sexual values, is familiar with resources for GLBT-Q youth, is willing to accept and support GLBT-Q youth even when they struggle to accept themselves, and is willing to identify and challenge heterosexism and other forms of sexual prejudice. Gay-affirmative professionals must be willing to do what others and GLBT-Q youth may not be able to do—be proud, supportive, and a strong voice for *all* sexual orientations and gender variations.

CONCLUSION

As I have thought about closing this chapter, I have struggled with summarizing so many important issues regarding GLBT-Q youth. Since I began with the murder of Matthew Shepard, I leave you with the words of Dennis Shepard spoken to the one who murdered his son. In my opinion, there is no greater act of social advocacy, kindness, and respect for all people than what was demonstrated by Mr. Shepard (1999) in the following:

> Mr. McKinney, one final comment before I sit and this is the reason that I stand before you now. At no time since Matt was found at the fence and taken to the hospital have Judy and I made any statements about our beliefs concerning the death penalty. We felt that would be an undue influence on any prospective juror. Judy has been quoted by some right wing groups as being against the death penalty. It has been stated that Matt was against the death penalty. Both of these statements are wrong. We have held family discussions and talked about the death penalty. For example, he and I discussed the horrible death of James Byrd, Jr. in Jasper, Texas. It was his opinion that the death penalty should be sought and that no expense should be spared to bring those responsible for this murder to justice. Little did we know that the same response would come about involving Matt. I, too, believe in the death penalty. I would like nothing better than to see you die, Mr. McKinney. However, this is the time to begin the healing process. To show mercy to someone who refused to show any mercy. To use this as the first step in my own closure about losing Matt. Mr. McKinney, I am not doing this because of your family. I am definitely not doing it because of the crass and unwarranted pressures put on by the religious community. If anything, that hardens my resolve to see you die. Mr. McKinney, I'm going to grant you life, as hard as it is for me to do so, because of Matthew. Every time you celebrate Christmas, a birthday or the fourth of July, remember that Matthew isn't. Every time you wake up in that prison cell, remember that you had the opportunity and the ability to stop your actions that night. Every time that you see your cell mate, remember that you had a choice and now you are living that choice. You robbed me of something very precious and I will never forgive you for that. Mr. McKinney, I give you life in the memory of one who no longer lives. May you have a long life and may you thank Matthew every day for it.
>
> Your Honor, Members of the Jury, Mr. Rerucha, Thank you.

Toolbox for Change

Issue: Images/ perceptions	Change at individual level	Change at community level	Advocating change in mental health/educational systems
Homophobia	Become aware of internalized homophobia.	Have hate-crime reporting mechanisms and strong hate-crime laws. Train legal professionals on the legal, medical, and health consequences of homophobia.	Train health professionals and educators in the dynamics of individual, family, and institutional prejudice resulting from homophobia.
Heterosexism	Become aware of how one reinforces gender-stereotypical roles and notions of "acceptable" sexual identity	Eliminate use of exclusionary language; support equal rights for same-sex relationships (such as marriage, health benefits, legal rights).	Educate people about diverse forms of relationships and sexual development. Support comprehensive sexual education. Utilize inclusive language in counseling and educational settings.

Anti-gay hate crimes	Confront use of defamatory language (gay-bashing) and threats of physical harm toward GLBT-Q youth/adults.	Support penalties for discrimination and hate crimes based on sexual orientation. Support organizations that work to stop anti-gay hate crimes (human rights campaigns)	Educate people on the destructiveness of oppressing and marginalizing groups based on sexual orientation. Train educators on the seriousness of teasing and aggression based on homoprejudice. Provide support groups for victims of anti-gay crimes.
"Normal" sexual development	Be knowledgeable of biological, psychological, emotional, and social factors in sexual development. Be accepting of diverse sexual orientations and sexual self-identities.	Support sex education and research. Advocate for non-heterosexist research on typical sexual development (for example, rather than research the "cause" of homosexuality, research on the emergence of all sexual orientations).	Do research on sexual issues and create avenues for dissemination of sexual research to the public.

APPENDIX: ADDITIONAL RESOURCES

There are a number of helpful books, articles, videos, pamphlets, web sites, and organizations covering GLBT-Q issues. The following list, while not exhaustive, emphasizes resources that may be of particular interest to professional school and mental health counselors, families of GLBT-Q youth, school personnel, and GLBT-Q youth. The references are separated into their most relevant targeted population. Many of the references may be of interest across all categories.

School Counselors and Mental Health Professionals

Brown, M. L., & Rounsley, C. A. (1996). *True selves: Understanding transsexualism for families, friends, coworkers, and helping professionals.* San Francisco: Jossey-Bass.

Capuzzi, D., & Gross, D. R. (Eds.). (2001). *Introduction to the counseling profession.* Boston: Allyn & Bacon.

Chen-Hayes, S. F., & Banez, L. (2000). *LBGT youth counseling in schools and families leader guide.* Amherst, MA: Microtraining Associates.

Chung, Y. (1995). Career decision making of lesbian, gay and bisexual individuals. *Career Development Quarterly, 44*(2), 178–190.

Creighton, A., & Kivel, P. (1992). *Helping teens stop violence: A practical guide for counselors, educators, and parents.* Alameda, CA: Hunter House.

DeCrescenzo, T. (Ed.). (1994). *Helping gay and lesbian youth.* New York: Haworth Press.

Dworkin, S., & Gutierrez, F. (Eds.). (1992). *Counseling gay men and lesbians: Journey to the end of the rainbow.* Alexandria, VA: American Association for Counseling & Development.

Elia, J. P. (1993). Homophobia in the school: A problem in need of a resolution. *The High School Journal, 77*, 177–185.

Gay, Lesbian, and Straight Education Network (GLSEN). (1997, January 1). Staff development on homophobia issues. Retrieved February 12, 2002, from http://www.glsen.org/templates/resources/record.html?section=18&record=382

Gay, Lesbian, and Straight Education Network (GLSEN). (2000, April 1). The GLSEN lunchbox: A comprehensive training program for ending anti-gay bias in schools. Retrieved February 12, 2002, from http://www.glsen.org/ templates/resources/record.html?section=18&record=767

Gay, Lesbian, and Straight Education Network (GLSEN). (2001, October 30). Lesson plan: What do "faggot" and "dyke" mean? Retrieved February 12, 2002, from http://www.glsen.org/templates/resources/record.html?section=18&record=1049

Harris, M. B. (1997). *School experiences of gay and lesbian youth: The invisible minority.* New York: Haworth Press.

Herdt, G. H. (Ed.). (1989). *Gay and lesbian youth.* New York: Haworth Press.

Hershberger, S. L., Pilkington, N. W., & D'Augelli, A. R. (1997). Predictors of suicide attempts among gay, lesbian and bisexual youth. *Journal of Adolescent Research, 12*(4), 477–497.

Hunter, S. (Ed.). (1998). *Lesbian, gay and bisexual youth and adults: Knowledge for human services practice.* Thousand Oaks, CA: Sage Publications.

Irvine, J. (Ed.). (1994). *Sexual cultures and the construction of adolescent identity.* Philadelphia, PA: Temple University Press.

Namaste, V. K. (2000). *Invisible lives: The erasure of transsexual and transgendered people.* Chicago: University of Chicago Press.

O'Connor, A. (1994). Who gets called queer in school? Lesbian, gay, and bisexual teenagers, homophobia, and high school. *The High School Journal, 77*, 71–72.

Owens, R. E. (1998). *Queer kids: The challenges and promises for lesbian, gay, and bisexual youth.* New York: Harrington Park Press.

Robinson, K. E. (1994). Addressing the needs of gay and lesbian students: The school counselor's role. *The School Counselor, 41*, 326–332.

Savin-Williams, R. C. (1990). Gay and lesbian adolescents. *Marriage and Family Review, 14*(3–4), 197–216.

Savin-Williams, R. C. (1990). *Gay and lesbian youth: Expressions of identity.* New York: Hemisphere.

Schneider, S. G., Farberow, N. L., & Kruks, G. N. (1989). Suicidal behavior in adolescent and young adult gay men. *Suicide and Life-Threatening Behavior, 19*, 381–394.

Smolinsky, T. (2001, December 14). What do we really think? A group exercise to increase heterosexual ally behavior. Retrieved February 12, 2002 from http://www.glsen.org/templates/resources/record.html?section=18&record=1093

Tolan, P. H., & Choler, B. J. (Eds.). (1993). *Handbook of clinical research and practice with adolescents.* New York: John Wiley & Sons.

Williamson, I. (1999). Why are gay men a high risk group for eating disturbance? *European Eating Disorders Review, 7*(1), 1–4.

Parents, Families, and Friends

Bernstein, R. (Ed.). (1995). *Straight parents, gay children.* New York: Thunder's Mouth Press.

Casper, V., & Schultz, S. B. (1999). *Gay parents/straight schools: Building communication and trust.* New York: Teachers College Press.

Clark, D. (1990). *Loving someone gay.* Berkeley, CA: Celestial Arts.

Dew, R. F. (1995). *The family heart: A memoir of when our son came out.* New York: Ballantine.

Evelyn, J. (1998). *Mom, I need to be a girl.* Imperial Beach, CA: Walter Trook.

Fairchild, B., & Hayward, N. (1989). *Now that you know: What every parent should know about homosexuality.* (2nd ed.). San Diego, CA: Harcourt Brace Jovanovich.

Gottlieb, A. R. (2000). *Out of the twilight: Fathers of gay men speak.* New York: Haworth Press.

Parents, Families, and Friends of Lesbians and Gays. (1995). *Our daughters and sons: Questions and answers for parents of gay, lesbian and bisexual people.* Washington, DC: Author.

Patterson, C. J., & D'Augelli, A. R. (Eds.). (1998). *Lesbian, gay and bisexual identities in families: Psychological perspectives.* New York: Oxford University Press.

Savin-Williams, R. C. (2001). *Mom, dad. I'm gay. How families negotiate coming out.* Washington, DC: American Psychological Association Press.

GLBT-Q Youth

Bass, E., & Kaufman, K. (1996). *Free your mind: The book for lesbian, gay, and bisexual youth and their allies.* New York: HarperCollins.

Bean, J. (Ed.). (1986). *In the life: A black gay anthology.* Boston: Alyson Publications.

Borhek, M. V. (1993). *Coming out to parents: A two-way survival guide for lesbians and gay men and their parents.* Cleveland, OH: Pilgrim.

Fricke, A. (1981). *Reflections of a rock lobster: A story about growing up gay.* Boston: Alyson Publications.

Gray, M. (1999). *In your face.* New York: Haworth Press.

Harris, M. B. (Ed.). (1998). *School experiences of gay and lesbian youth.* Binghamton, NY: Haworth Press.

Heron, A. (Ed.). (1994). *Two teenagers in twenty: Writings by gay and lesbian youth.* Los Angeles: Alyson Publications.

Kay, P., Estapa, A., & Dessetta, A. (Eds.) (1996). *Out with it: Gay and straight teens write about homosexuality.* New York: Youth Communications.

Marino, T. W. (1995). To be young and gay in America. *Counseling Today, 37*(11), 1–8.

Rench, J. E. (1992). Understanding sexual identity: A book for gay teens and their friends. Lerner Publishing Group.

Stanley, J. P., & Wolf, S. J. (1980). *Coming out stories.* Boston: Persephone.

Williams, W. (1985). *The spirit and the flesh: Sexual diversity in American Indian culture.* Boston: Beacon.

Teachers and School Administrators

Chasnof, D., & Cohen, H. (1996). *It's elementary: Talking about gay issues.* Alexandria, VA: American School Counselor Association.

Comstock, G. D. (1991). *Violence against lesbians and gay men.* New York: Columbia University Press.

Gay, Lesbian and Straight Teachers Network (GLSTN). Retrieved April 21, 2003 from http://www.qrd.org/qrd/www/orgs/glstn/

Harbeck, K. M. (Ed.). (1997). *Coming out of the classroom closet: Gay and lesbian students, teachers, and curricula.* Binghamton, NY: Harrington Park Press.

Harris, L. (1993). *Hostile hallways: The AAUW survey on sexual harassment in America's schools.* Washington, DC: American Association of University Women Educational Foundation.

Herek, G., & Berrill, K. (Eds.). (1992). *Hate crimes: Confronting violence against lesbians and gay men.* Newbury Park, CA: Sage Publications.

Jennings, K. (Ed.). (1994). *One teacher in ten: Gay & lesbian educators tell their stories.* Los Angeles: Alyson Publications.

Kessler, S. J. (1998). *Lessons from the intersexed.* New Brunswick, NJ: Rutgers University Press.

Letts, W. J., & Sears, J. T. (1999). *Queering elementary education: Advancing the dialogue about sexualities and schooling.* Lanham, MD: Rowman & Littlefield Publishers.

Pinar, W. F. (Ed.). (1998). *Queer theory in education.* Mahway, NJ: Lawrence Erlbaum.

Sexuality Information and Education Council of the United States (SIECUS) NationalGuidelines Task Force. (1996). *Guidelines for comprehensive sexuality education: Kindergarten–12th grade* (2nd ed.). New York: Author.

Swartz, K. J. (1996). *The price of non-existence: Psychosocial risk factors in gay and lesbian adolescents.* Doctoral dissertation, Wright State University, Dayton, OH.

Unks, G. (Ed.). (1995). *The gay teen: Educational practice and theory for lesbian, gay and bisexual adolescents.* New York: Routledge.

Uribe, V. (1991). *Project 10 handbook: Addressing lesbian and gay issues in our schools* (3rd ed.). Los Angeles: Friends of Project 10.

Woog, D. (1995). *School's out.* Boston: Alyson Publications.

Woog, D. (1998). *Jocks: True stories of America's gay male athletes.* New York: Alyson Books.

Magazines

Some magazines would be useful to display in the school counseling office so that students can become more educated on GLBT-Q issues and GLBT-Q students can feel more comfortable with their sexuality. The magazines *Inside Out, OUT, The Advocate, OutYouth, Rethinking Schools,* and *Y.O.U.T.H.* all would be useful in creating safer schools.

Videotapes

There are numerous videos addressing a broad range of sexual orientation and gender identity/expression issues that can be purchased online from GLSEN, PFLAG, or Microtraining Associates. The following is a brief list of recommended videos for school counselors, teachers, parents, guardians, administrators, and students.

All God's Children, produced by Woman Vision, the National Gay and Lesbian Task Force, and the National Black Lesbian and Gay Leadership Forum (1996). Purchase item #VHS-AGC-WV2. *All God's Children* is a documentary regarding the black church's acceptance of black lesbian women and gay men as a unique component of the church body. This video highlights the role of the church and its members' commitment to equal rights and social justice for all people. A classroom study guide accompanies the video.

Both My Moms Are Named Judy: Children of Lesbians and Gays Speak Out, produced by the Lesbian and Gay Parents Association (1994). Purchase item #VHS-BMM-PR1. Designed for elementary-school educators and administrators, this video presents a diverse group of children (ages 7–11) who have lesbian and/or gay parents. These children openly discuss their family relationships and their feelings about being teased because of their parents' homosexual orientation. They reveal insight on secrecy and silence about homosexuality in the classroom, and they provide practical suggestions on how to effect positive change.

Gay Youth, an Educational Video, produced by Pam Walton (1995). Purchase item #VHS-GAY-PW. This video compares the unfortunate suicide of twenty-year-old Bobby Griffith with the remarkable life of seventeen-year-old Gina Guiterrez. It demonstrates how LBGT-Q youth are at great risk in our society. More importantly, it shows that through proper education and information coupled with acceptance and support, LBGT-Q youth can overcome the obstacles faced by sexual minorities.

I Just Want to Say, produced by GLSEN (1998). Purchase item #VHS-JWS-GL1. Tennis champion Martina Navratilova discusses the anti-gay climate in schools across the nation and its devastating impact on gay youth. She reveals how educators and school personnel can effectively teach respect and dignity for all students. Two very important

Public Service Announcements follow the main feature with Judy Shepard.

Youth OUTLoud! Addressing Lesbian, Gay, Bisexual and Transgender Youth Issues in Our Schools, produced by Sun & Moon Vision Productions (2000). Purchase item #VHS-YOL-GL1. Promoting safety is a must for all students, particularly for lesbian, gay, bisexual, transgendered, and questioning youth of color in our schools. This documentary reveals the stories of several high school students who initiate positive change from local school district policies to state and federal laws.

Counseling LBGT Youth in Schools and Families: I, II, produced by Microtraining Associates (http://www.emicrotraining.com/) (2000). Video series by two counselor-educators (Stuart Chen-Hayes and Lynn Banez) that teaches professional counselors how to work effectively with LBGT issues in schools. Multiracial vignettes throughout; leader guide and transcript in addition to the two videotapes.

It's Elementary, produced by Women's Educational Media purchase (1995). Purchase item #VHS-YOL-GL1, or the educational training version #VHS-IEM-HC. *It's Elementary* gives real-life examples of school activities, faculty meetings, and classroom discussions about lesbian and gay issues. There is an accompanying viewing guide designed to facilitate open constructive dialogue among the adults in school communities.

Internet Web Sites

There are many available web sites that are directly related to GLBT-Q students and families. The GLSEN web page (http://www.glsen.org/) stresses the organization's drive to create safe schools for GLBT-Q students. Training outlines, curriculum ideas, current laws, and articles regarding GLBT-Q education are downloadable. In-class activities are pre-made and age-appropriate, such as "Homophobia 101 and 201," as is the anti-homophobia curriculum for schools' staff and students. Professional contacts and a resource center are outlined to assist GLBT-Q people and allies in better understanding surrounding issues. Resources exist for parents of GLBT-Q youth to understand and accept their children's sexuality and create a safer home environment, thus further reducing psychosocial risk factors (Fairchild & Hayward, 1998).

The Parents, Families and Friends of Lesbians and Gays (PFLAG) web site (http://www.pflag.org/) promotes the health and well-being of gay, lesbian, bisexual, and transgendered persons and their families and friends through education and support, as well as advocating against discrimination. The site includes a complete listing of

PFLAG chapters by state, with links to local chapters, and numerous region-related products available for purchase, such as books, clothing, stickers, and other items supporting GLBT-Q lifestyles. Also available on this page is the pamphlet entitled, "Be Yourself: Questions and Answers for Gay, Lesbian and Bisexual Youth," at http://www.qrd.org/qrd/youth/be.yourself. The publication is especially helpful in helping youth to understand the issues surrounding their sexuality and other problems they may face.

The American Counseling Association division for Gay, Lesbian, and Bisexual Issues in Counseling (AGLBIC) (http://www.aglbic.org/index.htm) is dedicated to educating counselors about the unique needs of gay, lesbian, bisexual, and transgendered individuals while advocating for their social rights. The site provides contact information for therapists who are division members and specialize in counseling GLBT-Q clients. An online journal, division newsletter, and an information exchange listserver exist for those who want to become more competent in and inquisitive about GLBT-Q issues.

The American Psychological Association offers the Society for the Psychological Study of Lesbian, Gay, and Bisexual Issues (http://www.apa.org/divisions/div44/), promoting GLBT-Q lifestyles through research, education, and policy. Perhaps the most important tool for the counseling professional is a list of guidelines encompassing attitudes toward sexual minorities, relationships with family members, issues of diversity, and professional education. Additional links include journal articles, newsletters, conference information, and listserver subscriptions.

Information related to specific cultural and ethnic backgrounds include the following:

- National Latina/o Lesbian, Gay, Bisexual and Transgendered Organization: (www.llego.org)
- Gay Asian Pacific Support Network: (http://www.gapsn.org/)
- Lesbian, Gay, Bisexual, and Transgender South Asians: (http://www.trikone.org/)

Religious sites include the following:

- United Methodists for Lesbian, Gay, Bisexual, & Transgender Concerns: (http://www.umaffirm.org/)
- Gay and Lesbian Mormons: (http://www.affirmation.org/)
- Gay, Lesbian, Bisexual and Transgender Catholics: (http://www.dignityusa.org/)
- Lutherans Concerned for and Affirming God's Love for Gay and Lesbian People: (http://www.lcna.org/)

- Unitarian Universalists' queer-affirming association of congregations: (http://www.uua.org/obgltc/wcp/wc1expln.html)

Other web sites that offer GLBT-Q students, their families, and advocates information include the following:

- Out Proud: National Coalition for Gay, Lesbian and Bisexual Youth: (http://www.outproud.org/), where you can find numerous helpful brochures, links, classroom guidelines, and educational tools such as those mentioned above.
- Sex Education and Information Council of the United States (SIECUS): (www.siecus.org http://www.siecus.org)
- National Center for Lesbian Rights: (www.nclrights.org http://www.nclrights.org)
- Oasis Magazine: (http://www.oasismag.com/), for queer and questioning youth who want to write to each other.
- Outright: (http://outright.com/)
- The Cool Page for Queer Teens: (http://www.bidstrup.com/cool.htm).

Additional GLBT-Q Organizations and Internet Web Sites

- AGLBIC: The Association for Gay, Lesbian, and Bisexual Issues in Counseling (also includes transgender issues): (www.aglbic.org)
- BINET: Bisexual Network of the United States: (www.binet-usa.org)
- Bisexual Resource Center: (www.biresource.org http://www.biresource.org)
- Children of Lesbians and Gays Everywhere: (www.colage.org/)
- Dignity USA: (www.dignityusa.org/)
- IFGE: The International Foundation for Gender Education: (www.ifge.org)
- International Lesbian and Gay Association: (www.ilga.org/)
- PFLAG: Parents, Families, and Friends of Lesbians and Gays (and bisexuals and transgendered persons): (www.pflag.org)
- Gay & Lesbian Advocates & Defenders (GLAD): (www.glad.org/)
- Gender PAC: (www.gpac.org/)
- GLADD: Gay & Lesbian Alliance Against Defamation: (www.glaad.org/org/index.html)
- GLSEN: Gay, Lesbian, and Straight Education Network: (www.glsen.org)
- Human Rights Campaign: (www.hrc.org/)

- The International Gay and Lesbian Human Rights Commission: (www.iglhrc.org/)
- Lambda Legal Defense And Education Fund: (www.lambdalegal. org)
- Lesbian.com: (www.lesbian.com)
- LesbiaNation.com: (www.lesbianation.com/)
- National Black Gay and Lesbian Leadership Forum: (www.nblglf. org)
- National Center For Lesbian Rights: (www.nclrights.org)
- National Gay and Lesbian Taskforce: (www.ngltf.org/)
- National Latina/o Lesbian, Gay, Bisexual, and Transgender Organization: (www.llego.org)
- NYAGRA: New York Association for Gender Rights Advocacy: (www.nyagra.org)
- OUTPROUD: National Coalition of Gay, Lesbian, Bisexual, and Transgender Youth: (www.outproud.org)
- SIECUS: Sex Education and Information Council of the United States: (www.siecus.org)
- Triangle Foundation: (www.tri.org/)

ACKNOWLEDGMENTS

The author would like to thank Drs. Shannon Dermer and Stuart Chen-Hayes for their editorial comments and suggestions for this chapter.

REFERENCES

Adams, H. E., Wright, L. W., & Lohr, B. A. (1997). Is homophobia associated with homosexual arousal? *Journal of Abnormal Psychology, 105,* 440–445.

Allard, R., Beauchemin, J., Bedard, L., Dion, R., Tremblay, M., & Carsley, J. (2001). Hepatitis A vaccination during an outbreak among gay men in Montréal, Canada, 1995–1997. *Journal of Epidemiology and Community Health, 55,* 251–256.

Allen, L. B., Glicken, A. D., Beach, R. K., & Naylor, K. E. (1998). Adolescent health care experiences of gay, lesbian, and bisexual young adults. *Journal of Adolescent Health, 23,* 212–220.

Allen, L. S., & Gorski, R. A. (1992). Sexual orientation and the size of the anterior commissure in the human brain. *Proceeding of the National Academy of Sciences of the United States of America, 89,* 7199–7202.

Anderson, J. D. (1994). School climate for gay and lesbian students and staff members. *Phi Delta Kappan, 76,* 151–154.

Armesto, J. C., & Weisman, A. G. (2001). Attributions and emotional reactions to the identity disclosure ("coming out") of a homosexual child. *Family Process, 40*(2), 145–161.

Bailey, J. M., & Pillard, R. C. (1991). A genetic study of male sexual orientation. *Archives of General Psychiatry, 48*(12), 1089–1096.

Bailey, J. M., Pillard, R. C., Neale, M. C., & Agyei, Y. (1993). Heritable factors influence sexual orientation in women. *Archives of General Psychiatry, 50*(3), 217–223.

Bailey, J. M., et al. (1999). A family history study of male sexual orientation using three independent samples. *Behavioral Genetics, 29,* 79–86.

Baker, J. A. (1993). Critical issues and trends: Is homophobia hazardous to lesbian and gay health? *American Journal of Health Promotion, 7*(4), 255–256.

Bancroft, J. (1990). Commentary: Biological contributions to homosexuality. In D. P. McWhirther & S. A. Sanders (Eds.), *Homosexuality/heterosexuality: Concepts of sexual orientation.* New York: Oxford Press.

Bancroft, J. (1994). Homosexual orientation: The search for a biological basis. *British Journal of Psychiatry, 164,* 437–440.

Banks, A., & Gartrell, N. K. (1995). Hormones and sexual orientation: A questionable link. *Journal of Homosexuality, 28*(3–4), 247–268.

Beach, R. K., et al. (1993). Homosexuality and adolescence. *Pediatrics, 92,* 631–634.

Ben-Ari, A. (1995). Coming out: A dialectic of intimacy and privacy. *Families in Society, 76,* 306–314.

Bernstein, R. (Ed.). (1995). *Straight parents, gay children.* New York: Thunder's Mouth Press.

Bliss, G. K., & Harris, M. B. (1998). Experiences of gay lesbian teacher and parents with coming out in a school setting. *Journal of Gay & Lesbian Social Services, 8*(2), 101–109.

Bliss, G. K., & Harris, M. B. (1999). Teachers' view of students with gay or lesbian parents. *Journal of Gay, Lesbian, and Bisexual Identity, 4*(2), 149–171.

Boney-McCoy, S., & Finkelhor, D. (1995). Psychosocial sequelae of violent victimization in a national youth sample. *Journal of Consulting and Clinical Psychology, 63*(5), 726–736.

Boon, S. D., & Miller, R. J. (1999). Exploring the links between the interpersonal trust and the reasons underlying gay and bisexual males' disclosure of their sexual orientation to their mothers. *Journal of Homosexuality, 37,* 45–68.

Braford, J., Ryan, C., & Rothblum, E. D. (1994). National lesbian health care survey: Implications for mental health care. *Journal of Consulting and Clinical Psychology, 62,* 228–242.

Broderick, C. B. (1966). Socio-sexual development in a suburban community. *Journal of Sex Research, 2*, 1–24.

Broido, E. M. (2000). Constructing identity: The nature and meaning of lesbian, gay, and bisexual identities. In R. M. Perz, K. A. DeBord, & K. J. Bieschke (Eds.), *Handbook of counseling and psychotherapy with lesbian, gay and bisexual clients* (pp. 12–33). Washington, DC: American Psychological Association.

Buhrich, N., Bailey, J. M., & Martin, N. G. (1991). Sexual orientation, sexual identity, and sex-dimorphic behaviors in male twins. *Behavioral Genetics, 21*, 75–96.

Byne, W., & Parsons, B. (1993). Human sexual orientation: The biologic theories reappraised. *Archives of General Psychiatry, 50*, 228–239.

Cain, R. (1991). Relational contexts and information management among gay men. *Families in Society, 72*(6), 344–352.

Cass, V. C. (1979). Homosexual identity formation: A theoretical model. *Journal of Homosexuality, 4*(3), 219–235.

Centers for Disease Control and Prevention (CDC). (1998a). *Young people at risk—Epidemic shifts toward young women and minorities.* Atlanta, GA: Author.

Centers for Disease Control and Prevention (CDC). (1998b). Fact sheet: Youth risk behavior trends. Retrieved from http://www.cdc.gov/nccdphp/dash/yrbs/trend.htm. Atlanta, GA: Author.

Centers for Disease Control and Prevention (CDC). (1999). *HIV/AIDS Surveillance Report, 11*(1), 1–34.

Centers for Disease Control and Prevention (CDC). (2002). *HIV/AIDS Surveillance Report, 14*(1), 1–40.

Chapman, B. E., & Brannock, J. C. (1987). Proposed model of lesbian identity development: An empirical examination. *Journal of Homosexuality, 14*, 69–80.

Chen-Hayes, S. F. (2000). Social justice advocacy with lesbian, bisexual, gay, and transgendered persons. In J. Lewis & L. Bradley (Eds.), *Advocacy in counseling: Counselors, clients, & community* (pp. 89–98). Greensboro, NC: Caps publications (ERIC/CASS).

Chen-Hayes, S. F. (2001). Counseling and advocacy with transgendered and gender-variant persons in schools and families. *The Journal of Humanistic Counseling, Education, and Development, 40*(1), 34–48.

Chung, Y. B., & Katayama, M. (1996) Assessment of sexual orientation in lesbian/gay/bisexual studies. *Journal of Homosexuality, 30*(4), 49–62.

Clay, J. (1990). Working with lesbian and gay parents and their children. *Young Children, 45*(3), 31–35.

Coleman, E. (1987). Assessment of sexual orientation. *Journal of Homosexuality, 14*, 9–24.

Corliss, H. L., Cochran, S. D., & Mays, V. M. (2002). Reports of parental maltreatment during childhood in a United States population-based survey of homosexual, bisexual, and heterosexual adults. *Child Abuse & Neglect, 26,* 1165–1178.

Cramer, D. W., & Roach, A. J. (1988). Coming to mom and dad: A study of gay males and their relationships with their parents. *Journal of Homosexuality, 15,* 79–91.

D'Augelli, A. R. (1994). Identity development and sexual orientation: Toward a model of lesbian, gay, and bisexual development. In E. J. Trickett, R. J. Watts, & D. Birman (Eds.), *Human diversity: Perspectives on people in context* (pp. 312–333). San Francisco: Jossey-Bass.

D'Augelli, A. R. (1998). Developmental implications of victimization of lesbian, gay, and bisexual youths. In G. M. Herek (Ed.), *Stigma and sexual orientation: Understanding prejudice against lesbians, gay men, and bisexuals* (pp. 187–210). Thousand Oaks, CA: Sage Publications.

D'Augelli, A. R., & Dark, L. J. (1995). Vulnerable populations: Lesbian, gay, and bisexual youth. In L. D. Eron, J. H. Gentry, & P. Schlegel (Eds.), *Reason to hope: A psychological perspective on violence and youth* (pp. 177–196). Washington, DC: American Psychological Association.

D'Augelli, A. R., & Hershberger, S. L. (1993). Lesbian, gay, and bisexual youth in community settings: Personal challenges and mental health problems. *American Journal of Community Psychology, 21*(4), 421–448.

D'Augelli, A. R., & Hershberger, S. L. (1995). Lesbian, gay and bisexual youth and their families: Disclosure of sexual orientation and its consequences. *American Journal of Orthopsychiatry, 68,* 361–371.

D'Augelli, A. R., Hershberger, S. L., & Pilkington, N. W. (1998). Lesbian, gay, and bisexual youths and their families: Disclosure of sexual orientation and its consequences. *American Journal of Orthopsychiatry, 68,* 361–371.

D'Augelli, A. R., Hershberger, S. L., & Pilkington, N. W. (2001). Suicidality patterns and sexual orientation-related factors among lesbian, gay, and bisexual youths. *Suicide and Life-Threatening Behavior, 31,* 250–264.

D'Augelli, A. R., Pilkington, N. W., Hershberger, S. L. (2002). Incidence and mental health impact of sexual orientation victimization of lesbian, gay, and bisexual youths in high school. *School Psychology Quarterly, 17,* 148–167.

Dean, L. S., Wu, S., & Martin, J. L. (1992). Trends in violence and discrimination against gay men in New York City: 1984–1990. In G. M. Herek & K. T. Berrill (Eds.), *Hate crimes: Confronting violence against lesbians and gay men* (pp. 46–64). Newbury Park, CA: Sage.

Deevey, S. (1989). When mom or dad comes out: Helping adolescents cope with homophobia. *Journal of Psychosocial Nursing and Mental Health Services, 27*(10), 33–36.

Durby, D. D. (1994). Gay, lesbian, and bisexual youth. *Journal of Gay & Lesbian Social Services, 1,* 1–37.

Eckert, E. E., Bouchard, T. J., Bohlen, J., & Heston, L. L. (1986). Homosexuality in monozygotic twins reared apart. *British Journal of Psychiatry, 148*, 421–425.

Elia, J. (1993). Homophobia in the high school: A problem in need of a resolution. *The High School Journal, 77*, 177–185.

Eliason, M. J. (1996a). An inclusive model of lesbian identity assumption. *Journal of Gay, Lesbian, and Bisexual Identity, 1*, 3–19.

Eliason, M. J. (1996b). Identity formation for lesbian, bisexual, and gay persons: Beyond a "minoritizing" view. *Journal of Homosexuality, 30*, 31–58.

Eliason, M. J., & Randall, C. E. (1991). Lesbian phobia in nursing students. *Western Journal of Nursing Research, 13*(3), 363–374.

Elze, D. E. (2002). Risk factors for internalizing and externalizing problems among gay, lesbian, and bisexual youth. *Social Work Research, 26*(2), 89–100.

Fairchild, B., & Hayward, N. (1998). *Now that you know: A parents' guide to understanding their gay and lesbian children.* San Diego: Harcourt Brace.

Fassinger, R. E., & Miller, B. A. (1996). Validation of an inclusive model of sexual minority identity formation on a sample of gay men. *Journal of Homosexuality, 32*, 53–78.

The Federal Bureau of Investigation. (2000). *Crime in the United States, 2000: Uniform crimes report.* Washington, DC: U.S. Department of Justice.

Floyd, F. J., & Stein, T. S. (2002). Sexual orientation identity formation among gay, lesbian, and bisexual youths: Multiple patterns of milestone experiences. *Journal of Research on Adolescence, 12*(20), 167–191.

Fontaine, J. (1997). The sound of silence: Public school response to the needs of gay and lesbian youth. *Journal of Lesbian and Gay Social Services, 7*, 101–109.

Friedman, R. C., & Downey J. (1993). Neurobiology and sexual orientation: Current relationships. *The Journal of Neuropsychiatry and Clinical Neurosciences, 5*, 131–153.

Friedman, R. C., Green, R., & Spitzer, R. L. (1976). Reassessment of homosexuality and transsexualism. *Annual Review of Medicine, 27*, 57–62.

Fyfe, B. (1983). "Homophobia" or homosexual bias reconsidered. *Archives of Sexual Behavior, 12*, 549–554.

Gay, Lesbian, and Straight Education Network (GLSEN). (1999, January 1). Homophobia 101: Anti-homophobia training outline for school staff and students. Retrieved February 12, 2002 from http://www.glsen.org/templates/resources/record.html?section=18&record=248

Gentry, S. E. (1992). Caring for lesbians in a homophobic society. *Health Care for Women International, 13*(2), 173–180.

Ginsberg, R. W. (1998). Silenced voices inside our schools. *Initiatives, 58*, 1–15.

Gold, M. A., Perrin, E. C., Futterman, D., Friedman, B. F. (1994). Children of gay or lesbian parents. *Pediatric Review, 15*(9), 354–358.

Goldsmith, M. (1993). Invisible epidemic now becoming visible as HIV/AIDS pandemic reaches adolescents. *Journal of the American Medical Association, 270,* 16–19.

Gonsiorek, J. C. (1988). Mental health issues of gay and lesbian adolescents. *Journal of Adolescent Health Care, 9,* 114–122.

Gonsiorek, J. C., Sell, R. L., & Weinrich, J. D. (1995). Definition and measurement of sexual orientation. *Suicide and Life-Threatening Behavior, 25,* 40–51.

Gonsiorek, J. C., & Weinrich, J. D. (1991). The definition and scope of sexual orientation (pp. 1–12). In J. C. Gonsiorek & J. D. Weinrich (Eds.), *Homosexuality: Research implications for public policy.* Thousand Oaks, CA: Sage Publications.

Gourevitch, M. N. (1996). The epidemiology of HIV and AIDS. *Medical Clinics of North America, 80,* 1223–1228.

Greenberg, D. F. (1988). *The construction of homosexuality.* Chicago: University of Chicago Press.

Greene, J. M., Ennett, S. T., & Ringwalt, C. L. (1997). Substance use among runaway and homeless youth in three national samples. *American Journal of Public Health, 87,* 229–235.

Greene, J. M., Ennett, S. T., & Ringwalt, C. L. (1999). Prevalence and correlates of survival sex among runaway and homeless youth. *American Journal of Public Health, 89,* 1406–1409.

Grossman, A. H. (1994). Homophobia: A cofacotor of HIV disease in gay and lesbian youth. *Journal of the Association of Nurses in AIDS Care, 5*(1), 39–43.

Grossman, A. H., O'Connell, T. S., & D'Augelli, A. R. (2002). Transgender youth: Challenging traditional "girl-boy" activities-Implications of an exploratory study for new directions in research (pp. 83–104). In L. Lawrence & S. Parker (Eds.), *Leisure studies: Trends in theory and research.* Eastbourne, UK: Leisure Studies Association.

Hagga, D. (1991). Homophobia? *Journal of Social Behavior and Personality, 6,* 171–174.

Hamer, D. H., Hu, S., Magnuson, V. L., Hu, N., & Pattatucci, A. M. L. (1993). A linkage between DNA markers on the X chromosome and male sexual orientation. *Science, 261,* 321–327.

Harper, G. W., Contrearas, R., Correa, C., & Clack, H. L. (1999, June). *Gay/lesbian/bisexual youth of color: Juggling multiple identities.* Paper presented at the biennial meeting of the Society for Community Research and Action, New Haven, CT.

Harper, G. W., & Schneider, M. (2003). Oppression and discrimination among lesbian, gay, bisexual, and transgendered people in communities: A challenge for community psychology. *American Journal of Community Psychology, 31,* 243–252.

Harris, M. B. (Ed.) (1997). *School experiences of gay and lesbian youth: The invisible minority.* Binghamton, NY: The Hawthorn Press.

Harry, J. (1989). Parental physical abuse and sexual orientation in males. *Archives of Sexual Behavior, 18*(3), 251–261.

Harvey, M. J., Carr, C., Berrnheine, S. (1990). Lesbian mothers: Health care experiences. *Journal of Nurse-Midwifery, 34*(3), 115–119.

Henning, K. J., Bell, E., Braun, J., & Barker, N. D. (1995). A community-wide outbreak of hepatitis A: Risk factors for infection among homosexual and bisexual men. *The American Journal of Medicine, 99*(2), 132–136.

Herek, G. M. (1984a). Attitudes toward lesbian and gay men: A factor-analytic study. *Journal of Homosexuality, 10*, 39–51.

Herek, G. M. (1984b). Beyond "homophobia": A social psychological perspective on attitudes towards lesbian and gay men. *Journal of Homosexuality, 10*, 1–21.

Herek, G. M. (1988). Heterosexuals' attitudes toward lesbians and gay men: Correlates and gender differences. *The Journal of Sex Research, 25*, 451–477.

Herek, G. M. (1993). The context of antigay violence: Notes on cultural and psychological heterosexism. In L. D. Garnets & D. C. Kimmel (Eds.), *Psychological perspectives on lesbian and gay male experiences.* New York: Columbia University Press.

Herek, G. M. (2000). The psychology of sexual prejudice. *Current Directions in Psychological Science, 9*(1), 19–22.

Herek, G. M., Cogan, J. C., & Gillis, J. R. (2002). Victim experiences in hate crimes based on sexual orientation. *Journal of Social Issues, 58*(2), 319–339.

Herek, G. M., Gillis, J. R., & Cogan, J. C. (1999). Psychological sequelae of hate crime victimization among lesbian, gay, and bisexual adults. *Journal of Consulting and Clinical Psychology, 67*(6), 945–951.

Hershberger, S. L., & D'Augelli, A. R. (1995). The impact of victimization on the mental health and suicidality of lesbian, gay, and bisexual youths. *Developmental Psychology, 31*, 65–74.

Hetrick, E. S., & Martin, A. D. (1987). Developmental issues and their resolution for gay and lesbian adolescents. *Journal of Homosexuality, 2*(1/2), 25–43.

Hoyert, D. L., Kochanek, K. D., Murphy, S. L. (1999). *Deaths: Final data for 1997.* National Vital Statistics Reports, 47, 19. Hyattsville, MD: National Center for Health Statistics.

Hu, S., et al. (1995). Linkage between sexual orientation and chromosome Xq28 in males but not in females. *Nature Genetics, 11*(3), 248–256.

Hudson, W. W., & Ricketts, W. A. (1980). A strategy for the measurement of homophobia. *Journal of Homosexuality, 5*, 356–371.

Hunter, J. S. (1987). Stresses on lesbian and gay adolescents in school. *Social Work in Education, 9*, 180–190.

Hutchins, L., & Kaahumanu, L. (Eds.). (1991). *Bi any other name: Bisexual people speak out*. Boston: Alyson.

James, T., Harding, I., & Corbett, K. (1994). Biased care. *Nursing Times, 90*(21), 28–31.

Johnson, T. P., Aschkenasy, J. R., Herbers, M. R., & Gillenwater, S. A. (1996). Self-reported risk factors for AIDS among homeless youth. *AIDS Education and Prevention, 8*, 308–322.

Jordan, K. M., Vaughan, J. S., & Woodworth, K. J. (1997). I will survive: Lesbian, gay, and bisexual youths' experience of high school. *Journal of Gay & Lesbian Social Services, 7*, 17–33.

Kallman, F. J. (1952). Comparative twin study of the genetic aspects of male homosexuality. *Journal of Nervous and Mental Disease, 115*, 288–298.

Kenney, J. W., & Tash, D. T. (1992). Lesbian childbearing couples' dilemmas and decisions. *Health Care for Women International, 13*(2), 209–219.

Klein, F., Sepekoff, B., & Wolf, T. J. (1985). Sexual orientation: A multivariable dynamic process. In *Bisexualities: Theory and research* (pp. 35–49). New York: The Haworth Press.

Lafferty, W. E., Hughes, J. P., & Handsfield, H. H. (1997). Sexually transmitted diseases in men who have sex with men: Acquisition of urethral infections by fellatio and implications for STD/HIV prevention. *Sexually Transmitted Diseases, 24*, 272–278.

Lasco, M. S., Jordan, T. J., Edgar, M. A., Petito, C. K., & Byne, W. (2002). A lack of dimorphism of sex or sexual orientation in the human anterior commissure. *Brain Research, 936*(1–2), 95–98.

LeVay, S. (1991). A difference in hypothalamic structure between heterosexual and homosexual men. *Science, 253*, 1034–1037.

Mackereth, P. A. (1994). HIV and homophobia: Nurses as advocates. *Journal of Advanced Nursing, 22*, 670–676.

Malinsky, K. P. (1997). Learning to be invisible: Female sexual minority students in America's public high schools. *Journal of Gay & Lesbian Social Services, 7*, 35–50.

Martin, A. (1982). Learning to hide: The socialization of the gay adolescent. In S. Feinstein, J. Looney, A. Schartzberg, & J. Sorotsky (Eds.), *Adolescent psychiatry: Development and clinical studies* (Vol. 10, pp. 52–65). Chicago: University of Chicago Press.

Matchinsky, D. J., & Iverson, T. G. (1996). Homophobia in heterosexual female undergraduates. *Journal of Homosexuality, 31*, 123–128.

McCarn, S. R., & Fassinger, R. E. (1996). Revisioning sexual minority youth identity formation: A new model of lesbian identity and its implications for counseling and research. *Counseling Psychologist, 24*, 508–534.

McDonald, G. J. (1982). Individual differences in the coming out process of gay men: Implications for theoretical models. *Journal of Homosexuality, 8*, 47–60.

Meyer, I. H. (1995). Minority stress and mental health in gay men. *Journal of Health and Social Behavior, 36*, 38–56.

Meyer, I. H. (2003). Prejudice, social stress, and mental health in lesbian, gay, and bisexual populations: Conceptual issues and research evidence. *Psychological Bulletin, 129*(5), 674–697.

Miller, R. J., & Boon, S. D. (2000). Trust and disclosure of sexual orientation in gay males' mother-son relationships. *Journal of Homosexuality, 38*, 41–63.

Minton, H. L., & McDonald, G. J. (1984). Homosexuality identity formation as a developmental process. *Journal of Homosexuality, 9*, 91–104.

Morrissey, M. (1996). Attitudes of practitioners to lesbian, gay and bisexual clients. *British Journal of Nursing, 5*(16), 980–982.

Nelson, J. A. (1997). Gay, lesbian, and bisexual adolescents: Providing esteem-enhancing care to a battered population. *The Nurse Practitioner, 22*(2), 94–109.

O'Donohue, W., & Caselles, C. E. (1993). Homophobia: Conceptual, definitional, and value issues. *Journal of Psychopathology and Behavioral Assessment, 14*, 177–195.

Oswald, R. F. (2000). Family and friendship relationships after young women come out as bisexual or lesbian. *Journal of Homosexuality, 38*, 65–83.

Paroski, P. A. (1987). Health care delivery and the concerns of gay and lesbian adolescents. *Journal of Adolescent Health Care, 8*, 188–192.

Perrin, E. C., & Kulkin, H. (1996). Pediatric care for children whose parents are gay or lesbian. *Pediatrics, 97*(5), 629–639.

Pilkington, N. W., & D'Augelli, A. R. (1995). Victimization of lesbian, gay, and bisexual youth in community settings. *Journal of Community Psychology, 23*, 34–56.

Plummer, K. (1975). *Sexual stigma: An interactionist account.* London: Routledge & Kegan Paul.

Ponse, B. (1978). *Identities in the lesbian world.* Westport, CT: Greenwood.

Povinelli, M., Remafedi, G., & Tao, G. (1996). Trends and predictors of human immunodeficiency virus antibody testing by homosexual and bisexual adolescent males, 1989–1994. *Archives of Pediatric Adolescent Medicine, 150*, 33–38.

Reis, B., & Saewyc, E. (1999). *Eighty-three thousand youth: Selected findings of eight population-based studies as they pertain to anti-gay harassment and the safety and well-being of sexual minority students.* Seattle, WA: Safe Schools Coalition of Washington.

Reitman, D., St. Lawrence, J. S., Jefferson, K. W., Alleyne, E., Brasfield, T. L., & Shirley, A. (1996). Predictors of African American adolescents' condom use and HIV risk behavior. *AIDS Education and Prevention, 8*, 499–515.

Remafedi, G. (1985). Adolescent homosexuality: Issues for pediatricians. *Clinical Pediatrics, 24*, 481–485.

Remafedi, G. (1987). Homosexual youth: A challenge to contemporary society. *Journal of the American Medical Association, 258*, 222–225.

Remafedi, G. (1990). Sexually transmitted diseases in homosexual youth. *Adolescent Medicine: State of the Art Reviews, 1,* 565–581.

Remafedi, G. (1994). Predictors of unprotected intercourse among gay and bisexual youth: Knowledge, beliefs, and behavior. *Pediatrics, 94,* 163–168.

Remafedi, G., Farrow, J. A., & Deisher, R. W. (1991). Risk factors for attempted suicide in gay and bisexual youth. *Pediatrics, 87,* 869–875.

Remafedi, G., French, S., Story, M., Resnick, M. D., & Blum, R. (1998). The relationship between suicide risk and sexual orientation: Results of a population-based study. *American Journal of Public Health, 88*(1), 57–60.

Rich, J. D., Buck, A., Tuomala, R. E., & Kazanjian, P. H. (1993). Transmission of human immunodeficiency virus presumed to have occurred via female homosexual contact. *Clinical Infectious Disease, 17,* 1003–1005.

Robinson, B. E., Walters, L. H., & Skeen, P. (1989). Responses of parents to learning that their child is homosexual and concerns over AIDS: A national survey. *Journal of Homosexuality, 18*(1–2), 59–80.

Rose, L. (1994). Homophobia among doctors. *British Medical Journal, 308,* 586–587.

Rosenberg, P., Biggar, R. J., & Goedert, J. J. (1994). Declining age at HIV infection in the United States. *New England Journal of Medicine, 330,* 789–790.

Rotheram-Borus, M. J., Hunter, J., & Rosario, M. (1994). Suicidal behavior and gay-related stress among gay and bisexual male adolescents. *Journal of Adolescent Research, 9,* 498–508.

Rotheram-Borus, M. J., Koopman, C., Ehrhardt, A. A. (1991). Homeless youth and HIV infection. *American Psychology, 46,* 1188–1197.

Rotheram-Borus, M. J., Mahler, K. A., Koopman, C., Langabeer, K. (1996). Sexual abuse history and associated multiple risk behavior in adolescent runaways. *American Journal of Orthopsychiatry, 66*(3), 390–400.

Rotheram-Borus, M. J., O'Keefe, Z., Kracker, R., & Foo, H. H. (2000). Prevention of HIV among adolescents. *Prevention Science, 1,* 15–30.

Russell, S. T., Franz, B. T., & Driscoll, A. K. (2001). Same sex attraction and experiences of violence in adolescence. *American Journal of Public Health, 91*(6), 903–906.

Saunders, B., Villeponteaux, L., Lipovsky, J., Kilpatrick, D., & Veronen, L. (1992). Child sexual assault as a risk factor for mental disorders among women: A community survey. *Journal of Interpersonal Violence, 7,* 189–204.

Savin-Williams, R. C. (1994). Verbal and physical abuse as stressors in the lives of lesbian, gay male, and bisexual youths: Associations with school problems, running away, substance abuse, prostitution, and suicide. *Journal of Consulting & Clinical Psychology, 62*(2), 261–269.

Savin-Williams, R. C. (1998). Coming out to parents and self-esteem among gay and lesbian youth. *Journal of Homosexuality, 17*, 1–35.

Schneider, A. G., Farberow, N. L., & Kurks, G. N. (1989). Suicidal behavior in adolescent and young adult gay men. *Suicide Life Threatening Behaviors, 19*, 381–394.

Schwanberg, S. L. (1996). Health care professionals' attitudes toward lesbian women and gay men. *Journal of Homosexuality, 31*(3), 71–83.

Shepard, D. (1999, November 4). Dennis Shepard's statements to the court. Retrieved August 29, 2004, from http://www.matthewsplace.com/dennis2.htm

Shepard, J. (1999). An open letter to school administrators. Retrieved October 01, 2003, from http://www.pflag.org/education/schools/judyshepard.html

Sikand, A., Fisher, M., & Friedman, S. B. (1996). AIDS knowledge, concerns, behavior changes among inner-city high school students. *Journal of Adolescent Health, 18*, 235–328.

Smith, S. D., & Chen-Hayes, S. F. (2003). Leadership and advocacy for lesbian, bisexual, gay, transgendered, and questioning (LBGTQ) students: Academic, career, and interpersonal success strategies. In R. Perusse & G. E. Goodnough (Eds.) *Leadership, advocacy and direct service strategies for professional school counselors* (1st ed.). Belmont, CA: Brooks-Cole.

Spitzer, R. L. (1981). The diagnosis of homosexuality in DSM III: A reformulation of the issues. *American Journal of Psychiatry, 138*, 210–215.

Stevens, P. E. (1994). Lesbians' health related experiences of care and non-care. *Western Journal of Nursing Research, 16*(6), 639–659.

Strommen, E. F. (1989). "You're a what?": Family member reactions to the disclosure of homosexuality. *Journal of Homosexuality, 18*, 37–55.

Strommen, E. F. (1990). Hidden branches and growing pains: Homosexuality and the family tree. *Marriage and Family Review, 14*, 9–34.

Swaab, D. F., Gooren, L. J., & Hofman, M. A. (1995). Brain research, gender and sexual orientation. *Journal of Homosexuality, 28*(3–4), 283–301.

Swaab, D. F., & Hofman, M. A. (1990). An enlarged suprachiasmatic nucleus in homosexual men. *Brain Research, 537*, 141–148.

Telljohann, S. K., & Price, J. H. (1993). A qualitative examination of adolescent homosexuals' life experiences: Ramifications for secondary school personnel. *Journal of Homosexuality, 26*(1), 41–56.

Trippet, S. E., & Bain, J. (1992). Reasons lesbians fail to seek traditional health care. *Health Care for Women International, 13*(2), 145–153.

Troiden, R. R. (1979). Becoming homosexual: A model of gay identity development. *Psychiatry, 42*, 362–373.

Troiden, R. R. (1989). The formation of homosexual identities. *Journal of Homosexuality, 17*, 43–73.

Unks, G. (1994). Thinking about the homosexual adolescent. *The High School Journal, 77*, 1–6.

Uribe, V., & Harbeck, K. M. (1992). Addressing the needs of lesbian, gay, and bisexual youth: The origins of Project 10 and school-based intervention. *Journal of Homosexuality, 22,* 9–28.

Waldo, C. R., Hesson-McInnis, M. S., & D'Augelli, A. R. (1998). Antecedents and consequences of victimization of lesbian, gay, and bisexual young people: A structural model comparing rural university and urban samples. *American Journal of Community Psychology, 26,* 307–334.

Weinberg, G. H. (1972). *Society and the healthy homosexual.* New York: St. Martin's Press.

Weinberg, T. S. (1984). Biology, ideology, and the reification of developmental stages in the study of homosexual identities. *Journal of Homosexuality, 10,* 77–84.

Weinberg, T. S., Williams, C. J., & Pryor, D. W. (1994). *Dual attraction: Understanding bisexuality.* New York: Oxford University Press.

Wells, J., & Kline, W. (1987). Self-disclosure of homosexual orientation. *Journal of Social Psychology, 127*(2), 191–197.

Whitam, F., Diamond, M., & Martin, J. (1993). Homosexual orientation in twins: A report on 61 pairs and tree triplet sets. *Archives of Sexual Behavior, 22*(3), 151–170.

Whitman, J. S., Cormier, S., & Boyd, C. J. (2000). Lesbian identity management at various stages of the coming out process: A qualitative study. *International Journal of Sexuality and Gender Studies, 5*(1), 3–18.

Yates, G. L., MacKenzie, R. G., Pennbridge, J., & Swofford, A. (1991). A risk profile comparison of homeless youth involved in prostitution and homeless youth not involved. *Journal of Adolescent Health, 12,* 545–548.

Zea, M. C. (1999, November). *Latino HIV-positive gay men's narratives on disclosure of serostatus.* Paper presented at the 127th American Public Health Association Annual Meeting, Chicago, IL.

Zea, M. C., Reisen, C. A., & Diaz, R. M. (2003). Methodological issues in research on sexual behaviors with Latino gay and bisexual men. *American Journal of Community Psychology, 31,* 243–252.

CHAPTER 8

Socio-Spatial Experiences of Transgender Individuals

Kim D. Felsenthal

Western culture constructed sex, sexuality, and gender categories based on oppositional binaries, such as male/female, straight/gay, normal/deviant, that were to add structure and "normalcy" to our society. Now, because of advances in medical technology and changes in cultural and religious convention, these socially prescribed constructs are becoming more fluid and less defined. It is easier and more acceptable to question or even change who one is. This includes the act of "coming out" as gay or lesbian, "transitioning" to the other sex (either operatively or by cross-dressing), or by denying, thereby defying, all classification systems. One may now self-identify as transgender, transsexual, transvestite, gender bender, intersexed, drag, butch, queer, androgynous, gay, straight, lesbian, bisexual, or polymorphous. Therefore, the reductionist and restrictive binary taxonomies do not apply to today's gender-fluid society. Our society does not recognize the spectrum of genders and, therefore, individuals who are gender-variant have no "place" within our socio-spatial environment.

So, what happens when an individual does not fall within the two gender categories? Where does that person fit? Someone who is trans[1] challenges, even breaks, the rigid gender binary system and must grapple with these questions daily. Western society ensures trans people that there is no "place" for them by enacting biased, regulatory performances that fortify only the male and female constructs. By this I mean that through medical intervention, psychological diagnoses, governmental regulations, media interpretation, individual biases, and citizen policing, one is required to act, dress, and be only what their sex dictates.

When an individual transgresses the gender dichotomy, the repercussions are significant. The hostile environment that trans individuals face creates perilous conditions for them when they are "out" in public. Transphobic attitudes are played through acts of violence that considerably limit the use of public accommodations. If trans individuals are fearful when out in public, they will increase their tendency to stay close to home and will limit their capacity to use public space without fear of heterosexist violence. This has considerable consequences. When an individual does not have access to and use of public space, this will severely hinder identity development (Proshansky et al., 1983).

This chapter will look at the socio-spatial environment in which the trans individual lives. I will first discuss the construction and fortification of the gender binary of males and females. Thereafter, I will explore what happens when that binary is broken, and the socio-spatial implications of this fissure. Finally, I present some of the spatial strategies that trans individuals use to counter society's adverse reaction of them. Much of the information included here is from recent empirical work that has been performed either by the author, from a recent study on gender-variant individuals, or by other researchers in the burgeoning field of trans studies.

SOCIAL CONSTRUCTION OF MALE
AND FEMALE

Historically, sex has been referred to as biological—a chromosomal difference separate from culture or discourse. It has been defined by one's XY or XX chromosomes as well as by bodily differences, such as genital constructs and hair growth variations. Gender, however, is considered, according to the seminal work of psychologist Robert Stoller, an "overall sense of being male or female" and is present in a child's first year of life (Stoller, 1968). According to his theory, it is an internal experience that occurs within the individual's psyche. An infant, however, is born into a sexed society where heteronormative gender roles and behaviors are strictly taught and enforced. Thus, the social construction of gender is more rigidly defined by behavior as well as self-identification as either male or female, masculine or feminine.

John Money's research on the construction of gender in intersex individuals provided much of the groundwork for trans research. He found that once doctors declared the sexual identity of an intersex child (usually after several reconstructive surgeries), the child's gender development and expression would most likely be dictated by social influences (1994). In other words, if both the parents and the child's social circle treat the child like a boy, then the child will "learn" to become and behave as a boy.

Pierre Bourdieu's theory of *habitus* complements Money's findings on gender development (1977). Bourdieu posits that one's enactments, when played out repeatedly, become internalized and normalized. When the process is internalized in the collective, it becomes a societal norm. The proliferation of a binary gender system and the acts performed to fortify it (for example, violence against trans individuals), therefore, are the social habitus for gender norms in western society.

If we were to apply habitus to the development of the gender dichotomy, it would start with the parents' treatment of an infant when it was born. The elementary concept of using color to define gender, such as pink for girls and blue for boys, as well as differential behaviors with male and female infants (such as stimulating girls with talk and boys with rough play) initiates a social dynamic that will be mirrored in society. The gender distinctions are stratified further when parents threaten their child with punishments if they cross-dress or behave in a manner not deemed appropriate for their sex. Douglas Mason-Schrock's study on transsexual narratives (1996) describes the institutionalization of gender within various subcontexts. At home, for example, the trans participants explained, they were often punished or even sent to a psychologist for cross-dressing behaviors when they were young. These findings parallel those of Darryl Hill's empirical study on eighteen transgender individuals: "Parental prohibition of crossgender impulses and control of gender expression were fairly common [. . .]" (Hill, 2003, p. 132). As trans children grow, this negative reaction to atypical gender behavior continues in the schools. Often the teacher discourages the child from "inappropriate" behaviors, and the children themselves participate in gender-segregated play. A male-born participant in Mason-Schrock's study was discouraged from playing jump rope with the girls at school because that kind of play was not considered appropriate for boys (Mason-Schrock, 1996). For adults, gender norms proliferate in the workplace. In this setting, for example, trans individuals are pressured to socialize with same-gender colleagues as well as perform in a more "masculine" fashion. In addition, many trans individuals have difficulty finding jobs because of discriminatory hiring practices; in their studies on gender conformity, Gagne and Tewksbury found that when the individuals did work, they "have difficulty keeping [the jobs] because they had not yet perfected their ability to pass as women" (1998, p. 93). In addition, many transsexual individuals are fired or harassed once they "come out" at work. The work environment has strong fortifications of the gender binary. Therefore, for both men and women, the only place where feminine expression can safely be displayed is in the privacy of the home (Chusmir & Koberg, 1990). Public places remain places for gender-consistent behaviors and expression.

FORTIFICATION OF THE TWO GENDERS

Though gender is expressed in a multitude of ways, the "natural attitude" of gender in our society has spurred us to construct a gender system that consists only of males and females, not allowing for a third, fourth, or nth gender. These two genders are considered mutually exclusive and polar opposites or, according to common belief, are unchanging. This model is fortified and institutionalized through many regulatory processes, such as medical intervention, psychological diagnoses, governmental regulation, media interpretation, individual biases, and citizen policing.

Medical Intervention

Most scientists claim that gender is a social construction, but that sex is "real." This ideology supports the belief that there are only two genders, and it is substantiated by the two distinct biologies of male and female. Though some infants are born with genitals that are ambiguous or are born with both male and female organs, these biological differences are considered, by the medical profession, a problem to be "fixed" with "corrective" surgery. Physicians who specialize in the field of intersex conditions maintain that they try to ensure that, "the infant's true, natural 'sex' has been discovered, and that something that was there all along has been found. It also serves to maintain the credibility of the medical profession, [and] reassure the parents" (Kessler, 1998, p. 15). The infant's "true" or "natural" sex, therefore, must be male or female.

Psychological Diagnosis

The field of psychology also supports the gender binary by patholog-izing those individuals who transgress socially accepted sex-role norms. Although the American Psychiatric Association dropped homosexual-ity from its manual of disorders in 1973, it added the new diagnosis of gender identity disorder (GID) in its next edition. GID is defined as (a) a strong and persistent cross-gender identification, (b) a persis-tent discomfort with his or her sex or a sense of inappropriateness in the gender role of that sex, (c) no concurrence with a physical intersex condition, and (d) clinically significant distress or impairment in social, occupational, or other important areas of functioning (APA, DSM IV). This addition was highly controversial because of assertions pos-iting that GID was created to prevent possible behavioral manifesta-tions of homosexuality. Cross-dressing or atypical gender behavior in children, some assume, leads to homosexual adults; therefore, if a child is diagnosed with GID, then these behaviors can be "fixed" through therapeutic intervention. Evidence substantiating this proposition, though, is still inconclusive.

Government Regulation

Current legislation rarely acknowledges the existence of a third gender. Therefore, it does not provide gender-variant individuals pro-tections from discrimination and harassment. In New York state, for example, within two days of the birth, parents must declare on the birth certificate whether the infant is male or female. Additionally, the New York state assembly only recently, in 2002, voted on the Sexual Orientation Non-Discrimination Act (SONDA). This bill adds sexual orientation as a protected category under New York state's human rights law, but it still does not include language to protect individuals who are transgender or "other members of LGBT [lesbian, gay, bisex-ual, transgender] and other communities who don't conform to main-stream society's gender 'norms' and stereotypes because of their gender identity and/or expression—arguably those most at risk for daily dis-crimination and violence."[2] There are only four states that have laws that prohibit discrimination on the basis of gender identity and expres-sion. These are California, Minnesota, Rhode Island, and New Mexico. When gender-variant individuals are erased from legislative language, a precedent is set for the rest of society to condone the continued subordination and exclusion of those individuals who do not conform to society's standards.

Media

Media also plays a large role in the construction and enforcement of gender distinctions. Men and women are portrayed in television shows, movies, and advertisements in gender-appropriate clothing and are behaving in gender-consistent ways. Those who stray from this portrayal are seen as either comic deviants or pathologized psychopaths, as illustrated in the famous gender-ambiguous character Pat on *Saturday Night Live*, played by Julia Sweeney. The jokes came when the viewer struggled to figure out Pat's gender. In reality, the jokes about gender-ambiguous people or trans individuals escalate to increased tension and often end in anger and violence.

Humor is a common strategy used to sublimate the anger people feel about non-conforming gender performance. As Kate Bornstein, a male-to-female transsexual activist and writer, explains,

> we are the clowns, the sex objects, or the mysteriously unattainable in any number of novels. We are the psychotics, the murderers, or the criminal geniuses who populate the movies. Audiences have rarely seen the real faces of the transgendered. They don't hear our voices, rarely read our words. (1994, p. 60)

Darryl Hill's study reports similar findings supporting the supposition that the media constructs and fortifies the gender binary: "The clearest representation of genderism . . . is found in the portrayals of transgendered people in movies, on television talk shows and, in the news" (2003, p. 124).

There is a clear bias in the media against those who transgress gender-normative behavior and looks. Trans people are depicted with a skewed lens that often portrays them in deviant ways. Because of the influence media has on western culture, penetrating most homes throughout the United States, it makes a considerable contribution to the construction of "norms" for gender that support the dichotomy.

Individual Bias

This section relates to the personal instruments individuals use to fortify a gender binary system. Cognitive processes, psychological influences, self-image, and reliance on stereotypes can generate biased perceptions of others. These perceptions, when applied to gender norms, often result in heterosexist and transphobic violence and harassment. These individual acts of violence help to sustain the gender binary by sending a clear message to the trans population that their presence is not acceptable.

Cognitive theorists believe that in order for us to organize our thoughts more easily and have a frame of reference, schema congruence, or a correct situational interpretation and prediction, we must place like objects together. Therefore, a person with the physical attributes that match what is the norm for males will be grouped and associated with men. This process of social categorization is an organizational tool that helps to maintain gender distinctions because, cognitively, it is easier for a perceiver to place individuals into only two gender categories. If an individual does not perceptually fit into either of the two gender categories, thus causing difficulty for the perceiver to categorize that person, this may result in the perceiver feeling tension. In Kessler and McKenna's recent study on college students' perceptions of gender, they found that, "[a]lthough these students may consider gender extremely complex and allow for the possibility that it is not that important to categorize people by gender, in everyday life not knowing a person's gender still makes them very uncomfortable. They try to find out what the person 'really' is" (2000).

Social categorization also can lead to biased generalizations and misperceptions. Women, for example, are stereotyped as submissive, emotional, and maternal; therefore, when a person sees someone who has the physical attributes that match those of women, that someone will automatically be stereotyped in a similar fashion. If that person does not adhere to this social prescription, tension results between the woman and her perceiver. People may harass or attack the individual who is transgressing gender norms, hoping to force that person into a defined category because this will cognitively maintain category congruence. These adverse reactions will often compel transgressing individuals to sustain the gender binaries for fear of transphobic violence.

According to social identity theory, stereotyping and prejudicial acts are a means of maintaining one's self-image, self-worth, and self-integrity (Fein & Spencer, 1996; Turner, 1991). Fein and Spencer (1996) found, from their empirical studies, a strong link between self-affirmation and the perceptions of others. A person with a higher self-image, the researchers claim, will be less likely to have biased judgments of others, and vice versa. Likewise, when participants in their study received negative feedback regarding their own identity, acts performed to derogate others boosted their self-esteem. In other words, it boosts one's self-confidence and social status if they can diminish the status and esteem of others.

Performing prejudicial acts against others may also be a self-defense mechanism for individuals. According to many psychologists, the anger and hate we feel toward specific groups stems from our own self-hatred. Therefore, in order for us to maintain a healthy ego, we need to have enemies onto whom to project our self-hatred. Similarly, trans individuals become the target of this projection because they are often perceived as gay or lesbian (Deaux & Lewis, 1984; Madson, 2000). When individuals feel insecure about their own sexuality, rather than face the possibility of being gay, it is easier to project their fear and anger onto someone else they perceive as homosexual.

In addition, when people lack the experience of socializing with or just seeing people who are not like them, they are led to depend on the media to learn about other cultures and people. The media, though, as explained earlier, demonstrate warped perceptions of the trans population. If people construct their understanding of trans individuals from media images that portray gender variance as pathological or comic, then their attitudes toward people who trangress the gender categories will be negative. Violent or aggressive behavior could manifest from these skewed perceptions dictated to us through media images, thereby creating an environment in which it is impossible to deviate from the gender norms.

The sole identity of a trans person causes one to question a system that they have grown up believing in and proliferating. To suggest now that this system is inadequate causes individuals to re-evaluate their own identities and belief systems. This leaves them feeling vulnerable and possibly more open to an unstable self-esteem, elevated feelings of self-hatred, and a quicker acceptance of media information, each of which could trigger adverse reactions to those who deviate from their accepted social framework.

Citizen Policing

Citizen policing, for my purposes, is the collective process of fortifying gender dichotomy through self-policing. Like individual bias, group bias manifests feelings of tension and anger on a larger scale, which leads to violence against individuals who transgress gender norms.

Tarynn Witten and Evan Eyler research hate crimes and violence against gender-variant individuals and have surveyed over 300 transsexual, transgender, and cross-dressing people. They consider transphobic violence to be the following:

[G]ender terrorism whose underlying motivation is the maintenance of a social system in which males dominate females through emotional, verbal and physical acts of force and in which the line between the genders must be rigidly maintained in support of this social schema. (Witten & Eyler, 1999, p. 461)

The perpetrators, they continue, are misogynist and consider gender-variant people to be undermining male supremacy and the gender dichotomy. In other words, when trans people transition to the other gender or they defy gender categorization altogether, this action affects their social positioning within the power structure. Women, for example, can elevate their status by expressing themselves with a male identity. For many people, this poses a threat to their own power, and it dismantles a social structure that has been fortified for centuries.

Theorists in the field of social psychology explain prejudice as the result of ingroup/outgroup dynamics. Ingroup/outgroup dynamics are a social consequence of the cognitive process of social categorization. However, as Tajfel and Forgas assert, social categorization is thus much more than a purely cognitive task: it is central to social life. As such, it is subject to the pressures and distortions of the rich and variegated culture within which it arises (2000, p. 50).

They contend that the categories devised through our cognitive processes are not void of cultural meaning. Each has an associated value base that stems from societal inferences. Certain groups, for instance, have higher social value than others: men have more power than women, blacks and Latinos have lower status than whites, and so forth. These intergroup disparities, therefore, create feelings of tension and hostility that lead to acts of violence.

Social categorization within intergroup relations also elevates the position of the perceiver's own social group, the ingroup. Those who are outside their circle—the out-group—are then seen as subordinates. This is a social identity process that has the psychological effect of boosting the perceiver's self-esteem. In addition, when an ingroup feels a threat to its status, it exhibits greater prejudice toward others (Branscombe & Wann, 1994). This may include a perceived moral threat, such as homosexuality to a right-wing religious institution ingroup that considers same-sex love to be a sin. Similarly, to achieve "positive distinctiveness" for the ingroup, they proclaim, "We are what we are because *they* are not what we are" (Tajfel & Forgas, 2000, p. 114). This perceived value dissimilarity has been found to play an integral role in antigay prejudice (Haddock & Zanna, 1998).

Individual bias synthesized with citizen-group policing and institutionalization of gender dichotomies creates an insidious atmosphere filled with tension and violence. Trans individuals, therefore, feel forced to maintain the gender binary by suppressing their cross-gender identity desires and playing out heterosexual, gender-consistent behaviors while in public.

WHEN ONE IS NEITHER MALE NOR FEMALE

As stressed throughout this chapter, our society allows for only two genders—male and female. The gender binary is socially constructed and then fortified through the various regulatory agencies that have been described in the previous section. There are many individuals, though, who defy the system and do not conform to these gender constructs. These include people who do not fit within the prescribed categories and break society's model for gender, because of sex differences, autoerotic allures for cross-dressing, or gender identity conflicting with sex and identities. When individuals, by their appearance only, upset this model that society has tried so hard to promulgate and protect, this upsetting triggers strong emotions: "[P]erceivers may experience a range of negative affect, including embarrassment and anger" (Madson, 2000, p. 158). In fact, most people in the United States (over 93 percent) feel that cross-dressing is not "normal" or "all right" (Janus & Janus, 1993). These adverse, transphobic reactions directed toward those who defy gender categories lead to daily acts of discrimination, harassment, and violence. The findings from Witten and Eyler's surveys indicate that this group is more likely than the general population to experience violence against them because of this (1999). These daily stressors have profound impacts on trans individuals.

According to Hill, transgender violence is conceptualized through genderism, transphobia, and gender bashing (2003). Genderism, similar to the feminist concept of sexism, is considered "the system of beliefs that reinforces a negative evaluation based on gender nonconformity or an incongruence between sex and gender." Transphobia, on the other hand, is "the motivating force for negative reactions to transgendered people that involve fear and disgust in the observer" (Hill, 2003, p. 119). Gender-variant writer and advocate Leslie Feinberg maintains, "Gender-phobia targets women who are not feminine and men who are not masculine. Trans-phobia creates fear of changing sex" (Feinberg, 1996). The results of this biased attitude are discrimination, gender bashing, harassment, abuse, and assault.

According to Witten and Eyler's large-scale, transnational survey on the trans population, "transsexual, transgendered and cross-dressing individuals were more likely than their non-transgendered peers to experience multiple forms of violence and victimization across their lifespan" (1999, p. 464). In fact, roughly two transgender individuals are murdered each month in the United States, with at least two-thirds of all transgender people having experienced either physical or sexual assault (Isaacs, 2001), most of which happens in public space. Reported incidents against individuals who are trans, however, are lower than what is expected to be the reality of experiences, and they are often difficult to obtain due to the victims' hesitance to report an attack because of the often turbulent relationships with people in positions of authority, such as police officers and medical physicians: "Members of the transgender community rarely receive appropriate medical and criminal-justice interventions following a physical or sexual attack" (Witten & Eyler, 1999, p. 464).

In addition, violence against gender-variant individuals bears close resemblance to that against homosexuals because of the perceived sexuality of "butch" women and effeminate men. Roughly one-third of all hate crimes are against homosexuals (Isaacs, 2001), with nearly half of the incidents involving physical assault and 62 percent of those victims sustaining injury (National Center for Victims of Crime). Individuals who have physical characteristics that are inconsistent with their gender role behaviors are assumed to be homosexual by their perceivers (Deaux & Lewis, 1984) and could be vulnerable to these hate crimes against gays and lesbians. Heterosexist perpetrators also assume that an individual is gay or lesbian if the gender is illegible (Madson, 2000). The New York City Gay and Lesbian Anti-Violence Project reports in its annual *Hate Crimes Report* that more victims are being assaulted based on perceived sexual orientation.

Gender-phobic actions have significant consequences to one who digresses from the gender norms. They not only can result in physical harm to the person through violence and harassment, but the expected adverse reactions coming from society cause daily stressors that will impact the trans individual while navigating in public places. Daily hassles causing stress to an individual have psychological, somatic/physical, and behavioral outcomes: headaches, negative mood (such as depression), high-risk behavior, and so on (DiPlacido, 1998). For example, youth who have been victimized by assaults show more symptoms, post-traumatic stress reactions, and sadness (Bonney-McCoy & Finkelhor, 1995). Another effect of transphobic violence and rejection of the gender-nonconformist is a pressure to conform to the gender binary—many trans people feel they must decide to be either one gender or the other rather than keep a more fluid identity:

> Beginning in early childhood, and continuing throughout their lives, individuals learn to expect rejection, stigmatization, and the loss of relationships, should they violate gender norms. Fear of rejection acts as a pressure to establish and maintain "proper" gender. (Gagne & Tewksbury, 1998, p. 87)

When trans individuals challenge western culture's binary gender system by proving that there is a spectrum of genders and sexualities, there are considerable costs to be paid. Expressing gender behaviors or identities that are not consistent with their sex leaves trans people vulnerable to this homophobic and transphobic violence that permeates our society.

Socio-Spatial Implications of Living In-between

> Virtually anything on the other side of this door makes me uncomfortable [pointing to the adjacent front door to her home that leads to the outside world]. (42-year-old)

Historically, prejudice has been played out spatially, for example, with the ghettoization of the Jewish people to racially segregated schools and bathrooms. Spatial practices that reinforce prejudice against gender and sexuality continue to be played out today. According to philosopher Nancy Fraser, dominant groups use spatial tactics to fortify their social positions: "[W]here societal inequality persists, deliberative processes in public spheres will tend to operate to the advantage of the dominant groups and to the disadvantage of subordinates" (1993, p. 527).

In the late 1800s and the early 1900s, women were to be out in public alone only if they were engaging in a particular activity, such as shopping. If not, they were deemed nonrespectable or having sexual intentions. In public parks, women and girls over the age of ten were separated into areas that were often cordoned off with a fence or concealed behind shrubbery, and access to this space was restricted to certain hours of the day (Cranz, 1980). Today, women continue to be limited geographically, with travel remaining close to the home and conducted for targeted activities (Franck & Paxon, 1989).

Before the 1969 Stonewall revolt—the event that spurred lesbians and gay men to reclaim the streets, their commercial and recreational establishments, and their identities—much of gay and lesbian life was closely monitored through police raids and public surveillance. Individuals who were not wearing at least three articles of clothing consistent with their sex were arrested or harassed and beaten by police officers and the general public. Though today there are many gay and lesbian establishments flourishing throughout the country, space for those who are trans remains scarce.

The statement that opened this section renders a clear picture of the current socio-spatial experience of individuals who are gender-variant: everywhere outside the home is foreboding. In general, public places are uncomfortable environments for people not fitting into the gender "norms." In a study conducted by the author on the experiences of individuals not identifying as male or female (Felsenthal, 2001), all participants experienced some form of aggression against them, whether it was verbal harassment or physical attacks while "out" in public. One participant spoke of being chased out of the neighborhood at gunpoint, while others spoke of verbal threats and physical attacks:

I got stabbed in the neck, I got crap beat out of me a few times. I got beat up pretty bad for this [gender] issue. I had to put everything in a box for quite a few years. And just kept it as a private thing in my home. (46-year-old)

At one point we were getting followed around by men that were talking shit. It's like being a dog and making circles, looking to see who's following you. (37-year-old)

It has been made clear . . . that my presence can give offence, that they have not been happy with my appearance. They say nasty things to your face. (48-year-old)

Public bathrooms are particularly problematic for trans individuals. Most are gender-specific, designated for males or females, forcing individuals to choose a gender if they are to use the facility. This dilemma poses a problem not only for the gender-variant individual but for the patrons of the public bathrooms as well.

Public rest rooms are the worst. The last time I was in a woman's bathroom was 12 years ago. (37-year-old)

Sometimes I just pee outside to avoid that situation. (28-year-old)

I got arrested in Tuxedo, NY, got beat up by the cops there, harassed to no end. That was about not being allowed to use the bathroom anywhere so I pulled over to the side of the road. (46-year-old)

(Bathrooms) create a feeling of consternation, confusion to the point of paralysis. Confusion easily shapes into anger or hostility. Unisex bathrooms would be the smart thing to do. (48-year-old)

Dressing rooms also pose a problem for trans individuals. Some of the participants mentioned using the Internet to do their shopping just to avoid uncomfortable situations. Others buy their clothing in thrift shops where there are typically no dressing rooms and where the workers are also known to be "alternative."

Many of the places I go don't have dressing rooms, so I don't have to deal with it. (28-year-old)

One might assume that places designated for or that have been appropriated by the gay and lesbian community would be open and bias-free to the trans population. The words *transgender* and sometimes *queer* have even been added to the title of many gay and lesbian organizations to imply full acceptance and inclusion of those who are gender-variant. However, all of the participants in the author's study claimed that the gay and lesbian community still resisted full inclusion of the trans population. Many participants stated that they still were not able to find a community or place within these environments because of the built-in bias and social stigma attached to them.

We are the black sheep of the gay world. They are angry with us 'cause we are giving them a bad name . . . we are not maliciously stating anything against them, we're just being us. (37-year-old)

They feel that trans people are an unacceptable face of the community . . . because they are often thought of as outlandish or sex workers. (48-year-old)

These tensions by the gay and lesbian community toward those who are trans are played out geographically with the boundaries imposed to restrict access to public space by those who are trans:

They [gays and lesbians] look at us [gender-variant people] like we are infiltrators. (28-year-old)

I went into the men's bathroom at the gay expo and I got looks from people and I thought: "Shame on you!" (27-year-old)

There are lots of gay bars where I would not be accepted walking into looking like this. (48-year-old)

Part of [a video segment on gays and lesbians] was having an inclusive queer community and not to include trans people—how the fuck can you do that!?! (27-year-old)

This church around the corner [has] a very big sign out front that says they accept all people, including gays. But the preacher couldn't deal with transexuals at all. The MCC [a church for the GLBT community], that is a more interesting situation. They have a transgender group, the only thing is the first day I am there they want to dump me into this transgender group. Say you accept us and then you pen us off, segregate us, and with no distinctions. (42-year-old)

Most spaces that are specifically designated for the trans population are therapeutic organizations that provide social services such as group therapy or drug and rehabilitation counseling. There are very few places like bars, cafes, or clubs for trans individuals to go for social support, socialization, and networking. To a large extent, gay and lesbian space has allowed members of a subordinate group to be the majority where they establish their own social norms and maintain control over that environment:

The first thing one sees [on Fire Island Pines] is a charming skew of accustomed male mores. Everywhere men hug and smooch; couples walk, hands entwined or casually draped into the rear of a partner's cut-offs. . . . Everywhere an easy male affection suffuses the air. (Nimmons, 2002, p. 20)

This has not been the case for the trans population.

The experience of negotiating space within New York City's public spheres for the participants is complicated and poses relentless risks of intimidation or bodily harm. Both the heterosexual and homosexual communities resist inclusion of those who are gender-variant by remaining static in their compliance with the socially prescribed gender dichotomies.

SIGNIFICANCE OF BEING OUT OF "PLACE"

[T]he subjective sense of self is defined and expressed not simply by one's relationship to other people, but also by one's relationships to the various physical settings that define and structure day-to-day life. (Proshansky et al., 1983, p. 58)

Any social existence aspiring or claiming to be real but failing to provide its own space would be a strange entity, [without space] it would fall to the level of folklore and sooner or later disappear all together thereby immediately losing its identity, its domination. (Lefebvre, 1991, p. 53)

In the two excerpts above, Proshansky and LeFebvre highlight the significant role that place has in the construction and expression of individual and collective identities. Environmental psychologists explore this dynamic relationship between people and place, revealing a significant interplay between their two constructions. They assert that access to public places provides individuals with "links to the physical world" and helps one create and sustain a sense of self. Concepts such as place identity, place attachment, and placemaking demonstrate the significance of these person-place relations (Lynch, 1993; Hummon, 1992; Gerson, Stueve, & Fischer, 1977; Proshansky et al., 1983; Dixon & Durrheim, 2000).

The concept of place identity as described by Proshansky and others (1983) offers a link between defining the self and the lived experience in the context of the physical environment. According to Proshansky, place identity is a "substructure" of self-identity, and identities are defined by transactions with the physical environment. Environmental psychologists assert that appropriating and creating meaningful space are fundamental rights and part of what it means to be human. Without the ability to claim and form attachments to space, one's identity development and proclamation will be hindered. This is a critical point when thinking about the experiences of trans individuals in public spaces. Impending harassments and assaults by heterosexist and transphobic individuals and groups restrict a trans person's access to many public spaces.

Spatial restrictions placed on individuals because of prejudices, therefore, have significant outcomes on an individual's identity development and expression. Denying access to and use of space to particular individuals or groups will maintain their subordinate position and can erase or invalidate their identity. Conversely, owning and appropriating space help to define and proclaim one's individual and collective identities.

SPATIAL TACTICS FOR AFFIRMATION AND EMPOWERMENT

A poem by Maya Angelou (1978) states: "But still like air, I'll rise." This is a proclamation made to show the strength of black people to overcome a pernicious environment of extreme and overt racism. As described in the previous sections, the trans population has also faced hostile territories in western culture. They have also had to devise strategies to overcome this hatred that has been targeted toward them. A simple, yet very powerful way people who are trans "rise" from their oppressive, misogynist, homophobic, and transphobic environment is to appropriate and govern space—claim it as their own. Using Nancy Fraser's nomenclature, they create *subaltern counter publics*: "parallel discursive arenas where members of subordinated social groups invent and circulate counter discourses to formulate oppositional interpretations of their identities, interests and needs" (1993, p. 527). People who do not conform to the socially constructed cultural norms, therefore, will create their own spaces in which to construct, reproduce, and display their identities. Subaltern counter publics are essential to the proclamation and validation of collective identities.

Kevin Lynch's strategies for creating "meaningful space" (1993) coincide with the establishment of subaltern counter publics. He asserts that for a place to have meaning to an individual, certain conditions must be met. Two conditions Lynch proposes that are of particular importance to the GLBT community are that the place must not limit the activity of the user, and it should create a safe environment that allows for freedom of behavior. In other words, there must be places that afford outward affections between same-sex individuals, as well as places that offer space for gender-variant expression without fear of homophobic or transphobic violence. Per Gustafson developed a three-pronged factorial approach to placemaking that supports Lynch's ideas (2000). He posits that the self (one's subjective experience), others (inhabitants of the space), and the physical environment (built and naturally landscaped) are all interrelated factors that play significant roles in how one creates meaningful space. For example, a queer space will become a meaningful space to trans individuals if they have personal attachments and memories of it, positive social dynamics with other trans people there, and if particular aspects of the physical space itself, such as lighting and color schemes, appeal to them. Individuals who transgress the socially accepted gender binaries pose a unique challenge to "normative" use of, appropriation of, and attachment to space.

Appropriation is the act of making something one's own. When "we appropriate aspects of the world as anchors for self identity, . . . we change our environment and we are in turn changed by environmental experience." Appropriating and creating meaningful space, according to place attachment theory, are fundamental rights and part of what it means to be human. Without the ability to claim and form attachments to space, one's identity development and proclamation will be hindered. It is within this defined space that the users can feel they are able to move freely to meet their (individual and social) needs and drives (Proshansky, Ittelson, & Rivlin, 1976).

In gay and lesbian literature, the process of appropriating space is often termed "queering" space. Many queer theorists assert that "queering space" is the production and repetition of queer acts performed in heterosexual space (Desert, 1997; Valentine, 1996). For example, according to this idea, a woman kissing her girlfriend on the sidewalk would be creating a temporal lesbian space on that sidewalk. I question the reality of this supposition. To make heterosexual space queer is to appropriate it, to be the majority in that space, and have the ability to assert some kinds of regulatory controls over it. In other words, a queer space is one where many homosexuals and transsexuals can congregate, behave, and express a sexual identity freely without fear of homophobic violence. It is where their behaviors become the norm. The lesbians on the sidewalk are not the norm for that space and stand a good chance of facing harassment for their "deviant" performance.

In contrast, many groups of trans individuals do find ways to "queer" space. By reinterpreting, reclaiming, and reconstructing space that is trans, they, in turn, are queering space. The home, for example, is reinterpreted for many trans people. It serves as a multi-functional platform for working, socializing, and networking, in addition to providing a place for living (sleeping, eating, and relaxing). Dwelling thus contributes to supporting and grounding the various selves (as friend, worker, activist, etc.) for the participants. The participants use the home in ways that parallel bell hooks' "home of resistance":

> The homeplace was the one site where one could freely confront the issue of humanization where one could resist. Black women resisted by making homes where all black people could strive to be subjects, not objects, where we could be affirmed in our minds and hearts despite poverty, hardship, and deprivation, where we could restore to ourselves the dignity denied to us on the outside in the public world . . . it was about the construction of a safe place where black people could affirm one another and by so doing heal many of the wounds inflicted by racist domination. (hooks, 1990, p. 42)

Dwellings are also a place to break free of the gender role norms that are attached to it, such as the home being "women's space." When the residents of the house have gender identities that transgress the norms, there is more freedom to reinterpret and re-establish domestic rules (for example, the rule that the woman cleans and the man takes out the garbage). Domestic chores, then, can be more congruent to one's personality than to societal expectations.

More important, the home is the place where most cross-gender behaviors are initially played out. Men can, in the privacy and safety of their own home, dress in women's clothing without fear of embarrassment or transphobic violence. In Erving Goffman's (1959) terms, this *backstage* environment is the place where the performer "can relax; he can drop his front." It is also the place where performers can be schooled in frontstage identity expression (actions of politeness and *decorum* played out for "audiences"). This is where trans people learn to "do" gender and practice new gender-specific skills.

Reclaiming space gives trans individuals the opportunity to reposition themselves within the social hierarchy. For example, settings for music and sports allow trans people to excel, and possibly surpass, other participants in certain activities that give them the power to gain control over that environment. Sports, performance arts, and music have created that avenue for social movement.

> I go to jazz clubs where nobody cares what you are, if you like jazz, you're in. It's not about who you are, it's about what you do, your knowledge and expertise. (42-year-old)
>
> I could be who I was and excel and have the guys be more impressed with my skill. (28-year-old speaking about soccer)
>
> I was on a biker team and a very famous street fighter. Many transgenders were on biker teams. (30-year-old)
>
> I would move right in and start with the biggest guy fighting. I was a big fighter. (37-year-old)

Trans people also (re)construct alternative sites established exclusively for them. It is here that the individual who is gender-variant can appropriate, defend, and manage the space. The gender-variant population, who now become the majority, establishes the rules and norms to be followed. The True Spirit Conference (TSC), for example, is an annual conference established specifically for gender-variant people—a place that accepts and encourages gender expressions across the scale between male and female. Its venues not only offer entertainment, but education, socializing, and community-building as well. Like the home, TSC offers a space where gender-variant individuals are the majority and where regulatory policies are established by them.

By reinterpreting, reclaiming, and (re)constructing space, the trans population is able to "queer" space and create a meaningful environment that Proshansky, Lynch, and Gustafson assert are essential to developing and expressing one's identity.

DISCUSSION AND CONCLUSION

Michel Foucault proclaims that the most powerful "place" is in the body (1978). The body is our instrument for expressing who we are and who we want to be. It represents social status and positions us within social hierarchies. We have the power, though, to change our bodies and their expressions and thus to dismantle the power associations that are afforded to it. Individuals make alterations to their appearance that are as simple as changing the color of their hair, or they can be as complex as redefining their gender attributes through surgical procedures or wearing clothing inconsistent with their assigned sex. The possibilities of making our identities fluid can be endless, though. According to society's dictates, they must remain within the boundaries of our prescribed social framework. When one dares to transgress this system by expressing gender in a way that does not conform to accepted standards for males and females, the power that Foucault speaks of is then removed from that individual, leaving them no "place" to be within the socio-spatial structure of our society.

Our citizens ensure this placelessness of trans people by creating a volatile environment for them to live in. They leave them no space within the physical geography in which to safely be who they are without fear of homophobic or transphobic violence. Trans individuals, though, are not without agency. They reclaim their individual and collective identities, and thus their power, by defining their own space in which to develop and express their identities freely. Trans individuals use places such as arenas for competitive sports, the True Spirit Conference, and even the home for not only empowerment but also dominance within these subcultures. They actively create space for which to reposition themselves within the social structure from one of subordination to one of authority.

Though the trans population is actively taking steps to make a "place" for themselves in our socio-spatial environment, the problem of fortifying our socially accepted gender dichotomy still penetrates

Toolbox for Change

For	Images/perceptions	Strategies for change
Individuals	Individuals remain biased in their perceptions and actions toward transgendered individuals.	Not only does tolerance need to be practiced, but people need to welcome into their lives and work environments those individuals who do not fall within the two prescribed gender categories.
Community	Bias, discrimination, and violence against transgendered people still permeate our communities.	Just as collective action is taken against those who are transgendered, collective action can also be taken against those who perform prejudicial and harmful acts against transgendered individuals.
Practitioners	Design professionals continue to create environments that accommodate only males and females.	Nongender-specific space should be incorporated into the design plans of new construction and renovations. For example, unisex bathrooms and dressing rooms should be offered in places of public accommodation.
	People within the field of psychology . . .	People within the field of psychology need to reassess the utilization of the GID diagnosis.
Educators	Gender-bias and gender-conforming strategies are still played out in the classrooms.	Teachers need to be aware of how their pedagogy affects nongender-conforming children. Encouraging "gender-appropriate" or gender-segregated activities should be minimized if not eliminated from discourse and action.

continued

Toolbox for Change (continued)

For	Images/perceptions	Strategies for change
Legislators	The transgendered are virtually erased in the eyes and documents of our legislators.	Revise wording in existing legislation that protects homosexuals from hate crimes and discrimination to include transgendered individuals. In states where there are no current laws that protect either homosexual or transgendered individuals, create laws to ensure their safety and equal treatment in housing, jobs, etc.

our society at all levels, from individual bias to collective prejudicial actions. This condition will continue as long as we live in a culture that only *sees* gender attribute differences but does not accommodate those who are in-between the gender dichotomy—the struggle to find a "place" for people who are trans will continue, and pernicious crimes will proliferate.

How then do we deal with an environment that condones hate crimes against trans people? Discussing and reconceptualizing gender in theory or even crystallizing it in writing is the easy part. Having the tools to implement change is where the challenge rests. Though most can visualize what a third, fourth, or nth gender may look like, how do we make room for them in our society? Where do they fit within the rigid gender framework? Though there are no simple answers to these questions, the Toolbox for Change offers some suggestions on how to possibly address some of these complex issues.

NOTES

1. The term *trans* will be used here as an umbrella term for anyone who self-identifies as gender-variant, transgender, queer, androgynous; or who is a transsexual, either pre-, post-, or non-operative; or who is either intersexed (having ambiguous genitalia) or a hermaphrodite (having both male and female sex organs).

2. Audre Lorde Project Action Alert, February 7, 2002.

REFERENCES

Angelou, M. (1978). *And still I rise*. New York: Random House.

Bonney-McCoy, S., & Finkelhor, D. (1995). Psychosocial sequelae of violent victimization in a national youth sample. *Journal of Counseling and Clinical Psychology, 63*, 726–736.

Bornstein, K. (1994). *Gender outlaw*. New York: Vintage Books, Random House.

Bourdieu, P. (1977). *Outline of a theory of practice*. Cambridge: Cambridge University Press.

Branscombe, N. R., & Wann, D. L. (1994). Collective self-esteem consequences of outgroup derogation when a valued social identity is on trial. *European Journal of Social Psychology, 24*, 641–657.

Chusmir, L. H., & Koberg, C. S. (1990). Dual sex role identity and its relationship to sex role conflict. *Journal of Psychology, 124*(5), 545–556.

Cranz, G. (1980). Women in urban parks. *Signs: Journal of Women in Culture and Society, 5*(3), 579, 595.

Deaux, K., & Lewis, L. L. (1984). Structure of gender stereotypes: Interrelationships among components and gender label. *Journal of Personality and Social Psychology, 46*, 991–1004.

Desert, J. U. (1997). Queer space. In B. Ingram, A. M. Bouthillette, & Y. Retter (Eds.), *Queers in space: Communities/public places/sites of resistance* (pp. 17–27). Washington: Bay Press.

DiPlacido, J. (1998). Minority stress among lesbians, gay men and bisexuals: A consequence of heterosexism, homophobia, and stigmatization. In H. Herek (Ed.), *Stigma and sexual orientation: Understanding prejudice against lesbians, gay men, and bisexuals* (pp. 138–159). California, London, New Delhi: Sage Publications.

Dixon, J., & Durrheim, K. (2000). Displacing place-identity: A discursive approach to locating the self and other. *British Journal of Social Psychology, 39*, 27–44.

Fein, S., & Spencer, S. (1996). *Readings in social psychology: The art and science of research*. Boston: Houghton Mifflin.

Feinberg, L. (1996). *Transgender warriors: Making history from Joan of Arc to Dennis Rodman*. Boston, MA: Beacon Press.

Felsenthal, K. (2001). *Gender variance and the experience of place*. Unpublished manuscript.

Foucault, M. (1978). *The history of sexuality: An introduction* (Vol. 1). New York: Vintage Books.

Franck, K., & Paxon, L. (1989). Women and urban public space. In I. Altman & E. Zube (Eds.), *Public places and spaces* (pp. 121–146). New York/London: Plenum Press.

Fraser, N. (1993). Rethinking the public sphere: A contribution to the critique of actually existing democracy. In S. During (Ed.), *Cultural studies reader* (2nd ed., pp. 518–537). London/New York: Routledge.

Gagne, P., & Tewksbury, R. (1998). Conformity pressures and gender resistance among transgender individuals. *Social Problems, 45*(1), 81–101.

Gerson, K., Stueve, C. A., & Fischer, C. S. (1977). Attachment to place. In C. S. Fischer et al. (Eds.), *Networks and places* (pp. 139–161). New York: The Free Press.

Goffman, E. (1959). *The presentation of self in everyday life.* Garden City, NY: Doubleday.

Gustafson, P. (2000). Meanings of place: Everyday experience and theoretical conceptualizations. *Journal of Environment Psychology, 21,* 5–16.

Haddock, G., & Zanna, M. (1998). Authoritarianism, values, and the favorability and structure of antigay attitudes. In H. Herek (Ed.), *Stigma and sexual orientation: Understanding prejudice against lesbians, gay men, and bisexuals* (pp. 82–107). London: Sage Publications.

Hill, D. (2003). Genderism, transphobia, and gender bashing: A framework for interpreting anti-transgender violence. In B. C. Wallace & R. T. Carter (Eds.), *Understanding and dealing with violence: A multicultural approach* (pp. 113–136). London: Sage Publications.

hooks, b. (1990). *Yearning: Race, gender, and cultural politics.* Boston: South End Press.

Hummon, D. M. (1992). Community attachment: Local sentiment and sense of place. In I. Altman & S. Low (Eds.), *Place attachment* (pp. 253–278). New York: Plenum.

Isaacs, T. (2001). Domestic violence and hate crimes. *Criminal Justice Ethics, 20,* 31–43.

Janus, S. S., & Janus, C. L. (1993). *The Janus Report on sexual behavior.* New York: John Wiley.

Kessler, S. (1998). *Lessons from the intersexed.* New Brunswick: Rutgers University Press.

Kessler, S., & McKenna, W. (2000). Who put the "trans" in transgender? Gender theory and everyday life. *International Journal of Transgenderism, 4*(3).

Lefebvre, H. (1991). *The production of space.* Oxford, UK: Blackwell Publishing.

Lynch, K. (1993). Public space meanings and connections. In S. Carr et al. (Eds.), *Public space.* Cambridge, UK: Cambridge University Press.

Madson, L. (2000). Inferences regarding the personality traits and sexual orientation of physically androgynous people. *Psychology of Women Quarterly, 24,* 148–160.

Mason-Schrock, D. (1996). Transexuals' narrative construction of the "true self." *Social Psychology Quarterly, 59*(3), 176–192.

Money, J. (1994). The concept of gender identity disorder in childhood and adolescence after 39 years. *Journal of Sex and Marital Therapy, 20*(3), 163–177.

Nimmons, D. (2002, March/April). Communities of equals. *The Gay and Lesbian Review.*

Proshansky, H., et al. (1983). Place identity: Physical world socialization of the self. *Journal of Environmental Psychology, 3,* 57–84.

Proshansky, H., Ittelson, W., & Rivlin, L. (Eds.) (1976). *Environmental psychology* (2d ed.). New York: Holt, Rinehart & Winston.

Stoller, R. (1968). *Sex and gender: On the development of masculinity and femininity.* London: Hogarth Press.

Tajfel, H., & Forgas, J. (2000). Social categorization: Cognitions, values and groups. In C. Strangor (Ed.), *Stereotypes and prejudice* (pp. 113–140). Philadelphia, PA: Psychology Press.

Turner, J. C. (1991). *Social influence.* Buckingham, UK: Open University Press.

Valentine, G. (1996). (Re)negotiating the heterosexual street. In N. Duncan (Ed.), *Body space: Destabilizing geographies of gender and sexuality* (pp. 146–155). London/New York: Routledge.

Witten, T., & Eyler, E. (1999). Hate crimes and violence against the transgendered. *Peace Review, 11*(3).

CHAPTER 9

Black Men Who Have Sex with Men

Carlton W. Parks

More systematic attention is being paid by social scientists in the twenty-first century to subgroups within the general population who possess multiple identities that result in multiple oppressions. Such subgroups permit social scientists to uncover the cumulative impact of membership in multiple categories (such as race, gender, ethnicity, sexual orientation identity, religious identification, and age) on these individuals' phenomenological experiences as well as how others behave toward them (Adams & Kimmel, 1997). One subgroup empirically receiving increasing attention is black men who have sex with men. Why is such systematic attention important?

Landrine (1995) argues that explanations for overt behavior must be obtained from behavior in context. Thus, as a function of sociohistorical/cohort/contextual influences, the same behaviors expressed by different subgroups may yield different explanations for their occurrence. One can't presume to know without some verification or confirmation why people behave the way they do. Explanations for the behaviors of any subgroup are often tied to the sociohistorical/cohort/contextual influences associated with that specific subgroup. Thus, one cannot use white gay men as the "standard" to assess the psychological functioning and adjustment of men who have sex with men.

CROSS'S REVISED RACIAL IDENTITY DEVELOPMENT THEORY AND BLACK MEN WHO HAVE SEX WITH MEN

Racial group identity and sexual orientation identity from a lifespan perspective are two psychological constructs that shed some insight into the phenomenological experiences of black men who have sex with men across the life course. In 1991, William Cross discussed a number of revisions in his negrescence model. First, an individual's personal identity is now theorized to be separate and distinct from his or her reference group orientation. Reference group orientation incorporates the constructs of "salience," or the importance of race in one's life, as well as possessing a "valence" (a quality of objects that affects their attractiveness to organisms) that can be positive, negative, or neutral. The relationship between personal identity, reference group identity, and self-esteem is theorized to be varied across individuals with varying outcomes, since personal identity plays a minor role in the development of racial identity. For instance, a person who identifies strongly with his racial group doesn't necessarily have elevated self-esteem or positive mental health. There exists one exception to this proposed pattern: black self-hatred is believed to be associated with low self-esteem because it incorporates a negative reference group orientation into one's individual personal identity (Vandiver, Cross, Worrell, & Fhagen-Smith, 2002).

The five-stage model has been streamlined into four stages: pre-encounter, encounter, immersion-emersion, and internalization. These stages reflect the overarching themes of black racial identities. Within the pre-encounter stage there now exist three identities: assimilation, miseducation, and self-hatred. The immersion-emersion stage has two identities: intense black involvement, and anti-white sentiment. Finally, the internalization stage has three identities: black nationalist, biculturalist, and multicultural inclusive. These eight identities describe the expanded negrescence model with only six of the seven measurable identities (biculturalist excluded) measurable on the Cross Racial Identity Scale (Vandiver et al., 2000).

The distinction between being a "gay black" versus a "black gay," where one's sexual orientation identity or racial identity predominates one's self-concept, is still a speculative notion. Very little empirical data currently exist supporting the relationship between this distinction and psychological functioning. Etzhorn (1995) revealed that primarily race-identified (black gays) and non-primarily race-identified black men (gay blacks) did not differ on measures of sexual orientation or racial identities. Cross and Fhagen-Smith (2001) speculate that the modal black adolescent who is experiencing the development of a gay male or lesbian identity automatically chooses his/her sexual orientation identity to be more salient than the reference group orientation. We need empirical data with culturally diverse black adolescent males attempting to navigate and negotiate the development of their racial and sexual orientation identities to validate such a contention. Such data might possibly reveal the existence of multiple developmental trajectories among this group. It is premature to presume one "politically correct" sequence in the establishment of multiple identities.

THE POTENTIAL PITFALLS TO "COMING OUT," AND SEXUAL IDENTITY DEVELOPMENT THAT RESULTS IN BLACK MEN CHOOSING NOT TO SELF-LABEL AS GAY OR BISEXUAL

Similarly, when black men who have sex with men are involved in the coming out process, there exist a number of assumptions based on dichotomous thinking that concern the "appropriate sequence of events" of the coming out process that lead to psychological well-being and adjustment. It is assumed, based on the more "out" one is, that the more well adjusted they will be across contexts. There is seldom discussion of levels of coming out. Coming out is presumed to lead to problem reduction as well as elevated levels of self-esteem and self-worth. To remain "in the closet" is associated with elevated levels of shame, guilt, and internalized homophobia. When one closely examines the populations these assertions were based on, they were for the most part middle-class, college-educated, white gay men. Once again, context plays an important role here when discussing the impact of sociocultural influences on the coming out process for black men who have sex with men.

Morales (1990) asserts that the coming out process creates challenges for ethnic minority men who have sex with men with respect to their loyalties and prioritizing their allegiances to the following three communities: their ethnic minority community (presumed to be "heterosexual"), the white gay male community, and the society at large. To fully come "out" would possibly result in total ostracism and rejection from their ethnic minority community as well as the society at large. Moreover, abandonment by the white lesbian, gay male, bisexual, and transgendered (LGBT) communities is very likely to occur due to gay racism (Boykin, 1996a).

Given the frequent occurrences of gay racism that still exist between black men and white gay males (Boykin, 1996a), it is highly unlikely that the white gay male community would become the primary support system of black men. Given the above realities, it is not too surprising that many ethnic minority men who have sex with men choose instead to negotiate a relationship between them and their ethnic minority community that permits them to remain "a member in good standing." This compromise typically means negotiating a new arrangement with their extended family members, if they plan to remain active and integrated members. This becomes a particularly delicate negotiation, given how gender roles (particularly masculinity) are conceived and perceived among oppressed and marginalized populations (Hatchett, 1991; Marable, 1995; Staples, 1995). Coming out as a gay or bisexual male can often be considered the final public insult to an extended family constellation (Morales, 1996; Boykin, 1996b), since to be considered masculine is to be homophobic (Herek, 1987). If these negotiations are not handled with care and skill, then a new family constellation consisting of non-blood family members will need to be created. With the interaction of geographic region, socioeconomic status, and cohort influences added to the mix, the complexity inherent in the coming out process for men who have sex with men becomes even more apparent. That explains why many have decided, as a survival strategy within a hostile oppressive environment, to "remain in the closet" within different arenas of their lives. Once again, relying too heavily on the white gay male as the "standard" to assess ethnic minority men's psychological functioning and adjustment may lead to rather faulty assumptions and conclusions related to the coming out process (Smith, 1998).

Another illustration of this reality is in the area of self-labeling one's sexual orientation identity status. One major contribution of the HIV infection/AIDS literature focusing on risky sexual behaviors among men who have sex with men is the difference in the expression of sexual behaviors between various racial subgroups. For instance, black men, compared to whites, are more likely to report engaging in anal intercourse than oral sex. Similarly, men who have sex with men are more likely to self-label as bisexual compared to white men. Black men are far more likely to report concomitant substance use with unprotected intercourse (Heckman, Kelly, Bogart, Kalichman, & Rompa, 1999; Myers, Javanbakht, Martinez, & Obediah, 2003).

Male gender roles and sexuality have direct implications for the discussion of risky sexual behaviors between partners in black heterosexual close relationships. These discussions become even more sensitive when black males are secretly engaging in same-sex sexual behavior (Campbell, 1995). To address the risk factors related to risky sexual behaviors within the context of black couple relationships, one must begin conceptualizing the interpersonal dynamics (particularly patterns of communication) from a systemic perspective (Campbell, 1995; Wingood & DiClemente, 1997, 1998; St. Lawrence et al., 1998; Wyatt et al., 1997). The gender-role attitudes and behaviors of the male partner concerning risky sexual behaviors play a critical role in the couple dynamics of sexual decision-making.

ATTITUDES SURROUNDING THE GENDER ROLES OF BLACK MEN WHO HAVE SEX WITH MEN HAVE THEIR ORIGINS IN SOCIOHISTORICAL INFLUENCES DATING BACK TO SLAVERY

In the United States, the gender-role norms of black men are tied to historical issues dating back to the black male experience of slavery. These past experiences currently impact how the larger society conceives black male masculinity and sexuality as well as how members of the black community perceive one another (Marable, 1995; White & Cones, 1999). Survey findings have revealed that blacks tend to be more liberal with respect to gender-role norms, while other survey findings have found them to be more egalitarian in their gender-role attitudes. Finally, other studies are more likely to report more traditional or conservative gender-role attitudes. Black men have also been found to be more conservative than women, although fewer gender differences between black men and women have been found to exist compared to whites (Hatchett, 1991).

Given institutionalized racism, inequities in the economic arena as well as the criminal justice system result in black men being particularly vulnerable to gender-role identity concerns. Black males typically do not adhere to the traditional European model of masculinity, wherein men are perceived to be masters of their own fate (that is, being powerful, independent, decisive, and assertive) (Staples, 1995). This makes it even more difficult for them to be effective breadwinners for their families. Consequently, sexuality in the form of procreation becomes central to a black male's definition of a sense of self, in direct response to the issues mentioned above (Staples, 1995; Monteiro & Fuqua, 1996).

In contrast, the black male model of masculinity theorizes that the black male, on a spiritual level, is born with the spirit of both male and female. There is more of a balance in the behavioral characteristics associated with masculinity: strength with gentleness, independence with interdependence, and emotional control with emotional expressiveness. Masculinity is different from femininity in its style and form, not in its basic nature (Lewis, 1975). One needs to utilize the appropriate model/framework when interpreting behaviors associated with ethnically and culturally diverse groups.

In reaction to not being masters of their own fate, black males may adopt an interpersonal stance through behaviors, scripts, and posturing that suggests to the outside world that they are in control of the world surrounding them (Lazur & Majors, 1995). When one adds the variable of sexual orientation to the picture, the distorted gender-role image of black male masculinity becomes even more distorted, given the stereotype that all homosexual men behave and act like women. A careful examination of the interaction of race, sexual orientation identity, and gender roles reveals that of black males who have sex with other males, their ethnicity is typically far more central to their core identity than their sexual orientation identity. The opposite is often the case for white gay males.

Given these realities, it is presumed at times by both black and white scholars that homosexuality is non-existent in African or black societies, and if it does exist, it is a contaminant of white societies or a byproduct of oppression. The devaluation of homosexual behaviors among males within the black community seems to stem from two issues: whether the black male is "insertive" or "receptive" with his male sexual partner, and whether or not there is some conscious recognition/labeling by the partners that their sexual behaviors are "homosexual" in orientation. Based on AIDS-related research, public health epidemiologists are uncovering the reality that black men are more likely than white men to report engaging in same-sex behavior and to label themselves bisexual (Monteiro & Fuqua, 1996). These findings suggest that sexual expression as well as racial identity develop within a cultural context and should be examined accordingly using culturally sensitive models.

BLACK EXTENDED FAMILIES' FRAGILE AND AMBIGUOUS RELATIONSHIPS WITH BLACK MEN WHO HAVE SEX WITH MEN

The nuclear and extended family plays a pivotal role in nurturing the racial identity and socialization of its members. It becomes the major context for social support and the psychological well-being of its constituents. Based on the traditional African belief system, the individual owes his or her very existence to all the members of the family (living, dead, and yet-to-be-born). The individual realizes that he did not and could not exist alone and that he is an integral part of that collective (the family) (Nobles, 1996). These African traditions are reflected in the major strengths of contemporary black families, which include a strong achievement orientation, a strong work orientation, flexible family roles, strong kinship bonds, and a strong religious orientation (Hill, 1999). Coming out as a gay male within one's nuclear and extended family in the black community can lead to varied family reactions ranging from indifference to tolerance to ostracism. This can be extremely threatening to most men who have sex with men who rely on their extended families for their survival and well-being.

Black families can hold rather traditional family values that reflect their religious beliefs. Heterosexual lifestyle norms can be highly valued, since they serve to perpetuate the survival of the family: getting married and having biological children who take on the family name and their traditions. Thus, the family of a black male who has sex with men would have to adjust its expectations and value structure to successfully integrate such a family member. Other, more pressing concerns can vie for the attention and energies of the family, which can make such a task even more daunting. For instance, given the chronic and acute stressors associated with an extended family constellation, there is the real issue of whether there are enough emotional resources to expend on this matter, given the other, "more" pressing concerns.

It is incumbent upon ethnic minorities to maintain strong connections to their support systems as a way to buffer the continual stressors they face. Such connections serve as a lifeline to many men who have sex with men who are dealing with overt and covert racism, sexism, and/or sexual prejudice. Family members can provide comfort, aid, and assistance in the form of resources and nurturance. One's family becomes a "haven" from the storm. To jeopardize this type of support system indefinitely is no small matter to be dismissed lightly. There are serious consequences that will result from tampering with the equilibrium that has been developed with one's family. Great care and caution need to be taken before men who have sex with men seriously consider threatening such a support system, especially when there is nothing to replace it, and/or the individual in question doesn't have the skills necessary to recreate an alternative support system. For these reasons, it is not surprising that men who have sex with men have maintained their connections with their extended families.

EDUCATIONAL ISSUES THAT CAN POTENTIALLY SABOTAGE THE CAREER DEVELOPMENT OF BLACK MEN WHO HAVE SEX WITH MEN

Black males rely on schools to provide them access to social, economic, and political mobility within our technological society. Thus, the school environment needs to be safe and conducive to learning. It is becoming increasingly apparent that social and emotional adjustments are just as important as predictors of scholastic performance and persistence in school as academic preparation (Monteiro & Fuqua, 1996). Racial and sexual orientation identity formation are strongly related to social and emotional adjustment, which in turn impact school achievement. Carlson (1997) asserts that gay and ethnic minority students and their world views are typically marginalized within the school community. Their voices are seldom heard or taken seriously. Instead, they are perceived by the school establishment as being deviant, different, and disempowered.

Pilkington and D'Augelli (1995) revealed that in a school setting, 38 percent of youth of color felt uncomfortable disclosing their sexual orientation. Forty-six percent of youth of color reported hiding their sexual orientation from other students. Nineteen percent of youth of color revealed that they had been physically hurt by another student. Forty-five percent of youth of color have hidden their sexual orientation identity from their teachers, and 6 percent reported being hurt by a teacher because of their sexual orientation. Twenty-eight percent of youth of color admitted that their openness about their sexual orientation identity was affected by fears of being physically hurt by students and teachers. These findings reveal a rather hostile environment in the schools that is not necessarily conducive to learning and academic achievement. Without a strong foundation during the primary and secondary school years, it becomes more difficult to benefit from post-secondary educational experiences, which are critical in our current technological society.

One area where we have relatively minimal information is how men who have sex with men navigate and negotiate the career development process that starts in high school. It is clear that LGBT populations have unique challenges finding assistance in navigating this process (Crouteau, Anderson, Distefano, & Kampa-Kokesch, 2000). Family and societal messages play influential roles in socializing how LGBT individuals develop their occupational interests and choices. Gay and bisexual men are more likely to embrace non-traditional occupations than are heterosexuals due to the process during sexual orientation identity formation where the masculinity construct undergoes a major transformation. Due to sexual prejudice and employment discrimination, gay and bisexual men are also more likely to have restricted occupational choices, since they tend to pursue career lines where there have already been trailblazers before them. Gay and bisexual men also tend to internalize the broader society's vocational stereotypes pertaining to homosexual and occupational choice, which influences what career lines they perceive to be available to them and worth expending energy to attain. The external environment plays a major role in rewarding and shaping the career development process of black male youth. Racial discrimination and unfair labor practices still make it difficult for black males to establish and maintain full-time employment. Without a strong educational background, that is virtually an unattainable goal.

RELIGIOUS INVOLVEMENT AS AN AMBIGUOUS PROTECTIVE BUFFER AMONG BLACK MEN WHO HAVE SEX WITH MEN

Much of the research conducted documenting a positive association between religious involvement and life satisfaction/psychological well-being is based on black samples where sexual orientation identity was presumed but never directly assessed (Levin, Chatters, & Taylor, 1995; Ellison & Taylor, 1996; Ellison, 1993, 1995). Anecdotal data suggest that white gay men, bisexuals, lesbians, and transgendered adults perceive their religious and spiritual practices to be central to their overall sense of self (Barret & Barzan, 1996; Halderman, 1996; Ritter & O'Neill, 1989). Boykin (1996b) and Weatherford and Weatherford (1999) revealed the phenomenological experiences of black men and women engaging in same-sex sexual behavior who remain invisible with the black church for fear of possible expulsion. The yearly or biannual gay bashing, homophobic sermon where the minister preaches against homosexuality is routinely tolerated in silence. Everyone is clearly aware that homosexuals are present in the congregation, but there is still total silence. These sermons serve a purpose, as Ellison (1997) explains:

> There is also a coercive dimension to the role of religious groups that merits more detailed investigations in the future. Religious institutions are institutions of social control, and may have the capacity to levy negative sanctions against deviant members. Persons who neglect family responsibilities, engage in negative lifestyles (e.g. idleness, infidelity/ promiscuity, substance abuse, criminality), or both may bear the brunt of gossip, direct rebukes, and other forms of social pressure from other church members. . . . This threat of ostracism may deter some individuals from indulging in habits and behaviors that might undermine family harmony and stability. (p. 129)

The black church has the potential to provide black men who have sex with men the support necessary to foster their psychological adjustment. Unfortunately, there also exists strong pressure to have all of their parishioners conform to a rather rigid and dogmatic set of lifestyle guidelines.

Alternatively, the gay affirmative church (such as Unity Fellowship) has the potential to foster and nurture the integration of racial and sexual orientation identities through three basic functions, as posited by O'Neill and Ritter (1992): affirming the inherent goodness of every human being, developing a sense of community, and providing access to God and/or a creator. This environment also has the potential to create a "haven," or protective buffer, from the pressures (such as acute and/or chronic stressors) of the outside world and can create a type of "second family" for its constituents. Such an environment can facilitate the development of opportunities for psychological empowerment.

THE AMBIVALENT ATTACHMENTS TO INTERRACIAL INTIMATE PARTNERS AMONG BLACK GAY MEN

Peplau, Cochran, and Mays (1997) sampled black men and women about their same-sex close relationships. The men were in their early thirties and had completed an average of three years of college. Most were employed full-time, and 31 percent earned more than $30,000 a year. The median annual income was $22,000. Most of these men self-labeled as gay (84.6 percent) or bisexual (10 percent). Another

5 percent did not self-label as gay or bisexual. Forty-two percent of these black gay men reported being involved in interracial relationships with white gay male partners. Three factors that accounted for 57 percent of the variance shed some light on the personal factors that led participants to select their partners: instrumental resources, such as a job, residence, income, and friends; inner personal attributes, such as personality, cultural sophistication, and spiritual energy; and physical attributes of the partner, like sexual abilities, ethnic background, and physical attractiveness. The relationship duration for these black gay men varied from less than one month to more than thirty-five years. Sixty-one percent reported being in love with their partners. Overall, they described their relationships as close and satisfying. With respect to commitment, 44 percent were currently living with their partners, which was perceived as one indicator of commitment. The men were less satisfied sexually with their current partners than black lesbians were. About 50 percent of these men reported that their relationships were monogamous, but since their relationships began, two thirds had had sex outside of their relationships and had a greater number of partners than did their black lesbian counterparts. Ninety-one percent of the black gay men revealed that this extra activity involved a male partner. Only a minority (19 percent) had told their partners about their extra-relationship sex.

When the researchers examined the correlates of relationship satisfaction, they found that only the inner attributes of the partner (personality, intelligence, spiritual energy, etc.) were found to be significantly associated with relationship satisfaction. Similarly, feelings of love and feeling emotionally close were also found to be significant correlates of relationship satisfaction. Finally, perceptions that one's partner was equally satisfied with their relationship was a significant correlate of relationship satisfaction for this sample.

Interestingly, sexual behavior inside and outside of the relationship was found to be associated with personal satisfaction. Greater sexual frequency, higher sexual satisfaction, and monogamy were all significantly associated with overall relationship satisfaction for men who have sex with men. The men's HIV status was not related to their ratings of relationship satisfaction, to their frequency of sex with their partners in the previous month, or to their sexual satisfaction. Likewise, one's partner's HIV status was not associated with relationship satisfaction, frequency of sex with their partner in the previous month, or sexual satisfaction. These findings give us a window into the close relationships of black gay men. It is unclear whether or not black men who have sex with men were sampled here. If they were, would they have reported similar findings?

Hopson and Hopson (1995) asserted that black heterosexual couples dating back to slavery viewed their own relationships as tied to the social and psychological strengths of the entire black community. White and Parham (1990) link collectivism with egalitarianism within black male/female relationships. Masculinity and femininity from this perspective are not mutually exclusive, and individuals possessing dual qualities (masculine and feminine traits) were highly valued. These relationships always need to be viewed within their sociohistorical/sociocultural context. Thus, blacks' affectionate and respectful behavioral exchanges are not just a function of their partner's behavior but also a function of the specific value orientation emphasizing oneness with the larger black community. This resource exchange of love and esteem appears to be governed by socioeconomic influences (Staples, 1985). Gaines, Buriel, Liu, and Rios (1997) have called for more empirical attention to assess these interpersonal relationship dynamics among black partners within the context of black same-sex close relationships. Gaines (1994) revealed that neither affection nor respect was reciprocated to a significant degree among black male–male couples.

More concerted empirical attention needs to be paid to diverse types of same-sex relationships, including among ethnically and culturally diverse men. In particular, how do perceived power and influence or the lack thereof (for example, a partner's ethnic minority status within the external environment) negatively impact the interpersonal dynamics within a same-sex relationship? (Bingham et al., 2003). Poon (2000) discusses how gay men of Asian descent may be more vulnerable to relationship violence within same-sex relationships with white partners. Similarly, Williams (1994) discusses how power, status, and the lack thereof within the external environment get displaced onto the close relationship dynamics leading to relationship violence among heterosexual black couples. Similar work needs to occur to provide some insight into the interpersonal dynamics that occur within same-sex relationship violence among ethnically and culturally diverse men who have sex with men, particularly interracial, same-sex couples. Williams and his colleagues have begun to address this topic (Richie, 2002).

SURVIVING AND THRIVING IN THE
WORKPLACE AMONG BLACK MEN WHO
HAVE SEX WITH MEN

The workplace is another arena that provides real challenges to black men who have sex with men. The issue becomes whether or not to reveal their same-sex sexual behavior outside or within this environment to co-workers, superiors, and so on. What type of climates exist within the workplace for employees who are "different?" What types of feedback, along a number of dimensions, both verbal and nonverbal, are being communicated by the administration/employees/staff concerning cultural diversity issues within the workplace? To what extent have all the levels of the organizational staff been adequately prepared to deal effectively with cultural diversity issues as they appear on the scene? What impact have cultural diversity issues had on work productivity? Work environments vary considerably to the extent that they have begun to address these issues. Black men who have sex with men are in a rather delicate position once they enter the work environment, since they don't self-label as gay or bisexual. If this aspect of their identity is revealed, what types of reactions will occur? More importantly, will they be able to navigate and negotiate the varying outcomes that may occur if this work environment is not inclusive?

One case study that may shed some light onto these issues is the qualitative research of Friskopp and Silverstein (1995) that focused a portion of attention on black, Asian/Pacific Islander, and Latino gay professionals who were graduates of Harvard Business School's MBA program and were entering corporate America. Many of these ethnic minority gay professionals chose to remain closeted at work for fear of the consequences to their career paths and development if they came "out." These individuals felt that it was doubly difficult to fit in. They perceived that there were social and career obstacles to promotions that they believed were almost impossible to surmount. Their experiences coping with gay racism within the white gay male community as well as the heterosexism/sexual prejudice within their ethnic minority communities did not prepare them to integrate their racial and sexual minorities within their work environments. What was interesting was that the subgroup of black gay professionals who did decide to come "out" in corporate America did not experience the retribution that they expected.

It is important to note that this sample is clearly an atypical sample that cannot be generalized to ethnic minority gay men. It does provide some provocative qualitative data concerning the perceptions of individuals possessing multiple minority identities that result in multiple oppressions and how corporate America responds to such individuals' overt behavior. What is interesting from a longitudinal perspective is that many of these gay male professionals with Harvard MBA degrees eventually became self-employed, starting their own small businesses outside of corporate America. What would be interesting is to better understand how the process that evolved as they entered corporate America impacted that decision.

A long-standing myth that exists is that gay men and lesbians are economically and educationally elite and therefore don't deserve any special treatment. In an independent study released by the University of Maryland–College Park, researchers documented that the gay population was as economically and socially diverse as any other subgroup. The study reported an average annual income of $26,321 for gay men and $15,056 for lesbians, and concluded that they earned 11 percent to 27 percent less than heterosexual men and 5 percent to 14 percent less than heterosexual women, respectively (Winfeld & Spielman, 1995). When one adds race and ethnicity to this equation, variability in annual income and educational attainment become even more pronounced among gay men and lesbians.

MULTIPLE MINORITY STRESSORS EXPERIENCED BY BLACK MEN WHO HAVE SEX WITH MEN

Franklin (1999) has coined the phrase *the invisibility syndrome* to describe the inner struggles of black men who believe their talents, abilities, personality, and worth are not valued or recognized due to prejudice and discrimination. There are seven dynamic elements to the invisibility syndrome that are related to the repeated daily hassles black men encounter: (1) one feels a lack of recognition or appropriate acknowledgment, (2) one feels there is no satisfaction or gratification from the encounter, (3) one feels self-doubt and the lack of legitimacy, (4) there is no validation from the experience, (5) one feels disrespected, (6) one's sense of dignity is compromised and challenged, and (7) one's basic identity is shaken, if not uprooted. It is the social construction of racism that provided the foundation for these acts of prejudice and discrimination (Franklin, 1999; Davis, 1999).

Black men, as a result of this process, seldom feel a part of the mainstream culture, and this invisibility impacts their beliefs and attitudes as well as their sense of self and self-esteem. Similarly, being invisible also results in the need to manage elevated levels of stress and anxiety. Franklin (1998) defined these reactions as *microaggressions*—subtle acts or activities experienced as hostile and that fit a personal history and pattern of racial slights and disregard. These realities cut across the mainstream heterosexual culture as well as within the white gay male community (Boykin, 1996a). Black men who have sex with men experience the cumulative effects of these minority stressors (racism, gay racism, sexual prejudice, etc.) even more intensely than traditional black men due to their multiple minority identities resulting in multiple oppressions (DiPlacido, 1998).

SEXUAL PREJUDICE EXPERIENCED BY BLACK MEN WHO HAVE SEX WITH MEN WITHIN THE BLACK COMMUNITY IS STILL UNCLEAR EMPIRICALLY

It is commonly asserted that homosexuality is less tolerated within the black community than in the white community (Ernst et al., 1991). Unfortunately, there are very few empirical data sets that document this "reality." When Ernst et al. (1991) sampled state employees' responses to the statement "AIDS will help society by reducing the number of homosexuals (gay people)," it was not surprising that black females were more likely to endorse this statement than were white females. There were no differences between black males and white males in their endorsements of this item. These authors interpret these data as a reflection of the reality that gay black men are one more way to reduce the already shrinking pool of available, "eligible" (to women) black single men.

Interestingly, Herek and Capitanio (1995), in a two-wave telephone survey with a national probability sample of 391 black heterosexual adults, did not replicate Ernst et al. (1991). Sexual prejudice clearly exists within the black community, but it does not appear to be at elevated levels compared with whites. Based on anecdotal evidence from both gay black men as well as black men who have sex with men, it appears that there still exists sexual prejudice in the mainstream culture as well as the black community, and it inhibits everyone by limiting their choices and their opportunities to grow and integrate these different aspects of their identities. This inhibiting becomes even more problematic when one considers that black men, as a group, are still being viewed as an "endangered species" (Gibbs, 1988).

STRATEGIES FOR COMBATING PREJUDICE AND DISCRIMINATION AGAINST BLACK MEN WHO HAVE SEX WITH MEN

As one can tell from the toolbox for change below, from an ecological level of analysis, prejudice and discrimination need to be combated along a number of levels. Individuals need to begin to acknowledge their biases and begin the process of embracing human diversity. The social science literature is clear that the best way to induce attitude change is to establish and maintain relationships that challenge our pre-existing stereotypes and beliefs. This strategy works the best when the parties are involved in a cooperative activity where the outcome is important to both parties. This is a real challenge for this group, since black men who have sex with men tend to be invisible and are reluctant to come "out" to anyone, particularly relative strangers. A more accessible group to start off this process would be black gay men who are "out."

Work on the prevention of HIV infection/AIDS, here in the United States and now around the world, has taught that the adoption of viable prevention programs relies heavily on tailoring these programs to the needs of specific communities. Thus, one size does not fit all. As mentioned earlier in this chapter, the explanations for why one community engages in behavior can have no relevance whatsoever for another community. Thus, culturally informed programs tailored to the communities in need of services are the only way to directly impact attitudes and behavior (Brooks, Rotheram-Borus, Bing, Ayala, & Henry, 2003; Diaz, 1998). There are still many communities that resist such a notion. Their community leaders believe that all communities are alike and we are all human beings with the same needs. These leaders need to be comfortable in restructuring existing institutions to become more inclusive of the diversity within our midst and to service the populations that are presently in need of their services (Richie, 2002). Similarly, lawmakers need to become more inclusive when developing social policy. This means taking into consideration from the outset the considerable intra-individual differences that exist with groups and crafting social policy that acknowledges that reality. White and Cones (1999), Jones (1994), and Watts and Jagers (1997) have excellent suggestions and recommendations for community interventions that can dramatically improve the lives of black men.

Finally, practitioners and educators have a professional/ethical obligation to provide services to ethnically and culturally diverse populations that seek their assistance. This objective needs to permeate every aspect of the delivery of services and would necessitate retraining (both didactic and experiential) and restructuring existing interventions and treatment/curriculum protocols. This would mean conceptualizing case materials in radically different ways, providing quality multicultural supervision, and re-conceptualizing the process treatment/education and outcome (Schiele, 2000; de Anda & Becerra, 2000). There still exists considerable resistance by both practitioners and educators toward embracing human diversity in all of its forms. Once again, only through continued didactic and experiential training can this process successfully unfold in the twenty-first century.

Toolbox for Change

For	Images/perceptions	Strategies for change
Individuals	Clinging unconsciously to racist and homophobic beliefs (such as feelings of inferiority) about racial and sexual minorities. One's beliefs impact one's overt behavior.	Establishing and maintaining relationships over time with racial and sexual minorities who challenge one's pre-existing stereotypes and belief systems.
Community	Resistance to embracing human diversity. Resistance to the development of culturally informed primary, secondary, and tertiary prevention, as well as empowerment programs.	Dramatic changes in the structure and operation of institutions. Social policy that is more inclusive of racially and culturally diverse groups.
Practitioners/ educators	Resistance to multicultural education perspectives, and the heterogeneity that exists within racial and sexual minorities.	Exposure to didactic and experiential training based on the Afrocentric paradigm.

REFERENCES

Adams, C. L., Jr., & Kimmel, D. C. (1997). Exploring the lives of older African-American gay men. In B. Greene (Ed.), *Ethnic and cultural diversity among lesbians and gay men. Psychological perspectives on lesbian and gay issues* (Vol. 3, pp. 132–151). Thousand Oaks, CA: Sage Publications.

Barret, R., & Barzan, R. (1996). Spiritual experiences of gay men and lesbians. *Counseling Values, 41,* 4–15.

Bingham, T. A., Harawa, N. T., Johnson, D. F., Secura, G. M., MacKellar, D. A., & Valleroy, L. A. (2003). The effect of partner characteristics on HIV infection among African-American men who have sex with men in the young men's survey, Los Angeles, 1999–2000. *AIDS Education and Prevention, 15, Supplement A,* 39–52.

Boykin, K. (1996a). Gay racism. In K. Boykin (Ed.), *One more river to cross: Black and gay in America* (pp. 212–235). New York: Doubleday.

Boykin, K. (1996b). *One more river to cross: Black and gay in America.* New York: Doubleday.

Brooks, R., Rotheram-Borus, M. J., Bing, E. G., Ayala, G., & Henry, C. L. (2003). HIV and AIDS among men of color who have sex with men and men of color who have sex with men and women: An epidemiological profile. *AIDS Education and Prevention, 15, Supplement A,* 1–6.

Campbell, C. A. (1995). Male gender roles and sexuality: Implications for women's AIDS risk and prevention. *Social Science and Medicine, 41*(2), 197–210.

Carlson, D. (1997). Gayness, multicultural education, and community. In M. Seller & L. Weis (Eds.), *Beyond black and white: New faces and voices in U.S. schools* (pp. 233–255). Albany, NY: State University of New York Press.

Cross, W. E., Jr., & Phagen-Smith, P. E. (2001). Patterns of African-American identity development: A life-span perspective. In C. L. Wijeyesinghe & B. W. Jackson III (Eds.), *New perspectives on racial identity development: A theoretical and practical anthology* (pp. 243–270). New York: New York University Press.

Crouteau, J. M., Anderson, M. Z., Distefano, T. M., & Kampa-Kokesch, S. (2000). Lesbian, gay, and bisexual vocational psychology: Reviewing foundations and planning construction. In R. M. Perez, K. A. DeBord, & K. J. Bieschke (Eds.), *Handbook of counseling and psychotherapy with lesbian, gay, and bisexual clients* (pp. 383–408). Washington, DC: American Psychological Association.

Davis, L. E. (Ed.). (1999). *Working with African-American males: A guide to practice.* Thousand Oaks, CA: Sage Publications.

de Anda, D., & Becerra, R. M. (Eds.). (2000). *Violence: Diverse populations and communities.* Binghamton, NY: Haworth Press.

Diaz, R. M. (1998). *Latino gay men and HIV: Culture, sexuality, and risk behavior.* New York: Routledge.

DiPlacido, J. (1988). Minority stress among lesbians, gay men, and bisexuals: A consequence of heterosexism, homophobia, and stigmatization. In G. M. Herek (Ed.), *Stigma and sexual orientation: Understanding prejudice against lesbians, gay men, and bisexuals* (pp. 138–159). Thousand Oaks, CA: Sage Publications.

Ellison, C. G. (1993). Religious involvement and self-perceptions among black Americans. *Social Forces, 71*(4), 1027–1055.

Ellison, C. G. (1995). Race, religious involvement, and depressive symptomatology in a southeastern U.S. community. *Social Science and Medicine, 40*(11), 1561–1572.

Ellison, C. G. (1997). Religious involvement and the subjective quality of family life among African-Americans. In R. J. Taylor, J. S. Jackson, & L. M. Chatters (Eds.), *Family life in black America* (pp. 117–131). Thousand Oaks, CA: Sage Publications

Ellison, C. G., & Taylor, R. J. (1996). Turning to prayer: Social and situational antecedents of religious coping among African-Americans. *Review of Religious Research, 38*(2), 111–131.

Ernst, F. A., Francis, R. A., Nevels, H., & Lemeh, C. A. (1991). Condemnation of homosexuality in the black community: A gender-specific phenomenon? *Archives of Sexual Behavior, 20*(6), 579–585.

Etzkorn, J. P. (1995). Gay identity and involvement in the gay community among African-American and white gay men (Doctoral dissertation, University of Texas–Austin). *Dissertation Abstracts International 56,* 461A.

Franklin, A. J. (1998). Invisibility syndrome in the psychotherapy with African-American males. In R. L. Jones (Ed.), *African-American mental health* (pp. 395–411). Hampton, VA: Cobb & Henry Publishers.

Franklin, A. J. (1999). Invisibility syndrome and racial identity development in the psychotherapy and counseling of African American men. *The Counseling Psychologist, 27*(6), 761–793.

Friskopp, A., & Silverstein, S. (1995). Straight jobs, gay lives: Gay and lesbian professionals, the Harvard Business School, and the American workplace. New York: Scribner.

Gaines, S. O., Jr. (1994). Exchange of respect-denying behaviors among male-female friendships. *Journal of Social and Personal Relationships, 11,* 5–24.

Gaines, S. O., Jr., Buriel, R., Liu, J. H., & Rios, D. I. (1997). *Culture, ethnicity, and personal relationship processes.* New York: Routledge.

Gibbs, J. T. (Ed.). (1988). *Young, black, and male in America: An endangered species.* Westport, CT: Auburn House.

Halderman, D. C. (1996). Spirituality and religion in the lives of lesbians and gay men. In R. P. Cabaj & T. S. Stein (Eds.), *Textbook of homosexuality and mental health* (pp. 881–896). Washington, DC: American Psychiatric Press.

Hatchett, S. J. (1991). Women and men. In J. S. Jackson (Ed.), *Life in black America* (pp. 84–104). Newbury Park, CA: Sage Publications.

Heckman, T. G., Kelly, J. A., Bogart, L. M., Kalichman, S. C., & Rompa, D. J. (1999). HIV risk differences between African-American and white men who have sex with men. *Journal of the National Medical Association, 91*(2), 92–100.

Herek, G. M. (1987). On heterosexual masculinity: Some psychical consequences of the social construction of gender and sexuality. In M. S. Kimmel (Ed.), *Changing men: New directions in research on men and masculinity* (pp. 68–82). Newbury Park, CA: Sage Publications.

Herek, G. M., & Capitanio, J. P. (1995). Black heterosexuals' attitudes toward lesbians and gay men in the United States. *Journal of Sex Research, 32*(2), 95–105.

Hill, R. B. (1999). *The strengths of African-American families: Twenty-five years later.* Lanham, MD: University Press of America.

Hopson, D. S., & Hopson, D. P. (1995). *Friends, lovers, and soul mates: A guide to better relationships between black men and women.* New York: Fireside.

Jones, D. J. (Ed.). (1994). *African-American males: A critical link in the African-American family.* New Brunswick, NJ: Transaction Publishers.

Landrine, H. (1995). Cultural diversity, contextualism, and feminist psychology. In H. Landrine (Ed.), *Bringing cultural diversity to feminist psychology: Theory, research, and practice* (pp. 1–20). Washington, DC: American Psychological Association.

Lazur, R. F., & Majors, R. (1995). Men of color: Ethnocultural variations of male gender role strain. In R. F. Levant & W. S. Pollack (Eds.), *A new psychology of men* (pp. 337–358). New York: Basic Books.

Levin, J. S., Chatters, L. M., & Taylor, R. J. (1995). Religious effects on health status and life satisfaction among black Americans. *Journal of Gerontology: Social Sciences, 50B*(3), S154–S163.

Lewis, D. K. (1975). The black family: Socialization and sex roles. *Phylon, 36*, 221–237.

Marable, M. (1995). The black male: Searching beyond stereotypes. In M. S. Kimmel & M. A. Messner (Eds.), *Men's lives* (pp. 26–32). Boston: Allyn & Bacon.

Monteiro, K. P., & Fuqua, V. (1996). African American gay youth: One form of manhood. In K. P. Monteiro (Ed.), *Ethnicity and psychology: African-, Asian-, Latino- and Native American psychologies* (pp. 59–78). Dubuque, IA: Kendall-Hunt Publishers.

Morales, E. (1990). Ethnic minority families and minority gays and lesbians. In F. W. Bozett & M. B. Sussman (Eds.), *Homosexuality and family relations* (pp. 217–239). Binghamton, NY: Harrington Park Press.

Morales, E. (1996). Gender roles among Latino gay and bisexual men: Implications for family and couple relationships. In J. Laird & R. Jay-Green (Eds.), *Lesbians and gays in couples and families: A handbook for therapists* (pp. 272–297). San Francisco: Jossey-Bass Publishers.

Myers, H. F., Javanbakht, M., Martinez, M., & Obediah, S. (2003). Psychosocial predictors of risky sexual behaviors among African-American men: Implications for prevention, *AIDS Education and Prevention, 15, Supplement A,* 66–79.

Nobles, W. W. (1996). Africanity and the black family. In K. P. Monteiro (Ed.), *Ethnicity and psychology: African-, Asian-, Latino-, and Native-American psychologies* (pp. 100–113). Dubuque, IA: Kendall-Hunt Publishers.

O'Neill, C., & Ritter, K. (1992). *Coming out within: Stages of spiritual awakening for lesbians and gay men.* San Francisco: Harper and Row.

Peplau, L. A., Cochran, S. D., & Mays, V. M. (1997). A national survey of the intimate relationships of African-American lesbians and gay men: A look at commitment, satisfaction, sexual behavior, and HIV disease. In B. Greene (Ed.), *Ethnic and cultural diversity among lesbians and gay men. Psychological perspectives on lesbian and gay issues* (Vol. 3, pp. 11–38). Thousand Oaks, CA: Sage Publications.

Pilkington, N. W., & D'Augelli, A. R. (1995). Victimization of lesbian, gay, and bisexual youth in community settings. *Journal of Community Psychology, 23,* 34–56.

Poon, M. K. (2000). Inter-racial same-sex abuse: The vulnerability of gay men of Asian descent in relationships with Caucasian men. *Journal of Gay and Lesbian Social Services: Issues in Practice, Policy & Research, 11*(4), 39–67.

Richie, B. E. (2002). Lesbian, gay, bisexual and transgendered session. In O. Williams (Ed.), *Community insights on domestic violence among African-Americans: Conversations about domestic violence and other issues affecting their community* (pp. 26–29). St. Paul: University of Minnesota Press.

Ritter, K. Y., & O'Neill, C. W. (1989). Moving through loss: The spiritual journey of gay men and lesbian women. *Journal of Counseling and Development, 68,* 9–15.

Schiele, J. H. (2000). *Human services and the Afrocentric paradigm.* Binghamton, NY: Haworth Press.

Smith, A. (1998). Cultural diversity and the coming out process: Implications for clinical practice. In B. Greene (Ed.), *Ethnic and cultural diversity among lesbians and gay men. Psychological perspectives on lesbians and gay issues* (Vol. 3, pp. 279–300). Thousand Oaks, CA: Sage Publications.

Staples, R. (1985). Change in black family structure: The conflict between family ideology and structural conditions. *Journal of Marriage and the Family, 47,* 1005–1013.

Staples, R. (1995). Stereotypes of black male sexuality: The facts behind the myths. In M. S. Kimmel & M. A. Messner (Eds.), *Men's lives* (3rd ed., pp. 375–380). Boston: Allyn & Bacon.

St. Lawrence, J. S., Eldridge, G. D., Reitman, D., Little, C. E., Shelby, M. C., & Brasfield, T. L. (1998). Factors influencing condom use among African-American women: Implications for risk reduction intervention. *American Journal of Community Psychology, 26*(1), 7–28.

Vandiver, B. J., et al. (2000). *The Cross Racial Identity Scale*. Unpublished scale.

Vandiver, B. J., Cross, W. E., Jr., Worrell, F. C., & Fhagen-Smith, P.E. (2002). Validating the Cross Racial Identity Scale. *Journal of Counseling Psychology, 49*(1), 71–85.

Watts, R. J., & Jagers, R. J. (Eds.). (1997). *Manhood development in urban African-American communities*. Binghamton, NY: Haworth Press.

Weatherford, R. J., & Weatherford, C. B. (1999). *Somebody's knocking at your door: AIDS and the African-American church*. Binghamton, NY: Haworth Pastoral Press.

White, J. L., & Cones III, J. H. (1999). *Black man emerging: Facing the past and seizing a future in America*. New York: W. H. Freeman and Company.

White, J. L., & Parham, T. A. (1990). *The psychology of blacks: An African-American perspective*. Englewood Cliffs, NJ: Prentice-Hall.

Williams, O. (1994). Group work with African-American men who batter: Toward more ethnically-sensitive practice. *Journal of Comparative Family Studies, 25*(1), 91–103.

Winfeld, L., & Spielman, S. (1995). Straight talk about gays in the workplace: Creating an inclusive, productive environment for everyone in your organization. New York: American Management Association.

Wingood, G. M., & DiClemente, R. J. (1997). The effects of an abusive primary partner on the condom use and sexual negotiation practices of African-American women. *American Journal of Public Health, 87*(6), 1016–1018.

Wingood, G. M., & DiClemente, R. J. (1998). Partner influences and gender-related factors associated with noncondom use among young adult African-American women. *American Journal of Community Psychology, 26*(1), 29–51.

Wyatt et al. (1997). Adapting a comprehensive approach to African-American women's sexual risk taking. *Journal of Health Education, 28*(6), 52–59.

CHAPTER 10

Coping among Victims of Sexual Prejudice and Discrimination

Martin Kantor

W e cannot eliminate all the prejudice and discrimination in the world. Most of us are potential targets due to one characteristic or another. We hear a lot about prejudice and discrimination regarding race, ethnicity, gender, and sexual orientation. We hear less about other prejudice and discrimination that are just as commonly targeted to people based on their body size, disability, dress, and appearance. The overarching principle in the following discussion is that in coping with and managing prejudice and discrimination, knowledge is power that gives targets of prejudice and discrimination both the ability to succeed in life personally and professionally in the face of bigots' attempts to put obstacles in their way, and also the means to maintain their self-esteem in the face of bigots' attempts to lower it.

In my view, there are not just one but many types of prejudice and discrimination, and each requires a somewhat different corrective. My method for handling bigotry is a six-step approach that outlines a practical, doable method for handling the different types of prejudice and discrimination, based on understanding each specific type.

As a psychiatrist with over forty years of clinical experience with patients, I have seen literally hundreds of psychiatric patients for evaluation and therapy, some of whom have been hard-core bigots and others who have shown bigoted tendencies. I have previously addressed issues of psychopathology in general, and specifically the psychopathology of bigotry, in my books, particularly *Homophobia,* where the reader can find more clinical examples of bigotry, as well as references to the origins and sources of my theoretical assumptions.

The following discussion emphasizes methods for coping with and managing homophobia, but this is a generic method that may apply to all forms of bigotry, ranging from xenophobia to anti-Semitism, with the details varying only slightly according to who the targets of the moment are. For example, a mindset that is characteristic of all bigots is the need to stereotype by tarring all members of a class with the same brush, paradoxically discriminating against all members of a class by *failing* to discriminate between them. The following discussion also couples theoretical postulates with specific antitheses. When no specific antithesis is offered, the reader can safely assume that the general principles mentioned throughout apply.

IDENTIFY HIDDEN PREJUDICE AND SECRET DISCRIMINATION

Denying prejudice and discrimination can temporarily spare a target's feelings, but this denial will not solve the serious and often permanent emotional and practical problems that prejudice and discrimination create. Therefore, the targets are better off spotting prejudice and discrimination when and where they exist. They need to know when and where they have been discriminated against, and that they are not just imagining it or thinking that they are paranoid when in fact they are being persecuted. The following detailed discussion of bigotry can provide the targets of bigotry with the raw material they need to identify prejudice and discrimination, thereby distinguishing reality from imagination.

UNDERSTAND THE BIGOT'S ILLOGIC

To protect themselves against the inroads bigots make on their emotions and in their lives, targets of prejudice and discrimination should try to understand scientifically how bigots think. They can profitably identify the cognitive errors that make up bigoted theories. Understanding these cognitive errors highlights how irrational bigotry is. Knowing that bigotry is irrational helps targets of prejudice and discrimination cope by strongly suggesting that the rationale for the bigotry is seriously flawed.

Bigots are often sophists who, like all sophists, reason well though falsely. They can often reason more effectively than all but those victims best prepared to spot the fallacy of their thinking. They can do this because they tend to be shrewd, preoccupied with their bigotry, and have an emotional need to devalue others. Here are some of the specific logical fallacies (cognitive errors), both gross and subtle, that contribute to the sophistry that is inherent in bigotry.

Delusional Thinking

The thinking of many bigots, especially those who are paranoid, is characterized by what are called *primary delusions*. Just as some emotionally troubled individuals think that they are Napoleon and make their case for being Napoleon by announcing "I am he," then refusing to entertain rational arguments to the contrary, bigots deem their bashing to be right and justified because they "just know" that their targets are defective. Like people who think that they are Napoleon, bigots, when asked how they know that what they say is so, respond, "because I know it." As bigots see it, they are right to devalue you because you are devalued by their definition of things. Showing no willingness to brook even the best evidential argument to the contrary, they instead respond to even the most cogent counterarguments by repeating themselves. It does not fluster the anti-Semite to be reminded that Albert Einstein was a Jew any more than it flusters today's "Napoleon" to learn that we have the original's dead body. Their confident assertions lend their bigotry an air of expertise, and their self-deception makes it possible for them to stun and mesmerize their targets.

Paranoid Thinking

Bigots tend to condemn others for doing the same things that they themselves think and do, after conveniently forgetting that they themselves also think and do them. They tend to be hypocritical individuals who project their own unacceptable attitudes and desires, like the patient who denied that he had homosexual feelings, which he felt guilty about, by condemning others for being homosexual. Disappointment around a sense of personal failure is also externalized, as in "The reason I am not working is not that no one will hire me because I do not have the skills, but that all the immigrants around here took all the good jobs," or "Who can get anywhere in Hollywood when the Jews, gays, and lesbians control the whole town?" Such bigots scapegoat others so that they can deny that their problems are due to their own shortcomings. They also rationalize their victim-bashing this way, making it okay to "beat up faggots and foreigners."

Antithesis

Targets of these bigots can help counter the effects of the prejudice and discrimination by realizing the impersonal nature of the attacks. They can reframe the statements of bigots as the self-statements that they in fact are. They can realize, "He is not talking about me," or "She is talking about herself." They can remind themselves that behind every bigoted criticism of another is a criticism of oneself, that, in the vernacular, "It takes one to know one."

Backward Reasoning

Here bigots start with a conclusion, then collect only that evidence that supports their initial premise.

Part-to-Whole Thinking

Here bigots take a slice of reality and make it the entire thing by a process of magnification. The stereotyping that characterizes bigotry involves viewing rare, uncharacteristic, exotic, or nonexistent behaviors as typical of a whole class, and as serious and widespread. In the view of bigots, *all* Irish are complete sots who drink and talk too much; *all* Jews are cheap, money-grubbing hoarders; *all* blacks (but especially those encountered on a dark street) are dangerous; *all* Puerto Ricans are lazy and shiftless; *all* Italians are gangsters and buffoons who wear gold chains or dark-colored Zegna suits; and *all* Asians are sinister individuals not to be trusted. Practically speaking, a class is defined according to one or more assumed *negative* (not positive) characteristics of that class, forgetting that within any class there are many subclasses, and within subclasses there are many different individual styles, so that in effect the class itself does not really exist.

Selective abstraction is a form of part-to-whole thinking that, according to Beck (1985), involves drawing conclusions about a situation or event based on "a [single] detail taken out of context[,] ignoring other, more salient features of the situation, and conceptualizing the whole experience on the basis of this element" (p. 1437).

Assigning Guilt by Association

Bigots put their targets in an excessively negative light by grading them based on the people who sometimes surround them, for example, viewing all gay men as sissified.

Paralogical Predicative Thinking

According to Jules R. Bemporad and Henry Pinsker (1974), in paralogical predicative thinking, "the slightest similarity between items or events becomes a connecting link that makes them identical" (p. 532). The purpose is to create a new reality along desired lines. For example, many bigots reason falsely that if A can be meaningfully equated with B in any respect, and C can be meaningfully equated with B in any respect, then A = C. Thus, I (A) am a virgin (B). The Virgin Mary (C) is a virgin (B). Therefore I (A) am the Virgin Mary (C). In similar manner, homophobes who want to avoid recognizing that gay men and lesbians can be soldiers and sailors just as well as anyone else use the slightest (justified, or in this case, unjustified) similarity and force it into a connective link, concluding that gay (A) = feminine (B), girl (C) = feminine (B), so gay (A) = girl (C) (and girls can't fight).

Ad Hominem Reasoning

In ad hominem reasoning, criticism of the producer leads to falsely negative evaluation of the product, so that the work is judged by a preinstalled negative opinion of the worker. As one troubled veteran said to me, "What do gay men do in the trenches? Their nails."

Tangential Thinking

Tangential thinkers use minor, incremental, logical distortions to create large, major, illogical leaps. Their logical distortions are each so small, their falsifications each so gradual, and their shifts each so imperceptible that the process as a whole becomes convincing. Bigots use tangential thinking to strike fear into the hearts of the general public by creating the illusion that those they target are poised to get out of control. For example, they might "prove" that gay marriage is unacceptable because it breaks the currently accepted social mold, which breaks with tradition, which creates a generation of nontraditionalists, who will create a new, nontraditional society, which will overthrow the old, established world order—a familiar example of how bigoted tangential thinking crawls rather than leaps from false premise to false conclusion.

Absolutistic and Dichotomous Thinking

In this black and white thinking, an individual is, or groups of individuals are, divided into all-good and all-bad, pigeonholed, and judged accordingly.

Emotional Thinking

According to Robert J. Ursano and Edward K. Silberman (1988), emotional thinking leads to inexact labeling, which involves labeling "events in proportion to one's emotional response to them rather than according to the facts of the situation" (p. 870).

However, not all bigotry is the product of illogical thinking. Some is pure dissimulation for effect, as when a politician makes a certain group a common enemy in an election year just so that he or she can win an election. This kind of bigotry is manipulative, and its goal is to obtain a specific advantage, such as a competitive edge. Also, some bigotry is due to ignorance, which can in turn be due to inadequate schooling or poor briefing.

Antithesis

Targets of bigotry need to analyze the bigots' logic to uncover the logical errors. They might start a journal with two columns on the page—on the left, the bigoted reality, and on the right, the comparative truth. That way, the irrationality behind prejudice and discrimination will become clear, and the targets will realize that since bigots make very little sense, the exact details of what they say are of very little importance. A sample journal entry might show on the left, "If you are gay, you will make a bad soldier," and on the right, "Lawrence of Arabia." Another might show on the left, "If you are a woman, you will make a bad soldier," and on the right, "Joan of Arc."

RECOGNIZE THE DIFFERENT MODELS OF BIGOTRY

Different models of bigotry tend to be favored by different bigots depending on each bigot's individual personality and profession. The following discussion focuses on homophobia not only for itself but also as a paradigm of bigotry—that is, it generally applies equally to all forms of bigotry, ranging from xenophobia to anti-Semitism. Distinguishing among the types is corrective, for there is a different antithesis for each. Thus the antithesis of religious bigotry may involve joining a different church; the antithesis for sociocultural/political bigotry may require activism; and the antithesis for medical-model bigotry may require understanding that people who are emotionally troubled need to be cured, not taken seriously.

The Religious Model

The *religious* model supposedly tells us that homosexuals are sinners. Persons who espouse that model are not merely religious but *scrupulously* religious individuals. They may be grandiose proselytizers who "know" that they know right from wrong. Sometimes they even consult with God so that they can act as His emissary to spread the Word. This model is ingrained in much of society, and it is a very dangerous one because many gays and lesbians, already self-homophobic for some of the same reasons that others are homophobic about them, imagine themselves to be sinners and take such accusations seriously and personally.

Antithesis

Gays and lesbians or other targets of religious bigotry need to tell themselves over and over again that they are hearing only from the minority: scrupulously religious people are, in reality, just fanatics and extremists with a religious bent, who additionally like the public eye and know how to get it focused on them. Many observers would agree that *truly* religious people either have few thoughts on matters bigoted or view gays and lesbians like they view everyone else: as people with flaws and virtues in the usual proportion.

Targets of those religious homophobes who regularly quote the Bible should take a few moments and read the Bible to see what it actually contains. They should also remember that there are problems of translation that might warp the original Biblical messages that come down to us. Who is to say, for example, that the translation we are reading is not the work of an original homophobe who has taken words with multiple meanings and bent them to his or her will?

In summary, targets of religious prejudice and discrimination should understand that truly religious people are out to discover God's intent and to spread His word, but bigoted fanatic religious people are not out to mouth God's word, but to put words into God's mouth.

Those who seriously buy into the concept that they are sinners, that is, those who introject the bigot's words and cannot shake loose from them, may have an underlying emotional problem such as obsessionalism or depression. They may for that reason benefit from seeking personal therapy.

The Sociocultural/Political Model

In the *sociocultural/political* model of homophobia, gays and lesbians are forced into the role of participating in the bigot's game of playing a special card, for example, the race card. They might hear, "Gays and lesbians are a threat to the legitimate family, so vote for me and I'll take care of that problem" just as Latinos might hear that they "are entirely responsible for California going broke, so vote for me and I'll bridge the budget gap on their backs."

Often in this model, gays and lesbians are perceived to be eccentrics, that is, not part of the mainstream. There is a good deal of condescension here, usually for the purpose of keeping the target in his or her place. In this view, "it is okay to be gay, but not in my family," just as "it is okay to be a Jew, but I wouldn't want my daughter marrying one."

Antithesis

This consists chiefly of social activism, such as disseminating information about what minority groups are really like and getting out the vote. Of course all individuals, minority group or not, have a social responsibility to act locally in a way that gives the group they belong to a good reputation in the community.

The Medical Model

In the *medical* model of homophobia, the homosexual is not well but sick and needs to be cured. Some therapists—called reparative therapists—espouse this model of homosexuality and set about to cure gays and lesbians of their homosexuality. They often present case examples of what they call successful cures, which they may be able to do because they treat a select group—gays and lesbians who apply for therapy to go straight and are therefore by definition already in conflict about their homosexuality. In my professional experience, the patients they "cure" are not committed homosexuals but straights just going through a gay phase—bisexuals of the moment who might easily have tipped anyway even without therapy.

Antithesis

Targets of this medical model need to realize that they are not sick. Except for those who are homosexuals in serious conflict about their homosexuality and those who are really bisexual, the best idea is to not get involved in any form of therapy that is primarily geared to changing sexual orientation.

It is the view of many therapists today that while homosexuals do sometimes need psychotherapy like anyone else, the treatment should be directed not to the homosexuality itself but to the manifestations of emotional disorder that exist in the person who is homosexual, often for reasons that are unrelated to the homosexuality itself.

The Biological Model

A subtype of the medical model is the *biological* model, where individuals such as gays and lesbians, gypsies, Jews, or aborigines are viewed not as sinners, objects of political convenience, deviates, or sick, but as defectives, inferiors, or mutants. Those who espouse this model mention genetic issues often and proclaim that their only concern is that their targets will breed and destroy society as we know it. In extreme cases, they go beyond genetics to eugenics, and we hear of camps and sterilizations for the greater good.

Antithesis

Gays and lesbians should clearly recognize that no one group is genetically inferior to another and that no transmissible "inferior" gene characterizing a whole group has ever been discovered.

TREAT BIGOTS AS IF THEY WERE EMOTIONALLY TROUBLED INDIVIDUALS

While the medical model of homosexuality is a form of bigotry, the medical model of bigotry offers useful insight that can help victims avoid being intimidated. It does so by revealing that *serious* bigots are troubled individuals with emotional problems diagnosable even without formal psychological training and manageable according to diagnosis-based therapeutic methods worked out over the years and easily adopted for laymen. The operative principle here is that someone who is seriously emotionally disturbed is likely to be wrong about many things.

As mentioned in the book *Homophobia* (1998), homophobia goes far beyond being simply a sociopolitical matter. It is not only learned or something that all those healthy guys down at the sports bar are saying and doing, and it is more than fear based purely on ignorance and unfamiliarity. *Serious* bigotry of the homophobic kind is profitably viewed as a symptom of one or more underlying emotional problems. That is, much bigotry that passes as intellectual is in fact emotional. Prejudice, like neurosis, serves a defensive purpose, relieving anxiety and enhancing self-esteem, which is why Henry Pinsker says, "Prejudice, serving an adaptive function, will not go away" (2003). The inescapable conclusion is that since serious bigotry is in structure and content akin to an obsession or a delusion, it is appropriate to manage serious bigotry as one would manage any other deeply rooted emotional disorder, giving it the same clinical understanding and therapeutic care that one might lavish on any other psychological illness: applying familiar therapeutic methods to influence the masses, or one by one the individuals who make up those masses. Bigotry targets who know this have a whole new method for handling the homophobes, xenophobes, anti-Semites, and others of like kind who trouble them.

However, it must be emphasized that the equivalency is a rough one, that is, while there are distinct similarities between bigotry and emotional disorder, there are also some differences, and so the analogy at some point breaks down. For one thing, any bigoted person is part of and a reflection of his or her society. As Mautner notes (2003), we all learn attitudes and behaviors from media (print, television), and there is observational learning as children learn attitudes and behaviors from their parents. For another thing, the psychopathology in question may in effect be the psychopathology of everyday life. That is, while the bigotry is structurally psychopathological, the psychopathology does not rise to the level of a full emotional disorder and so does not constitute one. However, the differences should not obscure the similarities and lead to the blanket assertion that homophobia is purely a socially learned behavior that can be socially unlearned via better education of the individual and the greater enlightenment of social institutions. This is because you cannot unlearn mental illness easily, and that in turn partly accounts for why prejudice and discrimination rarely yield simply to confrontation and arguments to the contrary.

Paranoid Bigotry

Most serious students of homophobia recognize that paranoid mechanisms are causative in at least some cases. Homophobes who use paranoid mechanisms condemn the homosexual desires of others in order to deny that they have homosexual feelings of their own.

Antithesis

At least theoretically, managing paranoid homophobia involves cognitive restructuring—focusing on the homophobe's erroneous projective beliefs and conclusions to get the homophobe to identify them and then start dealing with and resolving his or her own problems by methods other than attributing them to others. Therefore, the proper reply to paranoid homophobes is the personal equivalent of, "It takes one to know one"—meaning that "queers wouldn't upset you so if they didn't push one of your very personal buttons," then adding, "Don't take it out on me, but instead, bigot, heal thyself."

Two caveats apply. First, the target should participate in the bigot's disillusionment, not in the bigot's therapy. Second, confrontation can be dangerous, especially with paranoid homophobes who can even become violent when told in so many words that they hate queers only because on some level they are queer themselves. Therefore, Mautner (2003) suggests that with these homophobes, one should mostly write the scenario out in a personal journal as a catharsis, quietly recognizing the projection involved in order to be in a better position to take the angry words and deeds less personally, along the lines of, "There is nothing wrong with me. You, not I, are the one with the problem." The targets of homophobes should then join relevant groups and leave it up to these groups to change the world.

Depressive Bigotry

Just as it is depressive to be excessively and unfairly critical of oneself, it is also depressive to be excessively and unfairly critical of others—and being homophobic, or otherwise bigoted, suits that purpose all too well. A troublesome thing about depressive bigots is that they know how to hurt not only themselves but also others. They know exactly how to go for the jugular and where to stick the knife in, thus rendering the other individual's self-esteem very low the same way that they render low their own.

Antithesis

Targets can at least theoretically manage depressed homophobes the same way that they can manage anyone else who is depressed, but few would feel comfortable with that approach. Very few would want to take steps to alleviate a depressed homophobe's depression by giving him or her a pep talk along the lines of "none of us, you included, is as bad as you make me, and us all, out to be"; and then, for the more charitably inclined, recommend a consultation with a therapist. Therefore, a good general supportive measure involves not taking the bigot's criticisms quite so personally after following what is perhaps the most useful of all the mantras for targets of bigots: "Consider the source."

Manic Bigotry

Manic bigotry is malignant narcissistic grandiosity associated with feelings of superiority combined with easy irritability, leading to a tendency to irrationally devalue others with very little provocation and on almost any grounds.

Antithesis

Theoretically at least, targets who spot manic bigots and understand that their problem is predominantly uncontrolled, speeding, high-pressure, irrational anger, will want to put their foot down and set limits—demanding that the bigots control their words and actions. However, once again, these bigots may be dangerous or violent, so instead of a vocal "stop it," a personal "I refuse to listen to this" mindset may be the "intervention" of choice.

Dissociative Bigotry

An important characteristic of dissociative bigotry is that it allows contrary ideas to exist side by side. For example, a bigot says, "All lesbians hate men," then contradicts himself and says, "All lesbians want to be men," two postulates that are both inherently incorrect and entirely incompatible. Anyone who stereotypes is effectively in a state of dissociation, because to stereotype, it is necessary to ignore facts that do not fit. There is little substantive difference among the amnesiac who ignores true facts about his or her identity, the patient with a multiple personality disorder who ignores who he or she actually is or was just a few minutes ago, and the anti-Semite who ignores the possibility that Albert Einstein was not genetically inferior.

Antithesis

A remedy for targets of dissociative bigots (and for therapists treating such people) is to integrate contradictory beliefs and fantasies the same way patients with a multiple personality disorder, a fugue, or amnesia need to integrate the various parts of their personalities. In simple terms, it behooves the targeted person to ignore all scenarios that constitute a picture that distorts due to having left some of the important pixels out.

Obsessional Bigotry

Obsessionals see defined groups as falling short of an excessively high ideal that characterizes not reality but obsessive, perfectionistic thinking. As a result, they condemn whole groups of people as "lazy and shiftless and unreliable," "money-grubbing," and "filthy dirty." Obsessional bigots neither shun nor bash their victims. Instead they simply both literally and figuratively wash their hands of them.

Antithesis

The target who is aware of the dynamics of the bigoted response will save his or her energy by not trying to talk these particular bigots out of their pathological, ritualistic thinking and behavior. He or she will recognize that talking to such bigots is about as unproductive as ordering a compulsive hand-washer to stop the process. Therefore, the remedy involves giving up and staying away. Fortunately, these bigots are usually private miniaturists who can be safely ignored.

Malignant Narcissistic Bigotry

Narcissistic individuals personalize, coming to believe that everything their targets do is relevant to them, the bigots. Not surprisingly, they then become controlling individuals, having made their target's behavior not only their source of anxiety but also their business, personal concern, and mission in life.

Malignant narcissistic bigots feel superior to their targets and believe that they have both the ability and right to abuse them. Theirs is the troublesome combination of being overly self-confident individuals convinced that only they have the truth and that their way is the one and only right way, and being self-deluding, self-congratulating individuals who are convinced that they are pure and others foul. They may become fanatics who proselytize and demand to be heard because they, and only they, have the "word." Presuming themselves deep and brilliant thinkers, they accept no input and brook no argument from others. Instead, they respond to others' legitimate protests by digging in and simply restating their cherished beliefs. They also demand an uneven playing field where they have rights and privileges that others should not be given. In a way, many resemble idiot savants whose so-called intellectual formulations appear as brilliant islands in a sea of the general ignorance and dysfunctionality they manifest in most other areas of their lives. That is, not only are these bigots prejudiced, they are often not as smart as they may claim to be.

Antithesis

An important remedy involves being skeptical of self-proclaimed experts. Instead of being cowed by the malignant narcissist's self-proclaimed expertise, targets simply should dismiss these individuals' contentions as products of a self-appointed expert status that overlooks how they in fact are amateurs often with little or no real training, who almost certainly know less than they say and think that they do, who rarely have first-hand experience with the matters of which they speak, and who proclaim a so-called universal wisdom that is little more than their personal opinion. It is fair to question the expertise of such bigots and to demand to see their "credentials."

Phobic Bigotry

The often-heard argument that homophobia is not a true phobia is generally sustainable—but not always, for some forms of homophobia do in fact follow the same structural patterns followed by true phobias. In phobic bigotry, the target of the bigotry is in some ways just a symbol of what is truly feared and hated—someone who stands in for a specific conflict-laden issue for the bigot. The bigot, after displacing his or her inner conflict onto the target, shuns the target because it represents an internal fear in much the same way a true phobic shuns his or her "trivial prompt": because it has come to symbolize an inner conflict. For example, imagine a homophobe who is in conflict about his forbidden sexual desires. Like some phobic bigots, he condemns sexuality because of a personal history of serious primal-scene exposure associated with intense masturbation and incest guilt. Next he displaces this entire conflict onto the homosexual so that instead of criticizing himself for his own unacceptable sexual longings, he shuns all homosexuals for theirs, in order to avoid being in any way reminded of their, and so of his own, "perverse sexuality." Homophobia like his is less "condemn and attack" than "fear and avoid." The bigot's familiar cry, "Don't let him be a pastor in your church" is then the approximate psychological equivalent of the dog-phobic's cry, "Don't let that beast anywhere near me." Homophobia, anti-Semitism, racism, or xenophobia is the phobic bigots' fear of flying, with gays, Jews, blacks, or foreigners their trivial prompts, chosen "well" as symbols of individual conflicts about sex and hostility.

Finally, as with the plane phobia, the fear and avoidance are secondarily rationalized to become "It makes sense to stay away from people who do frightening and disgusting things." Now the bigot views him or herself not as a bigot. He or she is, or at least thinks he or she is, just a good citizen acting responsibly and doing his or her social duty.

Antithesis

Coping with and managing phobic bigots involves refusing to be shunned, that is, meeting the avoider head-on and refusing to be excluded, instead demanding one's civil right to be there, and any affirmative action that is necessary to ensure that one can stay. The correct response to the phobic bigot is, "I don't care if you fear or disdain me. You have to include me, and if you won't, I'll see you in court." Once again, and this always applies even when not stated explicitly, the target should not put himself or herself in any danger. Therefore, it is often best to accomplish one's ends impersonally, that is, by joining an organization with clout rather than personally through direct confrontation. Of course, as with depressive bigots, the goal is to stop bigotry, not to become a part of the bigot's therapy.

Psychopathic Bigotry

We all know that bigotry can be a way to accomplish some specific end and achieve a certain, often political, goal. Often homophobia and xenophobia enhance one's credentials, helping politicians win a certain vote or get a specific civil appointment.

Antithesis

The challenge becomes one of keeping the bigot from achieving his or her ends as a reward for his or her unacceptable behavior. Social mechanisms, including the educative-behavioral methods Mautner describes (below), are an effective way to do that. The general public should never replace thinking for themselves with buying into a psychopath's persuasive but narrowly focused arguments. These arguments are meant to stir the masses up to shared passions entirely for the benefit of the psychopathic striver, who is eager to realize selfish ambitions. The general public should avoid being pawns in the frontline of the bigot's distractive game.

Personality-Disordered Bigotry

Bigots express their bigotry in different ways, at least three of which are consistent with the different interpersonal styles of histrionic, passive-aggressive, and sadomasochistic disorders. In such cases, managing bigots involves using methods derived from accepted therapeutic interventions geared to managing the equivalent personality disorder.

The Histrionic Style

Histrionic bigots overdo themselves, as when they make invidious comparisons among homosexuality, incest, bigamy, and bestiality, reacting with an intensity that is inappropriate given the relative unimportance of what they are concerned about.

Antithesis

One proper response to hysterical bigotry is "Calm down, take it easy, stop sounding the alarm, and just forget about it." Another, espoused in Mautner's transcendentally calming book *Living La Dolce Vita* (2002), involves living one's own sweet life regardless, and to the hilt, no matter what others say or do—in the vernacular, this means refusing to "let the bastards get you down."

The Passive-Aggressive Style

Homophobes who choose the passive-aggressive style are still homophobic, although they are "nice" homophobes who express their homophobia in more subtle ways than most. They do not come out and say that they hate homosexuals. Instead they ask loaded questions that are in fact assertions, such as "Don't you think that you are ruining your life by moving in with a male lover?" Or, they protest too much that they love homosexuals, as in the familiar "Some of my best friends are gay." Often they precede their condemnation with a diversionary compliment whose true intent is easily decipherable—for example, the much-overused and patently obvious "Love the sinner, hate the sin."

Antithesis

Passive-aggressives of all kinds, bigoted or not, need to be asked either to say what they mean, openly and honestly so that one can deal with it directly, or to not say anything so that one does not have to think about it at all.

The Sadomasochistic Style

Sadomasochistic bigots always seem to hurt themselves in the process of hurting the intended targets of their hatred. They have a need for self-destruction, which they live out, for example, in the form of a Freudian slip that gets them fired as they momentarily forget and condemn someone unfairly for his or her race, creed, color, or sexual orientation. It is not uncommon for them to condemn gays or lesbians to someone who has a family member who is gay or a lesbian, only to themselves wind up being excluded from the family the way they had planned to have the family exclude their target.

In conclusion, prejudice and discrimination are in effect transference reactions that involve projecting one's personal agenda onto the blank screen of the target and making that target into what one wants him or her to be for one's own emotional or practical reasons. As such, the words the bigots speak about others actually speak volumes about themselves. For as Levinson (1982) suggests, "[I]f bigots

say the same thing about blacks and Jews as they say about all victims, and about all their targets from the same class even though the
targets are a heterogeneous group, then what they say has to come
from within, not from without, i.e. that what they say depends . . .
upon their own psychology" (p. 57). It follows that the operative action
for targets of bigots is to recognize that they as targets are little more
than inkblots. That means that what bigots say is not about *you* but
about *them*, projected onto you. Therefore, targets should not take
personally what is said. After not taking it personally, they might also
insist on being viewed as individuals in their own right. However, the
response must not be one that evokes violence. A good idea is to respond
in an assertive way without being aggressive, and one way to do
that is to not be demanding or hostile by saying "shut up," but instead
saying something firm but noncontentious, like "this is what works
best for me."

PASSIVITY VERSUS ACTIVITY VERSUS COMPROMISE

Passivity

Targets who choose the passive approach ignore, avoid, or otherwise silently come to terms with bigotry.

Passivity involves what O'Connell (1993) calls "agreement." Here
the target handles judgmental bigots by deciding that "some things
just aren't worth getting upset about" (p. E1). This is the counterstrike
of choice on those occasions, however few these may be, when it is
the better part of valor to retain one's perspective or sense of humor
and let things pass, not accepting intolerance by acting unperturbed
about it.

Of course, everyone knows that there are dangers involved in being
too passive with bigots. Targets who allow themselves to be passive
stay beaten down until they become too weak to care anymore.
Besides, they let bigots get away with their bigotry, and that usually
inspires the more sadistic among them to even higher transports of
bigotry. Now the bigot goes from hating a defined group for all the
usual reasons to hating them even more in the belief that they can
be hated with impunity. True, going along with bigots who devalue
women and emasculate men pleases the bigots on one level, but on
another, more important level, they just smell blood and attack,
inspired to devalue and emasculate even more. Another reason why

passivity is an imperfect solution is that targets who vocally agree with bigots just for the sake of peace will likely experience cognitive dissonance that can ultimately lower their self-esteem further (Mautner, 2003).

This said, there are a few positive aspects to remaining passive in the face of bigotry. Here are some practical reasons for going along— right for some but hardly for all. Bigotry targets who accept being targeted coddle those who target them and on that account may be spared further punishment. For those who confound being assertive with being aggressive, being passive also helps deal in a general way with feeling guilty about speaking up. Activism can sometimes be a waste of effort, for, as the previous discussion has suggested, protesting prejudice can be to as little avail as protesting mental illness. All these things when taken together help explain why some gays and lesbians I have talked to feel that protesting loud and long is sometimes a waste of time. Therefore, they decide that for them the best idea is to live with a bad situation since they are unlikely to make it any better. They feel that since they cannot change the world, they might as well live with the world as it is. So they accept the inevitable and focus not on changing other people but on changing themselves, so that while they are still *targets* they are no longer *victims* of bigotry, for the bigotry now bounces off them.

Activity

Mautner (2003) recommends activity, that is, fighting back. As she puts it,

> What I am learning is that it is not easy to fight group defamation and discrimination through legal means. The courts have made it difficult in order to avoid the likelihood of frivolous cases, and also because it is hard to award any kind of damages to a large group (e.g., Italian Americans, blacks, gays). My best advice to combat negative stereotyping (which is really at the root of all bigotry—because as Albert Bandura found in his famous observational learning theory experiments in the 60's, the media has a causal effect on behavior) is to be our own ambassadors and not simply turn the other way when the media or individuals portray a particular group in a defamatory way involving a false generalization that reduces the group in the eyes of society. Our job as members of a negatively stereotyped group is to raise awareness, sensitize, and educate. Therefore we must do the following:
>
> 1. Do NOT let derisive humor get past us without informing the joke-teller that it is offensive (if they want to know why, explain, if not, let it stand at that).

2. Write letters to media personnel if they have portrayed a particular group in a negative stereotypical way. Contemporaneously send a copy to the organization that best represents the defamed group (ADL [Anti-Defamation League], AIDA [American Italian Defense Association], etc.)

3. Educate wherever you can. If you are blessed with a brain, you have to use it. Write to newspapers and magazines. Talk to local schools, libraries, etc. There are many organizations and institutions who love a free speaker. Put this in your calendar to do at least twice a year. It is the best type of pro-bono work there is.

4. Once armed with information and facts, make sure you use them whenever the opportunity presents itself in social circles, in the home, and in the workplace. As individuals, we can do a lot to start changing societal attitudes by enlightening and informing those around us.

I myself might add: While targets cannot always convince or cow individual bigots into no longer hating them, they can almost always help pass laws that keep bigots from acting on their hatred. Education and psychoanalysis are among the best ways to change a bigot's mind. But legislation is probably the best and fastest way to change a bigot's behavior.

The activism suggested here has mostly positive attributes. Activism is not only a good way to alert certain bigots to the fact that their negative views are unjustified, it is also a good way for the target to improve his or her self-esteem, for self-esteem often gains from the pride ordinarily associated with successfully defending oneself and the pleasure that comes from knowing one has actually had a hand in reducing the amount of bigotry in the world.

However, there are some negative aspects of activism, too. As previously mentioned, activism can present a personal danger to targets of victims. Many bigots are quick on the trigger and armed, especially the paranoid ones who keep guns in case of what is, dynamically speaking, an "attack from the rear." Targets sometimes get killed when they "assault" such people. In the case of homophobes who bash gays and lesbians to cope with their own unacceptable homosexual desires, the wrong countermeasures can simultaneously inflame their deepest desires and touch on their worst fears. As Mautner (2003) clearly states, activism may be "risky so you must judge the situation for yourself, and be prepared for the consequences. One Italian American woman was recently fired from an international company when her co-workers referred to their Italian clients as 'dagos.' When she complained she was fired for not getting along with her co-workers." Therefore, two important distinctions must be made. The first is the one between impersonal and personal assertion, for example, letters to the editor versus direct confrontation. The second is the one between assertion and aggression ("That upsets me, so I would appreciate it if you would stop, please," versus "I am going to talk to my lawyer and see what I can do to get you fired for that").

Compromise

Compromise, which is the least risky though probably also the least satisfying and least effective approach of them all, is worth considering when faced with opposition from bigots that is so overwhelming that what is ideal may not be achievable, leading to the inevitable conclusion that "half a loaf is better than none." In this approach, one acts with silent strength and without cloying passivity, discouraging abuse while avoiding passive submission on the one hand and dangerous confrontation on the other; in effect, saying "please" and "thank you" but "I mean what I say."

Sometimes targets compromise by setting their sights lower. Some gay men and lesbians feel that they should consider accepting civil unions rather than full marriage. Some workers are well advised to consider resisting their ambition and not climbing up too far in the corporate ladder. Would-be politicians who are in some ways person ally vulnerable (due to a certain past history) might want to think twice about entering the public arena. Thus Hal Lancaster ("Managing Your Career," 1996) advises targets of prejudice in the workplace when he quotes a business consultant, saying that some individuals offered a promotion should at least consider staying in their present jobs because they might be "better off where they are" (Tod White, as cited on p. B1).

Compromise does not mean masochistically abdicating, such as quitting one's job due to on-the-job prejudice, without at least first trying to work things out. Compromise means going along at least enough to avoid shouting matches between those on the offensive and those on the defensive. Yet targets still remove the pleasure of the kill from those sadists who are absolutely inspired by the masochistic screams of pain and attack even more when they see the red eyes of their weeping victims.

SELECTING THE RIGHT COUNTERSTRIKE

Here are some generic counterstrikes to supplement the above-mentioned antitheses to specific types of bigotry. The *passive-aggressive* counterstrike involves attacking with one's wits, not fists. The *hypo-manic* counterstrike involves living well as the best revenge. Here, targets in response ignore the putdowns and the glass ceilings and thrive and prosper regardless, or deliberately out of spite. This is *being defiantly generative*. The *aggressive* counterstrike involves using offense as the best defense, once again mindful of the dangers involved. Loraine O'Connell (1993), using mental health counselor Chris Rosenthal as her source and describing ways to handle judgmental people, calls this aggressive form of counterstrike *confrontation* and suggests that "aggressive counterstrike" might be helpful because "judgmental people are at their worst with those who allow them to get away with it" ("Sitting," 1993, p. E1). Mautner (2003) also refers to the "door in the face" technique as well as semi-aggressive techniques that involve persuasion, if that is the desired end, such as the "broken record technique" that starts with advertising's "foot in the door" technique. However, as Mautner also warns, "That is only a good idea if you have an arsenal at home. Sometimes you can tell who is a threat and who is just a bigot-wimp, but not always. With the bigot-wimp, aggression is cathartic and effective, but with the macho-bigot you might have a problem."

The *narcissistic* counterstrike involves what O'Connell (1993) calls the "fogging technique" (p. E1) and what can also be called the "gay-pride counterstrike." Here the individual counters that what you criticize me for is "one of the things I like best about myself" ("Sitting," p. E1). Using this technique, targets can counter prejudice by citing the advantages of being exactly what they are being condemned for.

The following is a list of caveats pertaining to counterstrikes, some of which have already been mentioned.

1. A counterstrike should never be a first strike. That is not protection against, but provocation of, bigots.

2. The aim of counterstriking is actual accomplishment, not mere emotional satisfaction. With bigots, the primary goal is not to be liked but to be left alone.

3. Direct counterstrikes are dangerous with bigots who are unstable. Here, roundabout confrontation is the best idea.

4. The timing must be right. Targets should try to avoid having to think on their feet, which often involves thinking reactively and emotionally. They can respond most effectively after they have thought out their approach carefully and given consideration to the best time and place for their counterresponse.

AVOIDING CERTAIN PITFALLS

Trying to Win Bigots Over

It is masochistic to focus on trying to convert, or bringing around and winning over, only the people who cannot and will not love one, as if that were the only way that one could feel lovable and as good as the next person.

Imagining Bigotry in Its Absence

People who belong to a defined class should not respond to constructive criticism as if it were a sign of bigotry. A supervisor had to discipline a gay psychiatry resident because he was having sex with patients in the clinic. The resident called this supervisor a homophobe, but it had nothing to do with the specific acts involved and everything to do with the exact place and time where the resident was performing them. A caveat for targets of bigotry is to never fight the irrationality of bigotry by becoming equally irrational oneself.

Being Self-Homophobic

As previously mentioned, the bigoted seed grows best on fertile ground, and it is further fertilized by low self-esteem and extreme self-doubt. It is an unfortunate truth that some gays and lesbians and other targets of bigotry are, at bottom, ashamed of themselves. Already convinced that they are somehow defectives or sinners, they buy into what the bigot has to offer them, then treat themselves in much the same shabby and even bigoted way that bigots treat them. Therefore, to some extent, managing the bigotry of others involves managing one's own self-bigotry, or any other form of self-cruelty, by developing a positive self-view that does not let another's negative assessment in.

Antithesis

The treatment principles of self-homophobia and other forms of self-bigotry follow closely the principles of treating any form of low self-esteem, and there are many self-help books that can assist and many therapists out there who can help when called upon.

Toolbox for Change

For	Images/perceptions	Strategies for change
Individual	Depression, low self-esteem, lack of functionality and creativity, suicidality.	Understanding bigots' illogic and confronting their irrationality.
		Viewing bigotry as a product of mental illness and therefore not to be taken at face value.
		Setting up internal firewalls (becoming inured to bigotry).
		Developing personal pride.
		Joining groups for strength in numbers.
		Living well as the best revenge.
Community	Mediocrity due to inhibition/destruction of some of the finest, highest-functioning, most creative members of the community.	Education of the leaders. Countering and correcting stereotypes factually.
	Loss of power, multidimensionality, and range of talent of the community.	Popularization of distortive nature of bigotry in the media.
	Divisiveness and infighting between pros and anti's (homophobes and homophiles).	Passing anti-bigotry laws. Activism by members of the community who are being targeted by bigots.
		People of the stigmatized groups should be educated and stay informed about bigotry so they can correct misinformation when they hear it—be it in the home, at social clubs, churches, or schools. People of the stigmatized groups need to raise awareness by writing editorials, giving public workshops, and conducting research.

Toolbox for Change

For	Images/perceptions	Strategies for change
		Hit bigotry where it hurts—in the pocketbook. That is, do not buy products from advertisers who sell by portraying false negative stereotypes, do not frequent businesses owned and run by bigots, etc.
Practitioners/ Educators	Prophetic, self-fulfilling negativity due to treating and educating differently based on preconceived notions that lead people to behave in the very way that is expected of them. This creates the very problems that were initially wrongly identified as intrinsic.	Education of educators. Passing laws that assure equality for patients and students. Affirmations making certain in a practical way that there will be across-the-board fairness regardless of sexual orientation, age, race, and the like.

CONCLUSION

In conclusion, this chapter presents a six-step guide to help individuals cope with prejudice and discrimination. It emphasizes three main approaches:

- Growth—through self-exploration and self-improvement.
- Coping—through self-defense via understanding where the bigot is coming from, and through making it easier to discount his or her contentions by appreciating the flaws in his or her logic and the emotional underpinnings of his or her behavior.
- Community action—enlisting the community's help to influence the bigot directly and quash the bigotry sociopolitically.

This chapter has emphasized that while bigotry does not usually tailor itself to one particular target but is more or less the same whether the targets are gays and lesbians, Jews, blacks, or foreigners, there are different types of bigotries that vary according to the personality and profession of the bigot and according to what emotional problem(s) prevail and generate the bigoted ideation. It offers both generic and specific countermaneuvers directed to the specific type of bigotry, according to the primary cognitive errors in the bigot's thoughts, and the primary emotional disorder that generates the bigoted notions and his or her prejudiced and discriminatory behavior.

REFERENCES

Beck, A. T. (1985). Cognitive therapy. In H. I. Kaplan & B. J. Sadock (Eds.), *Comprehensive textbook of psychiatry/IV.* Baltimore, MD: Williams and Wilkins.

Bemporad, J. R., & Pinsker, H. (1974). Schizophrenia: The manifest symptomatology. In S. Arieti & E. B. Brody (Eds.), *American handbook of psychiatry* (2nd ed., Vol. 3). New York: Basic Books.

Kantor, M. (1998). *Homophobia: Description, development, and dynamics of gay bashing.* Westport, CT: Praeger.

Lancaster, H. (1996, September 10). The job that's open might be a step up but a bad step for you. *The Wall Street Journal,* p. B1.

Levinson, D. J. (1982). The study of anti-Semitic ideology. In T. W. Adorno, E. Frenkel-Brunswik, D. J. Levinson, & R. N. Sanford (Eds.), *The authoritarian personality* (Abr. ed.). New York: W. W. Norton.

Mautner, R. (2002). *Living la dolce vita.* Naperville, IL: Sourcebooks.

Mautner, R. (2003). Personal communication.

O'Connell, L. (1993, August 12). Sitting in judgment. *Asbury Park Press,* p. E1.

Pinsker, H. (2003). Personal communication.

Ursano, R. J., & Silberman, E. K. (1988). Individual psychotherapies: Other individual psychotherapies: Cognitive therapy. In J. A. Talbot, R. E. Hales, & S. C. Yudofsky (Eds.), *The American psychiatric press textbook of psychiatry.* Washington, DC: American Psychiatric Press.

Index

About the Series and
the Series Editors

It is expected that nearly half of the entire U.S. population will be of nonwhite ethnic and racial minorities by the year 2050. With this growing diversity, clinicians, researchers, and, indeed, all Americans need to understand that the Eurocentric psychological views particular to Caucasians may or may not be relevant or adequate to address mental health issues in racial and ethnic minorities. This series addresses those issues, aiming to better understand how these factors affect mental health, and what needs to be done, or done differently, to heal disorders that may arise.

JEAN LAU CHIN is a licensed psychologist and systemwide dean of the California School of Professional Psychology at Alliant International University. She is also president of CEO Services, which offers clinical, educational, and organizational development services emphasizing cultural competence and integrated systems of care. She holds a doctorate from Teacher's College of Columbia University. Dr. Chin's past positions include associate professor of psychiatry at the Center for Minority Training Program, Boston University School of Medicine; regional director of the Massachusetts Behavioral Health Partnership; executive director of the South Cove Community Health Center; and codirector of the Thom Child Guidance Clinic. She has authored, coauthored, or edited books including *Relationships among Asian American Women* (2000), *Community Health Psychology*

(1998), and *Diversity in Psychotherapy: The Politics of Race, Ethnicity and Gender* (1993).

VICTOR DE LA CANCELA is associate clinical professor of medical psychology at the College of Physicians and Surgeons, Columbia University. He is also deputy executive director of Tremont-Crotona Child Development Center, and a clinical psychologist serving with the United States Army Reserve.

JOHN D. ROBINSON is a professor in the Departments of Psychiatry and Surgery at the College of Medicine and Hospital at Howard University. He is a fellow of Divisions 1, 12, 38, 44, 45, 49, 51, and 52 of the American Psychological Association. In 1998, he received a letter of commendation from the president of the United States for teaching excellence. Robinson is a distinguished visiting professor at the Walter Reed Army Medical Center and at the Tripler Army Medical Center. He earned his EdD in counseling psychology at the University of Massachusetts–Amherst, completed a clinical psychology residency at the University of Texas Health Sciences Center at San Antonio, and earned an MPH at Harvard School of Public Health. Robinson worked earlier as chief of interdepartmental programs in the Departments of Psychiatry and Surgery at Howard University, and has also served as dean of the Division of Graduate Studies and Research at the University of the District of Columbia, clinical professor in the Department of Psychiatry at Georgetown University School of Medicine, and clinical attending faculty in the Department of Psychiatry at Harvard University School of Medicine at the Cambridge Hospital.

About the Advisers

JESSICA HENDERSON DANIEL is an assistant professor of psychology in the Department of Psychiatry at Harvard Medical School, and both director of training in psychology and associate director of the LEAH (Leadership Education in Adolescent Health) Training Program in Adolescent Medicine at Children's Hospital of Boston. She is also an adjunct associate professor of psychology in the clinical psychology program at Boston University. Daniel is the past president of the Society for the Psychology of Women, Division 35, APA; and is coeditor of *The Complete Guide to Mental Health for Women* (2003). Her awards include the 1998 A. Clifford Barger Excellence in Mentoring Award from Harvard Medical School; the 2001 Education Distinguished Alumni Award from the University of Illinois; the 2002 Distinguished Contributions to Education and Training Award from APA; and the 2003 Professional Award from the Boston & Vicinity Club, Inc., National Association of Negro Business and Professional Women's Clubs, Inc.

JEFFERY SCOTT MIO is a professor in the Department of Behavioral Sciences at California State Polytechnic University–Pomona, where he also serves as the director of the master of science in psychology program. He received his PhD from the University of Illinois–Chicago in 1984. He taught at California State University–Fullerton in the counseling department from 1984–1986, then taught at Washington State University in the Department of Psychology from 1986 to 1994 before accepting his current position at CSPU–Pomona. His interests are in the teaching of multicultural issues, the development of allies, and how metaphors are used in political persuasion.

NATALIE PORTER is vice provost for academic affairs systemwide at Alliant International University. She is also an associate professor of psychology. She received her PhD from the University of Delaware. Porter's research interests include feminist and anti-racist models of clinical training and supervision, cognitive and emotional developmental changes in individuals abused or traumatized as children, and feminist therapy supervision and ethics.

JOHN D. ROBINSON is a coeditor of *Race and Ethnicity in Psychology*, a Praeger series.

JOSEPH EVERETT TRIMBLE is a professor of psychology at the Center for Cross-Cultural Research at Western Washington University. Trimble was a fellow in the Radcliffe Institute for Advanced Study at Harvard University in 2000 and 2001. He is a research associate for the University of Colorado Health Sciences Center, in the Department of Psychiatry, National Center for American Indian and Alaska Native Mental Health Research. He is also a scholar and adjunct professor of psychology for the Colorado State University Tri-Ethnic Center for Prevention Research. In 1994, he received the Lifetime Achievement Award from the Society for the Psychological Study of Ethnic Minority Issues, Division 45, American Psychological Association. In 2002, he was honored with the Distinguished Psychologist Award from the Washington State Psychological Association. He has authored eighty-two journal articles, chapters, and monographs, as well as authored or edited thirteen books, including the *Handbook of Racial and Ethnic Minority Psychology* (2002).

MELBA J. T. VASQUEZ is in full-time independent practice in Austin, Texas. A past president of APA Divisions 35 (Society for the Psychology of Women) and 17 (Society of Counseling Psychology), she has served in various other leadership positions. She is a fellow of the APA and a diplomate of the ABPP. She publishes in the areas of professional ethics, psychology of women, ethnic minority psychology, and training and supervision. She is coauthor, with Ken Pope, of *Ethics in Counseling and Psychotherapy: A Practical Guide* (1998, 2nd ed.). She is the recipient of several awards including Psychologist of the Year, Texas Psychological Association, 2003; Senior Career Award for Distinguished Contributions to Psychology in the Public Interest, APA, 2002; Janet E. Helms Award for Mentoring and Scholarship,

Columbia University, 2002; John Black Award for Outstanding Achievement in the Practice of Counseling Psychology, Division 17, APA, 2000; and the Distinguished Leader for Women in Psychology Award, Committee of Women Psychology, APA, 2000.

HERBERT Z. WONG has provided management consulting, diversity training, and organizational assessments to over 300 government agencies, businesses, and other organizations. He was the cofounder and president of the National Diversity Conference, Inc., which presented contemporary issues and future directions of workforce diversity. He was a consultant to the President's Commission on Mental Health (1977), the White House Conference for a Drug Free America (1989), and the President's Initiative on Race–White House Office of Science and Technology (2000). In the past twenty-five years, Wong has written extensively on multicultural leadership, cross-cultural communication, and diversity issues. Wong received his PhD in clinical and organizational psychology from the University of Michigan.

About the Contributors

BETTINA J. CASAD is a doctoral student in social psychology at Claremont Graduate University. Her current research program examines theories and consequences of stereotype violation.

CAROLE BAROODY CORCORAN earned her PhD and her MA in social psychology from Miami University, after having received her BA summa cum laude in psychology from Wittenberg University. In 1991 Dr. Corcoran was appointed to the Lt. Governor's Task Force on the Prevention and Early Intervention to Reduce the Incidence of Sexual Assault, and in 2002 she was named to the Virginia Attorney General's Advisory Council on Domestic Violence and Sexual Assault. She is a co-founder of the Rappahannock Council Against Sexual Assault, as well as co-chair of a National Task Force on Feminist Psychology for Division 35 (Society for the Psychology of Women) of the American Psychological Association. Dr. Corcoran has researched how to integrate race and gender into the curriculum and has helped coordinate several grants from the State Council of Higher Education for Virginia for developing programs in that area. She also co-founded the Race, Class, Gender Awareness Project and won Mortar Board's Outstanding Faculty Member Award. Nominated by Mary Washington College for the State Council of Higher Education's Faculty Awards Program in 1995 and 1996, Carole Baroody Corcoran was promoted to full professor of the psychology faculty in 1998. Dr. Corcoran was co-investigator on a $1 million grant awarded by the National Institute of Mental Health to investigate the outcomes of different types of traumatic life experiences in college women. She serves as an organizational development, training, and assessment consultant for creativity, leadership, and diversity. Dr. Corcoran is also involved in coordinating a pilot project using theater, dance, and spoken word with at risk adolescents. Presently, she is a Visiting Scholar at the University of Virginia Women's Center.

KIM D. FELSENTHAL is an adjunct professor of psychology at St. Joseph's College in Brooklyn, at the Fashion Institute of Technology, and at the New York City College of Technology. Felsenthal is a graduate student at the City University of New York Graduate Center in its environmental psychology program. She holds a master's degree in urban planning and in environmental psychology. Her dissertation investigates the use of the home in the development and expression of gender and sexuality of transsexual women. She has also conducted research and presented papers on the experience of gender-variant individuals in public space, as well as their subsequent (re)construction of place. She maintains that the physical environment plays a crucial role in the production of gender and sexuality.

MICHELLE KAMINSKI is an assistant professor of labor and industrial relations at Michigan State University. She conducts workshops for union members and leaders on a variety of topics, including increasing member involvement in local unions, the union role in high-performance work organization, basic economics, and the Family and Medical Leave Act (FMLA). She researches teams in unionized settings, workplace health and safety, and the development of union activists. Previously, Michelle was a bargaining unit chair with the Washington-Baltimore Newspaper Guild, Local 35. She received her PhD in organizational psychology from the University of Michigan.

MARTIN KANTOR is a psychiatrist who has been in full private practice in Boston and New York City, and active in residency training programs at several hospitals, including Massachusetts General and Beth Israel in New York. He also served as assistant clinical professor of psychiatry at Mount Sinai Medical School and as clinical assistant professor of psychiatry at the University of Medicine and Dentistry of New Jersey–New Jersey Medical School. He is the author of twelve other books, including *Distancing: Avoidant Personality Disorder Revised and Expanded* (2003); *Passive-Aggression: A Guide for the Therapist, the Patient, and the Victim* (2002); *My Guy: A Gay Man's Guide to a Lasting Relationship* (2002); *Treating Emotional Disorder in Gay Men* (1999); and *Homophobia* (1998). His newest book is *Understanding Paranoia: A Guide for Professionals, Families and Sufferers* (2004). Dr. Kantor earned his medical degree at Harvard Medical School and performed his internships and residencies in the early 1960s at Stanford University Medical Center, the Massachusetts General Hospital, and the University of Chicago Clinics. He practices now in New Jersey.

JUDITH LeMASTER is a licensed psychologist and earned her PhD in social and personality psychology at the University of California–Riverside. Her past positions include associate professor of psychology at Scripps College, assistant professor of psychology at Pitzer College, visiting assistant professor at the University of California–Riverside, and instructor at California State University.

AMY MARCUS-NEWHALL is associate dean of the faculty at Scripps College. She is also associate professor of psychology at Scripps College and a member of the graduate faculty at Claremont Graduate University. She received faculty fellowship research funding to lead a study from March 2003 to March 2004 on working and stay-at-home mothers. She is chair of the Society for the Psychological Study of Social Issues Membership Committee and consulting editor for the *Psychology of Women Quarterly*. She earned her PhD in social psychology at the University of Southern California.

LENA WRIGHT MYERS is a professor of sociology at Ohio University. With a specialty in social psychology, she has received numerous honors and awards for her national reputation in research and scholarship. Meyers's research has resulted in many articles published in professional journals. She has been a contributing author to *Another Voice: Feminist Perspectives on Social Life and Social Science, The Black Woman,* and *Violence in the Black Family: Correlates and Consequences.* She is the author of *Black Women: Do They Cope Better?* which was published in two later-revised editions. Her book *Black Male Socialization Revisited in the Minds of Respondents* was published in the Contemporary Studies in Sociology series. Her most recent book is *A Broken Silence: Voices of African American Women in the Academy.* She is a member of numerous national professional organizations, three of which she served as president.

ROBERTA L. NUTT is the founder and director of the counseling psychology doctoral program, which emphasizes family psychology and women's/gender issues at Texas Woman's University. She is coauthor of "The Division 17 Principles Concerning the Counseling/Psycho-therapy of Women: Rationale and Implementation" and the APA book *Bridging Separate Gender Worlds: Why Men and Women Clash and How Therapists Can Bring Them Together.* Nutt has written and presented extensively on gender and family issues; served in a number of leadership roles in psychology including president of the family psychology division of the American Psychological Association (APA), chair of the Texas State Board of Examiners of Psychologists, offices in both the women's and men's divisions and the counseling psychology division of the APA; and holds the ABPP diplomate in family psychology. She is currently cochairing an APA interdivisional task force developing new guidelines for psychological practice with girls and women.

JUDITH A. PARKER, associate professor of English and Linguistics at the University of Mary Washington, earned her PhD in linguistics from Brown University (1992). Her research has focused on speech processing and dyslexia and the oral narratives of children and sexual assault survivors. Dr. Parker co-directs an interdisciplinary research program on linguistic and psychological approaches to narrative and sexual assault trauma. Recent papers and presentations have reported on implications of this research for sexual assault survivors and for pedagogy in writing and teaching communication. In the past year, Dr. Parker's presentations have focused on anti-female messages perpet-uated through the "Powerpuff Girls" empire, power and politeness in the workplace, and the successful model of undergraduate linguistics at UMW. In her newest workshops, Dr. Parker has introduced activist and experiential theater techniques to explore inequities in ability and health, class, ethnicity, gender, language, and race. Dr. Parker's courses include psycholinguistics; the advanced seminar in speech, narrative, and emo-tion; linguistic approaches to discourse and text; and women's studies. Students participating in The Life Stories Project and The James Farmer Scholars Project engage in community service-learning with elderly residents and middle school students in Fredericksburg, Virginia.

CARLTON W. PARKS is professor and coordinator of the Multicul-tural Community-Clinical Psychology Emphasis Area at the California School of Professional Psychology, Los Angeles, at Alliant International University; and the campus program director of the graduate programs in educational psychology: school psychology concentration, in the Graduate School of Education at Alliant International University, Los

Angeles. Dr. Parks is a site visitor for the Committee on Accreditation of the American Psychological Association and was a clinical associate at the Lesbian and Gay Community Services Center in Minneapolis, Minnesota.

NICOLE SILVERMAN is an undergraduate honors student at Scripps College, majoring in psychology with a minor in Jewish studies. Her primary research interest lies in social psychology.

SHANNON D. SMITH completed his MA in pastoral counseling at the University of Ashland in Ashland, Ohio, and his PhD in counseling from Oregon State University–Corvallis. He has worked as a child and family therapist in community mental health and as a school counselor in the public school system (K–12). Currently he is an assistant professor in the Department of Educational Psychology at the University of Nevada–Las Vegas. His research interests include school counseling, counselor education, child and family therapy, play therapy, and the use of technology in counseling. Of particular interest to Shannon is social advocacy for underrepresented people groups.

SUZETTE L. SPEIGHT is an associate professor of counseling psychology in the Department of Leadership, Foundations, and Counseling Psychology at Loyola University–Chicago, where she has been since 1991. She received her PhD in counseling psychology from Ohio State University in 1990. Dr. Speight teaches courses including Multicultural Counseling, Ethics and Legal Issues in Counseling Psychology, Identity and Pluralism, Psychology of Oppression, and Professional Issues for Counselors. Her scholarly interests include multicultural training, perceptions and evaluations of similarity and difference, Afrocentric psychology, and identity development issues.

ANITA JONES THOMAS is a counseling psychologist with specializations in multicultural counseling and family therapy. Thomas received her BS in human development and social policy from Northwestern University, and an MA in community counseling and a doctorate in counseling psychology at Loyola University, Chicago. Thomas is an associate professor at Northeastern Illinois University, where she teaches courses in multicultural issues, family therapy, professional identity, and ethics. Her research interests include racial identity, racial socialization, and parenting issues for blacks. She has also conducted training seminars and workshops on multicultural issues for state and national professional organizations in counseling and psychology, and for hospitals and corporations.

KAREN M. WITHERSPOON is an associate professor of psychology at Chicago State University. She primarily teaches courses in the graduate program in counseling. Her research interests are in identity, mental health, and cognitive self-appraisal. Her current research program is funded through a National Institute of Mental Health grant to study the role of oppression in the mental health issues of black Americans. As a licensed psychologist, Dr. Witherspoon maintains her clinical expertise through part-time consulting with various public schools and social service agencies. Her clinical interests are in psychological assessment and mental health and oppression. Dr. Witherspoon is a national member of the American Counseling Association, the Association for Multicultural Counseling and Development, and the Association of Black Psychologists. She also serves on the board of the Chicago chapter of the Association of Black Psychologists.